Enemy of the People

—

'The narrative advances a theory backed by evidence that the Guptas, having captured President Jacob Zuma through becoming his close friends and family bankrollers, are using the president and his son to capture and repurpose state-owned enterprises and other key organs of state as vehicles for their own economic gain. Zuma himself has captured and repurposed public agencies such as the National Prosecuting Authority, the Hawks, the State Security Agency and the South African Revenue Service seemingly to protect him, his family, the Guptas and other associates.'

– Thuli Madonsela, former Public Protector

To Schalk, Lukas and Michiel,
young lions of a new dawn.

Enemy of the People

—

*How Jacob Zuma stole South Africa
and how the people fought back*

ADRIAAN BASSON & PIETER DU TOIT

Jonathan Ball Publishers
Johannesburg & Cape Town

First published in South Africa in 2017 by
JONATHAN BALL PUBLISHERS
A division of Media24 (Pty) Ltd
PO Box 33977
Jeppestown
2043
Reprinted once in 2017
ISBN 978-1-86842-818-2
ebook 978-1-86842-819-9

Twitter: www.twitter.com/JonathanBallPub
Facebook: www.facebook.com/JonathanBallPublishers
Blog: http://jonathanball.bookslive.co.za/

Cover by publicide
Front cover image: President Jacob Zuma on a three-day official visit to Germany in 2015.
Photo by Sean Gallup/Getty Images.
Photos courtesy of Media24, except for Salim Essa © Gallo images/Andrew Brown
Design and typesetting by Triple M Design
Printed and bound by CTP Printers, Cape Town
Set in 11/15pt Sabon MT Pro

'Let's tell the truth to ourselves even if the truth coincides with what the enemy is saying. Let us tell the truth.'

– Oliver Tambo, Solomon Mahlangu College, Tanzania, 2 May 1984

'Stealing the public money tends to make you an enemy of the people, that's what happened.'

– Tshepo Morajane, @tshepomorajane6 Twitter, 8 February 2017

'All of us there in the NEC have our smallanyana skeletons and we don't want to take out all skeletons because all hell will break loose.'

– Bathabile Dlamini, President of the ANC Women's League, 19 March 2016

Contents

——

Acronyms and abbreviations

—

ACTT   Anti-Corruption Task Team
ANC   African National Congress
ANCYL   ANC Youth League
BEE   black economic empowerment
CIA   Central Intelligence Agency
Cosatu   Congress of South African Trade Unions
DA   Democratic Alliance
EFF   Economic Freedom Fighters
GCIS   Government Communication and Information System
GDP   gross domestic product
GEAR   Growth, Employment and Redistribution plan
ICT   Imperial Crown Trading
IPID   Independent Police Investigative Directorate
MEC   Member of the Executive Council
MKMVA   uMkhonto we Sizwe Military Veterans' Association
NDPP   National Director of Public Prosecutions
NEC   National Executive Committee
NGC   ANC national general council
NPA   National Prosecuting Authority
NUMSA   National Union of Metalworkers of South Africa
OUTA   Organisation Undoing Tax Abuse
Prasa   Passenger Rail Agency of South Africa
RDP   Reconstruction and Development Programme
RSG   Radio Sonder Grense

SAA	South African Airways
SACP	South African Communist Party
SAPS	South African Police Service
SARB	South African Reserve Bank
SARS	South African Revenue Service
Sassa	South African Social Security Agency
SCA	Supreme Court of Appeal
SIU	Special Investigating Unit
SOE	state-owned enterprise
SSA	State Security Agency
UAE	United Arab Emirates

Prologue

—

It was late at night and they have seen this movie enough times before to know it was game over. The ANC had just lost control of two of South Africa's largest cities: Johannesburg and Pretoria, the financial and administrative capitals of the country, respectively. As they were sipping cheap coffee from polystyrene cups, the lieutenants of the oldest liberation movement in Africa – the African National Congress – looked dishevelled, defeated and old. The neon numbers on the massive screens at the election centre confirmed their worst fears: the party of Oliver Tambo, Walter Sisulu and Nelson Mandela had just started to die on their collective watch, 22 years after the ANC had won the glorious democratic elections of 1994.

There was no one to turn to. Around them, analysts in brightly lit TV studios tried to make sense of the historic local-government election results of 2016. How was it possible that the residents of some of the ANC's most successful metros could vote the party out of power? But Gwede Mantashe, Jessie Duarte and Zweli Mkhize knew why. They didn't have to listen to any analyst or statistician or Twitter expert to tell them. They had known why since at least 10 December 2013, when thousands of mourning ANC supporters booed and jeered President Jacob Zuma in front of a world audience that included Barack Obama, Ban Ki-moon and Hillary Clinton as he attempted to deliver his eulogy during Mandela's memorial service at Soweto's FNB Stadium. The ANC faithful had used hand signals to tell the ANC leaders that they wanted Zuma replaced – the same signals used by Zuma's supporters to humiliate former president Thabo Mbeki at the ANC's watershed Polokwane conference in 2007. This time the leadership hadn't listened. And now they were paying the price.

There was only one reason why the ANC lost Johannesburg and Pretoria, and his name was Jacob Gedleyihlekisa Zuma, the president of scandals. Zuma, the ultimate political survivor, who became president because of a false narrative he and his supporters had created, which made him the victim and martyr of everything Thabo Mbeki, his predecessor, had created and stood for. Under Zuma, the ANC not only started dying at the ballot box, but also became a corrupt vehicle for crooked politicians and criminal syndicates to infiltrate and control the state. Yes, of course, there had been corruption under Mbeki and even Mandela, but the destruction of institutions and individuals who could keep this crookery in check will be the loathsome legacy of the Zuma era. To rebuild these systems of accountability will take years, if not decades.

The endemic and systemic corruption had reached such levels under Zuma's presidency that loyal ANC cadres, who had given up the largest part of their adult lives for the liberation struggle, now say the only way for the country to be saved is for the ANC to be voted out of power in 2019. The ANC simply couldn't stand up to Zuma, so Zuma (and his capturers) captured the ANC. And, like a battered wife, the party knew what the root of the cause was for shedding support, but refused to kick the abusive husband out of the door. History will judge them for this.

How did a man who swore on 9 May 2009 that he would commit himself 'to the service of our nation with dedication, commitment, discipline, integrity, hard work and passion' come to embody everything that is wrong with South Africa? Through his misrule, Zuma and his circle of rogue protectors broke not only the country's spirit and moral fibre, but also our hearts. By allowing his son and dodgy friends to run amok and operate what is effectively a parallel state, by appointing compromised individuals to protect him and his cronies from prosecution, by weakening the state's investigative capacities to the point of institutional collapse, and by allowing weak and incompetent sycophants to manage key service-delivery departments, Zuma broke his oath of office and became an enemy of the people he had promised to serve.

Adriaan Basson & Pieter du Toit
October 2017

Cast of characters

Duduzane Zuma

Atul Gupta

Ajay Gupta

Rajesh 'Tony' Gupta

Mosebenzi Zwane

Des van Rooyen

Malusi Gigaba

Nathi Nhleko

David Mahlobo

Bathabile Dlamini

Faith Muthambi

Lynne Brown

Nhlanhla Nene

Cyril Ramaphosa

Pravin Gordhan

Mcebisi Jonas

Ace Magashule

Baleka Mbete

Gwede Mantashe

Jessie Duarte

Vytjie Mentor

Nompumelelo Ntuli-Zuma

Julius Malema

Thuli Madonsela

Berning Ntlemeza

Richard Mdluli

Anwa Dramat

Shadrack Sibiya

Johan Booysen

Shaun Abrahams

Nomgcobo Jiba

Victoria Geoghegan

Mogoeng Mogoeng

Anoj Singh

Hlaudi Motsoeneng

Ben Ngubane

Brian Molefe

Tom Moyane

Lungisa Fuzile

Ivan Pillay

Johann van Loggerenberg

Themba Maseko

Salim Essa

Iqbal Sharma
© Gallo images/Andrew Brown

Johann Kriegler

Francis Antonie

Wayne Duvenage

Sipho Pityana

Introduction

'You don't need to be a genius to see the trend in the country.
I'm not going to interpret what this means, or what the urgency is.
What I am telling you is that you have history unfolding in front of
you ... I think South Africans have a responsibility to
connect these dots.'

– Pravin Gordhan, 31 March 2017, the day after President Zuma fired him
as Minister of Finance

In the early evening of 19 March 2014, we were standing in the largely deserted newsroom in the offices of *Beeld* in Johannesburg, surrounded by empty coffee mugs and hundreds of pieces of paper circled and highlighted in bright colours. Most of the staff had gone home and the first edition of this, the youngest and most progressive Afrikaans newspaper in the country was about to be put to bed.

For hours we had been poring over Public Protector Thuli Madonsela's thorough report into Zuma's controversial Nkandla homestead, titled 'Secure in Comfort', and were hurrying to finalise the first edition's lead story. It had been a draining day, with Madonsela's investigations delivering the 447-page bombshell that Zuma had received undue benefits from the multimillion-rand alterations and upgrades to his family's complex in KwaZulu-Natal, and that he was to be held liable for part of the costs.

I

It had been the culmination of years of investigative work, first by the media and later by Madonsela, and led to the head of state being put in this untenable position. He had clearly known about the millions of taxpayers' rands spent on installing non-security upgrades, like a cattle kraal, air conditioning, a swimming pool and various other amenities at his family's estate. Yet he denied it. This was our Watergate moment, we thought. Zuma could surely not justify the spending and survive the Public Protector's damning findings.

South Africa was a maturing democracy where the rule of law was respected and integrity prized. It had emerged from the darkness of apartheid, inequality and discrimination to attempt to build an equitable and just society, based on the Constitution and human rights. And based on a shared commitment by its citizens to transparent, inclusive and participatory democracy, something that can't be legislated or enforced from above.

By early 2014 Zuma had been head of state for nearly five years. His government's record was unremarkable, muddling through a series of unrealised growth plans, development initiatives and big promises. The Nkandla renovations had been revealed in November 2009 by the media, six months after Zuma became president. For four years, the scandal, like many others to follow, was all but ignored by the ANC, the Presidency and Parliament, until Madonsela began her investigations.

After the Nkandla report had been dissected and digested – with Zuma weaving and ducking any and all forms of accountability to its findings – South Africans were confronted with a president who refused to conform to democratic norms and standards, a president who believed himself to be beyond the reach of law and one who reconfigured the state to suit his own factional and selfish ends. He simply refused to accept Madonsela's findings and proceeded to recruit the ANC and two of the three arms of state to protect him.

Zuma has done enormous damage to the body politic and South Africa's political economy ever since 2009, when he assumed the country's highest constitutional office – one once occupied by Nelson Mandela. He has systematically undermined and hollowed out institutions of state, dismissed the rule of law and the spirit of democracy, and encouraged a network of patronage and impunity, which has led to the looting of public resources on an industrial scale. At the centre of the network is his favourite son, Duduzane, and the Gupta family.

The manner in which Zuma has gone about his business since becoming head of state is quite remarkable. There has been an all-consuming and singular focus on himself and his own desires since assuming office, with the need to avoid facing the law and thereby the possibility of being imprisoned being the prime driver behind most, if not all, of his tactical and strategic moves. Zuma captured the security cluster (the police, Hawks, State Security Agency and National Prosecuting Authority), disembowelled the finance family (the National Treasury and SARS) and maimed state-owned enterprises (including SAA, Eskom and Transnet). His brazen manipulation of the state and its machinery has enabled him to ascend to an almost impregnable position and has made his family, through Duduzane, very, very wealthy.

Interfering with state institutions has helped Zuma survive his fair share of scandals. He fired his finance minister, so that his cronies and associates could get access to the National Treasury; he was found by the Constitutional Court to be in violation of his oath of office; he led the governing party to its worst showing in any election since 1994; he oversaw the emergence of a shadow state; and he fired a second finance minister without consulting the party's senior members. Any one of those instances could, and probably should, have spelt his end. But Zuma has survived through a combination of strategic foresight and structural weakness in the ANC. He has always been two or three moves ahead of the pack, while the ANC has been unable and unwilling to rein in his excesses. The state has come to function like a protection racket within a vast network of patronage and corruption.

But Zuma has also been the catalyst for the mobilisation of civil society and the gradual emergence of a new South African consensus on corruption and the rule of law. There have been a number of tipping points during Zuma's misrule that have activated civil society – the protection of rogue crime-intelligence boss Richard Mdluli, Zuma's attempts to subvert and bury the Public Protector's Nkandla report and his firing of Gordhan as finance minister. These gave rise to unprecedented civil protests by hundreds of thousands of South Africans and led to South Africa's second coming of civil activism.

A whole raft of new non-governmental organisations was born, think tanks and pressure groups started beating a path to the nation's courts and ordinary South Africans increasingly took to the streets to voice their displeasure about the status quo under Zuma. The independent media, under pressure from commercial realities and challenged by a growing government-friendly media cohort, has remained at the forefront of exposing corruption and wrongdoing, showcasing South Africa's proud tradition of a fourth estate at work. So, although Zuma and his network have left a trail of destruction in the civil service, they have also seen the rise of a new type of public servant, fearless and committed to the rule of law, and whistle-blowers who believe in justice and the original ideals of the democratic project.

When *Beeld* went to the printing press in the early hours of 20 March 2014, we knew Zuma was not about to capitulate to the rule of law and constitutionalism. But we also knew that South Africans stood ready to defend those values, which they did with tenacity and verve.

This book is an effort to chronicle how Zuma became an enemy of South Africans and how the people fought back.

PART I

The capture of the ANC

CHAPTER I

The coalition of the wounded

—

'He'll never become president. He doesn't have enough support
and he cannot do the job. Besides, the women's lobby
will never allow it.'

– Naledi Pandor and Thoko Didiza, on Jacob Zuma,

during a Gauteng ANC media networking dinner, Sunnyside Park Hotel, 2006

'Comrades! Comrades! Can the comrades at the front please sit down, so the comrades at the back can see?'

Dren Nupen, the petite, white-haired elections officer from the EleXions Agency – the company that managed the leadership election at the ANC's 52nd national conference in Polokwane in December 2007 – was standing on an empty stage, struggling to make herself heard above the din in the hot, stuffy delegates' marquee. She almost willed them into submission because she could simply not be heard over the chanting, singing and dancing. The conference was held in the grounds of the former University of the North in Mankweng, during the humid rainy season, and was dominated by factional battles. The build-up to the gathering had been acrimonious, with the different camps planting disinformation, launching smear campaigns and using dirty tricks on each other. Thabo Mbeki was determined to succeed in securing a third term as leader, while the South African Communist Party (SACP), Congress of South African Trade Unions (Cosatu) and the ANC's leagues coalesced around Jacob Zuma.

'Zuma mustn't be allowed to win … he will destroy the country,' was the message from the Mbeki faction.

'Mbeki cannot get another term … he will become a dictator,' was the rallying cry from the other side.

Most of the 4 000 delegates that Tuesday evening, 18 December 2007, were chanting 'Zu-ma! Zu-ma!' – with the emphasis on '-ma' thundering around the enclosed space. Many were holding up a section of *City Press*, with a picture of a singing Zuma underneath the headline 'What the Zumafesto holds'. The outgoing National Executive Committee (NEC) had vacated the stage and were sitting on the left-hand side of the giant tent. Mbeki sat in the front row, wearing a navy golf shirt and a tan sports jacket. He was surrounded by his kitchen cabinet, Mbhazima Shilowa, the loyal Gauteng premier and former Cosatu boss, Essop Pahad, Minister in the Presidency and Mbeki's enforcer, his brother Aziz, the Deputy Minister of Foreign Affairs, and Mosiuoa Lekota, the Minister of Defence, who had been shouted down on the very first day of the conference. They were the people who told him what he wanted to hear: that he must stand for a third term as party leader, that Zuma cannot be allowed to win and that they had the numbers to ensure that.

When the delegates, who were almost apoplectic with excitement, had calmed, Nupen took to the microphone and read from a note: 'The number of votes received … by comrade Jacob Zuma: two thousand three …' The rest of her words – she was supposed to say 'two thousand three hundred and twenty-nine' – were drowned out by the absolute bedlam that had broken out. Zuma's supporters were dancing on the tables, singing and shouting, making the hand gesture that football coaches use when they want to substitute a player and which became symbolic of the conference. 'Zu-MA, Zu-MA, Zu-MA!' reverberated around the tent. 'Comrade Zuma received 2 329 votes,' Nupen repeated. 'Comrade Thabo Mbeki received 1 505 votes.'

Zuma was welcomed onto the stage amid raucous cheering and, wearing a brown leather jacket and ANC cap, turned to acknowledge his supporters. Mbeki, still sitting in his seat, was stunned. In an instant, he became old, his face creased, his skin grey, and his hair and goatee looked white. He tried to hold on to a smile and winked towards the media contingent, sitting cross-legged in front of the stage. To his left, Lekota leaned forward, clapping hands and smiling at Zuma. Essop Pahad, to his right, frowned, and Shilowa, behind Mbeki, sat stony-faced.

It was brutal – a disaster and utter humiliation for the Mbeki slate. Zuma's candidates defeated their opponents by roughly the same margin – 60% support to 40% – every time. Kgalema Motlanthe over Nkosazana Dlamini-Zuma for deputy president; Baleka Mbete over Joel Netshitenzhe for national chairperson; Gwede Mantashe over Lekota for secretary general, Thandi Modise over Thoko Didiza for deputy secretary general and Mathews Phosa over Phumzile Mlambo-Ngcuka for treasurer general.[1]

Mbeki went onto the stage and gave Zuma an awkward hug, shook his hand and returned to his seat as delegates shouted 'ANC! ANC! ANC!' in staccato. Outside the tent it was drizzling softly, inside it was steaming, heaving. The election for the 80-member NEC saw prizes for a number of Zuma backers. Winnie Madikizela-Mandela received the most votes; the SACP's Jeremy Cronin (ranked fifth) and Blade Nzimande (11th) were near the top; loyalists Jeff Radebe and Jessie Duarte received strong support, as did former ANC Youth League (ANCYL) leader Malusi Gigaba, Free State chairperson Ace Magashule and ANCYL president, Fikile Mbalula. Derek Hanekom came in at 23rd, Zweli Mkhize 24th, Bathabile Dlamini 29th and Cyril Ramaphosa – who had been out of politics for almost a decade – was ranked at 30.

Zwelinzima Vavi, then general secretary of Cosatu – along with the SACP's Nzimande and the ANCYL's Mbalula, Zuma's most loyal of operatives – was relieved at the victory but cautious. Days before the elections, Vavi had said, 'The media demonised Zuma terribly, they created a monster out of him.' If it wasn't for Cosatu and the workers, Zuma would either have been in prison or in his home town, Vavi said. 'Ideologically and otherwise, Zuma we like him because the fellow has some natural gifts: down to earth, humane, accessible. He is by nature a unifier. We have never seen Zuma be angry against anyone. He laughs off the most provocative statements made against him. He will never throw tantrums. We see ourselves in him, not a high-flying intellectual, arrogant who will not listen to anyone.'[2]

But there was a rider: Vavi refused an offer to take up a seat in the NEC, telling the media after Zuma's victory he was content to remain as Cosatu's general secretary. 'Our role will remain that of providing checks and balances. We can't be co-opted. We need to remain on the outside,' he said. Those were to prove prescient words.

At a media conference the day after the election, Mbalula, who at the age of 36 was technically too old to serve as ANCYL president and would hand over the reins of the organisation to Julius Malema in five months' time, was triumphant. He bounced around the room, talking to journalists and bragging about how they had plotted Mbeki's fall. 'Nobody believed us when we said Zuma will win ... well, you were all wrong!' he crowed.

'There are many kinds of denialism, you know. Aids is only just one sort,' said Jeremy Cronin,[3] the SACP second general secretary and a strident Mbeki critic, referring to the distance between the then president and the party's rank and file, and Mbeki's reviled policy on HIV/AIDS.

Zuma's ascension to the party leadership was the biggest political moment in the country since the advent of democracy in April of 1994. It signalled a change of course for the young democracy and introduced populism, cynical manipulation and organised corruption into the South African body politic. It also entrenched factionalism and division in the ANC. And although the governing Tripartite Alliance (the ANC, SACP and Cosatu) remained unified for a short period of time, it exposed the deep ideological cleavages between these organisations.

When Mbeki fired Zuma from his position as deputy president on 14 June 2005 during a speech to a joint session of Parliament, Zuma was not in the house. Two weeks earlier, Justice Hilary Squires had found Zuma's friend and associate Schabir Shaik guilty on three counts of corruption and fraud for soliciting bribes on behalf of the then deputy president. No specific finding against Zuma was made but, from the thousands of hours of expert testimony and forensic evidence put before the court, it was clear – Zuma had a case to answer for. His name appears a total of 474 times in the judgment, with the word 'corrupt' or 'corruption' appearing 14 times in the same sentence.

Squires said in his judgment:[4]

> Shaik is quite plainly anything but a fool. Our assessment of him over the prolonged period he spent in the witness box, supplemented by the tone of his letters and his contributions to shareholder and board meetings revealed in the minutes, show him as being ambitious, far-sighted, brazen, if not positively aggressive in pursuit of his interests and discernibly focussed on achieving his vision of a large successful multi-corporate empire; and moreover, someone who believed Zuma was destined for high, if not the highest, political office.

He continued:

> It would be flying in the face of common sense and ordinary human nature to think that he did not realise the advantages to him of continuing to enjoy Zuma's goodwill to an even greater extent than before 1997; and even if nothing was ever said between them to establish the mutually beneficial symbiosis that the evidence shows existed, the circumstances of the commencement and the sustained continuation thereafter of these payments, can only have generated a sense of obligation in the recipient.

Zuma could clearly not repay the money Shaik lavished on him and Squires wondered whether Zuma's only option was to lend Shaik his name and the influence of his political office to show his gratitude. 'And Shaik must have foreseen and, by inference, did foresee that if he made these payments, Zuma would respond in that way. The conclusion that he realised this ... seems to us to be irresistible.'

The judgment provided Mbeki with the ideal cover to rid himself of Zuma, whose legal troubles had become a burden to the Presidency ever since former National Director of Public Prosecutions (NDPP) Bulelani Ngcuka had announced on 23 August 2003 that he would not charge Zuma, even though there was prima facie evidence of corruption against him. Mbeki was by then an already unpopular president in ANC structures. He ruthlessly elbowed aside all challengers for the party leadership in 1997, including a challenge by Ramaphosa, and strengthened his position at the party's elective conference in 2002. By 2005 there was general disgruntlement in the alliance, with the SACP and Cosatu leading a campaign against the so-called 1996 Class Project. This referred to the conservative fiscal and macroeconomic policies pursued by the first democratically elected government, and championed by Mbeki, Trevor Manuel (Minister of Finance) and Tito Mboweni (Governor of the South African Reserve Bank (SARB)). The government's GEAR (Growth, Employment and Redistribution) policy dictated fiscal responsibility while narrowing the budget deficit, targeting inflation and reducing government debt – mostly associated with pension funds. This meant the Reconstruction and Development Programme (RDP), which entailed massive social spending on services, development and infrastructure, had to be curtailed. Mbeki, Manuel and Mboweni were accused of being sell-outs, of following neoliberal policies that harmed the poor and were dubbed the high priests of capital. The alliance partners wanted more public spending. The Mbeki government resisted.

'The political agenda that Mbeki has driven over the last decade has been premised on the assumption that the first priority was to stabilise the commanding heights of our capitalist system and return it to profitability,' Nzimande wrote weeks before the Polokwane conference. 'The original assumption was that a 6% growth rate (regardless of the trajectory and quality of that growth) was the tide that would lift all ships, a necessary and sufficient condition to produce the changes for which the ANC's mass base had been struggling for [for] decades.'[5]

Similarly, Vavi argued the Mbeki government had shifted to the right instead of implementing radical reforms:

> Over many years now, we have said the alliance and ordinary ANC
> members are not driving government policy processes. We have cau-
> tioned that the most important economic policies are coming from
> government, more so from the presidency; that the people who have
> influence are drawn from Harvard University and the President's
> Investment Council.[6]

The economic policies that shaped the Mbeki era had their origins
in the early days of the ANC government. Soon after it took power,
Nelson Mandela's government realised South Africa would not remain
the flavour of the month forever, feted across the globe as a victory for
democracy, and flooded with good wishes and foreign direct investment.
The previous government had run up a deficit of almost 9% of GDP in
1993/94[7] and government's biggest creditors were local pension funds.

'The country was facing huge difficulties,' Manuel said later.
'Fortunately because of sanctions the country's foreign debt was neg-
ligible. The last loan by the World Bank was in 1967. We spoke to the
president about debt, and he replied: "So we owe all this money to the
pension funds. Do you think I should call Harry (Oppenheimer) and
Anton (Rupert)?" Because the people who had money were those two.'[8]

All South African pension funds had been compelled to invest in government bonds, and if government reneged on its commitment to pay
back its loans, it would have had disastrous consequences for the fledg-
ling state. Manuel recalled the meeting:

> It was a fundamentally important discussion. It gave rise to the
> question how to reduce the deficit, how to do more with less. It cul-
> minated in a speech in parliament on 14 June 1996 where we tabled
> a new macro-economic policy [GEAR]. At that stage the projections
> were that in 1998 we would be spending more on servicing debt than
> any other item in the budget. And Madiba said: 'If we're spend-
> ing more on debt servicing, that's money already spent?' We said:
> 'That's right, Mister President.' He replied: 'But then we're spend-
> ing more on yesterday than we are on tomorrow? Can we do a deal

where we always spend more on education than on anything else because if we do that then we are focused on the future.'[9]

Manuel consistently rejected criticism of GEAR and held the line that government had no option but to implement policies that would reduce debt and reduce the deficit. 'Before we tabled GEAR, Madiba invited the alliance leaders over to his house in Houghton on a Sunday morning to discuss it,' said Manuel.[10]

The Mbekiites brooked no opposition. The Presidency became the centre of power, with government policy conceived and driven by the office of Policy Coordination and Advisory Services in the Union Buildings, headed up by Joel Netshithenzhe. Mbeki relied 'heavily on business advice'[11] and regularly convened his international investment council, consisting of internationally renowned economists and advisors, who drew up documents like the Harvard Reforms. He even doubted whether the alliance could survive, saying he expected it to break down into its constituent ideological parts.[12] This did not sit well with his alliance partners and the ANC-Cosatu-SACP relationship deteriorated, with leaders like Nzimande and Vavi bemoaning the fact that Luthuli House had ceded its power to the Presidency.

And it was into this maelstrom of ideological and factional battles that Zuma stepped after Mbeki dumped him. Mbeki had selected Zuma to be his deputy, believing he didn't have the ambition or gumption to succeed him, thereby negating fears of Machiavellian machinations. But the Shaik judgment exposed Zuma's failings. He was impressionable, open to manipulation – and unable to work with money, struggling to finance his lifestyle and support his many children.

The National Prosecuting Authority (NPA) believed it had enough on Zuma and charged him with fraud, racketeering and corruption. He was prepared to do anything to evade the courts, and the loose coalition of the wounded – Cosatu, the SACP and certain ANC leaders who felt slighted by the aloof Mbeki, including careerists, opportunists and chancers – saw in Zuma the vanguard of a movement that could remove a president. And they rallied around him. They appeared alongside him during every court appearance, first at the Durban Magistrate's Court and later at the Pietermaritzburg High Court, holding vigils, singing struggle songs and burning ANC T-shirts bearing the image of Mbeki's face. 'We will ensure that whenever comrade Zuma appears in court our people will demonstrate en masse,' Vavi declared.[13]

Nzimande said state institutions were being abused to prevent Zuma from becoming president: 'Then who are we if Zuma's rights can be abused? ... no-one will stop us in ensuring that we reclaim what is ours!'[14] Mbalula, one of Zuma's most ardent supporters, said those trying to prevent Zuma from ascending to the presidency would fail. 'Jacob Zuma has been subjected ... [to] a campaign of disinformation and a campaign of ill-administration of justice. This is just political malice of desperate people who are basically misusing the justice system ...'[15]

To add fuel to the fire, Zuma was charged with rape in December 2005, after having unprotected sex with the HIV-positive daughter of a family friend.

But Zuma is nothing if not a survivor. On 8 May 2006, he was acquitted of the rape charge, and then, on 20 September that year Judge Herbert Msimang, from the Pietermaritzburg High Court, struck the NPA's corruption case from the roll. And when the NPA, days after his Polokwane victory, decided to charge Zuma again, his coalition sprang to his defence, accusing Mbeki and the Scorpions, the elite corruption-busting unit, of improper interference in the criminal-justice system. Judge Chris Nicholson from the Pietermaritzburg High Court agreed, finding on 12 September 2008 that there was political meddling and he, too, dismissed the charges against Zuma. When that judgment was overturned on appeal on 12 January 2009, Zuma had already won the battle. Mbeki was dramatically recalled as president weeks after the Nicholson judgment. By then, the national mood had changed. Mokotedi Mpshe, the acting NDPP, announced on 6 April 2009 that the NPA, who had pursued Zuma relentlessly believing they had enough to secure a conviction, would drop charges against the ANC president, saying it was 'neither possible nor desirable' to continue with the prosecution after the so-called 'spy tapes' came to light.

A month later, on 9 May 2009, Zuma took the presidential oath of office. 'To achieve all our goals, we must hold ourselves to the highest standards of service, probity and integrity,' he told guests at the Union Buildings' amphitheatre. 'Together we must build a society that prizes excellence and rewards effort, which shuns laziness and incompetence.'

The Polokwane coup had been complete, and the coming together of shared, if temporary, interests worked a charm. Zuma was out of jail and the alliance was again the centre of power.

CHAPTER 2

Cracks in the coalition

——

'We are prepared to die for Zuma. We are prepared to take up arms and kill for Zuma.'

– Julius Malema, 16 June 2008, addressing a Youth Day gathering in Thaba Nchu,

Free State

Jacob Zuma is an affable man. His guffaws when he reacts to a wise-crack and the disarming ease with which he laughs at himself have led to many ardent critics softening their tone when attacking him. He is easy to get on with, he has invited ideological opponents to his home to talk and debate with him and he connects easily with people from all walks of life. Former Democratic Alliance (DA) leader Helen Zille, a fierce critic of the president, recounted how 'charming' and 'charismatic' Zuma could be. 'In fact, I almost feel embarrassed and I feel kind of bad about it ... the best weapon that he can use against me is his complete charm. Because every time I've been really, really tough on him in the public arena, he meets and greets me as if he's been dying to see me for a very long time and he couldn't be warmer and more generous,'[1] Zille said in 2009.

The national mood in the country during the first year of Zuma's presidency had changed from despair and tension over the destructive leadership battle between Zuma and Mbeki between 2005 and 2008 to one of relief and optimism with the new status quo. Zuma wasn't like

Mbeki at all. Where Mbeki was aloof, Zuma was personable; where Mbeki was distant, Zuma was warm; and where Mbeki was dismissive, Zuma was inclusive.

The Tripartite Alliance was also rejuvenated and a new sense of civic duty and responsibility was sweeping through the lobbies of Parliament. Suddenly ministers were available to portfolio committees and MPs took up their neglected oversight function. Open debate and (mild) dissent was even encouraged in the ANC caucus. Even though Zuma came into office with the dark clouds of corruption hanging over him after the NPA controversially dropped its charges a month before the 2009 election, the consensus was that the latter years of the Mbeki era – which had seen a suppression of internal debate in the ANC, a reduced Parliament, manipulation of state institutions and HIV denialism – had been a depressing period. Serious questions remained, but Zuma impressed many with the warm way in which he engaged voters during the campaign ahead of the election. Politically, the alliance was satisfied with the manner in which he approached the task of the new government, removing Manuel from the National Treasury and establishing a new department (economic development) as a counterweight to the powerful finance ministry. There was also a renewed emphasis on land and redistribution, and a reorganisation of law-enforcement agencies began, with the dissolution of the Scorpions and the establishment of the Hawks in 2008.

The grand coalition that swept Zuma to power in 2007 was a 'garish and motley carnival',[2] however, consisting of groups with divergent interests and often conflicting ideologies, and almost all with different objectives. Even though the different interest groups had the same goal ahead of the Polokwane conference and the 2009 general election, it was clear the unity of purpose could not last. Zuma never had a clear vision or mission for the ANC, or the country, when he agreed to front the assault on Mbeki. His mission was simply to sidestep the corruption charges. He positioned himself as unfairly targeted by a system that is rigged against the common man in a country where the common man is poor and black. Zuma and his supporters inflamed the narrative, steadfastly arguing that he was the victim of a 'political campaign'[3] and a 'conspiracy',[4] and that he was 'persecuted like Christ'.[5]

Those who backed the new ANC leader went all in, supporting him from his first appearance in court, through his rape trial, right up until Judge Nicholson's ruling on 12 September 2008, which confirmed their worst suspicions: there was meddling in the case against him. Their support, however, was conditional on Zuma making fundamental changes to the way the ANC-led government managed the economy, which they believed was beholden to the neoliberal and anti-worker policies of the 1996 Class Project. With Zuma's election, the time had come to jettison Mbeki, Manuel and GEAR.

Cosatu said in a statement shortly after the 2009 election, ratcheting up the pressure on Zuma to come good on his promises: 'Our priority now is to make sure that the ANC's commitments in its progressive elections manifesto are driven forward and turned into a program of action. We must take vigorous action to protect workers from the impact of the global economic crisis, create new, decent jobs, transform the lives of the poor majority of South Africans.'

But the signs for the economy were ominous. When the rand fell by 2,5% after Mbeki was recalled (and Manuel resigned as finance minister), the ANC reacted with horror at the economic consequences. Although Manuel stayed on after Kgalema Motlanthe took over as caretaker president, it was clear that government couldn't chop and change at a whim, especially in the middle of a global financial crisis. The ANC under Zuma had to find a balance between retaining international investor confidence and keeping their political allies in the tent. Mathews Phosa, the ANC's treasurer general, sought to calm international markets during a visit to London in April 2009, telling investors that the party's macroeconomic policies would not shift. Phosa added that good governance and sound policies 'make for better partnerships ... the South African government understands this.'[6]

Although the influential Manuel was shifted to the National Planning Commission – a consultative body located in the Presidency – Zuma couldn't discard the fiscal conservatives wholesale. Manuel was replaced with Pravin Gordhan, the commissioner of the South African Revenue Service (SARS), who had helped modernise and professionalise the tax authority and who came from the so-called 'finance family'. And even though Ebrahim Patel, a trade unionist who headed up the new Department of Economic Development, and Rob Davies, the Minister of Trade and Industry, were given powers to run economic ministries, they were unable to shift government policy to the degree that the leftists hoped for. The markets rejoiced at Manuel's new responsibilities – he was in charge of overarching government planning – and Gordhan's appointment.[7]

But the unions started almost immediately braying for change. Just two weeks after Zuma had taken the presidential oath of office, the National Union of Metalworkers of South Africa (NUMSA) staged a march to the reserve bank, where the Monetary Policy Committee was meeting. The union demanded a lowering of interest rates and the scrapping of inflation targeting, which the reserve bank refused to consider. Mantashe, the ANC's new secretary general and an SACP office bearer, was having none of it, warning unions not to pressurise government. 'You are projecting the Zuma leadership as weak and indebted to various constituencies. Some unions are creating the impression the ANC must react instinctively to demands,' Mantashe told a National Union of Mineworkers' congress.[8]

The ANCYL, ever more militant and aggressive since the election of Julius Malema at a chaotic conference in Bloemfontein in 2008, also started their signature campaign to nationalise the country's mines, arguing that they were merely lobbying for the full implementation of the ANC's Freedom Charter. 'As defenders of the revolution, we will have a permanent problem with any member or leader of the ANC who opposes the Freedom Charter in an attempt to please the minority owners of mines and mineral resources,' Malema said after a public outcry following the youth league's nationalisation bid.

Despite his initial support, Vavi was the first of Zuma's supporters to break ranks. As general secretary of the country's largest and most influential trade-union federation, Vavi commanded an organisation that was arguably better managed and wealthier than the ANC. He wielded enormous influence and his support to Zuma during the tribulations of 2005 to 2009 was invaluable. 'Any efforts to stop Jacob Zuma from becoming president would be like fighting against the big wave of the tsunami,' he had said back in 2005. But by 2010 Vavi had already become disillusioned. Besides his frustrations with the lack of change in economic policy and the continued influence of Manuel and Gordhan in directing it, the emergence of an elite enriched by black economic empowerment (BEE) – many with ties to influential political office bearers – grated with him.

On 26 August 2010, he broke with Zuma. 'We're headed for a predator state where a powerful, corrupt and demagogic elite of political hyaenas are increasingly using the state to get rich,' Vavi told a stunned media conference at Cosatu House, the federation's dilapidated headquarters in Braamfontein. 'We have to intervene now to prevent South Africa from becoming a state where corruption is the norm and no business can be done with government without first paying a corrupt gatekeeper.'[9] This followed revelations that a company in which Zuma's son Duduzane had an interest, Imperial Crown Trading (ICT), was to receive a 21% share in the Sishen iron-ore mine in the Northern Cape. The share belonged to ArcelorMittal, but the company had neglected to convert its old mining rights into new-order mining rights, as required by law. When these lapsed, they were snapped up by ICT. ArcelorMittal then offered to buy ICT for a cool R800 million to get the mining rights back, which would have made Zuma Jr and his partners – including the chief executive of the then relatively unknown Gupta family's Oakbay Resources – instant millionaires.[10] After a shareholder outcry, the deal collapsed.

The ICT–Sishen drama wasn't the only incident that riled Vavi. A year before, Zondwa Mandela, a grandson of Nelson Mandela, and Khulubuse Zuma, a nephew of the president, had bought the Pamodzi gold mines in Orkney and Grootvlei through their company, Aurora Empowerment Systems. They proceeded to run the mines into the ground, stripping the entities of their assets and neglecting to pay salaries. This, however, did not suppress their appetite for lavish consumption, both flaunting expensive cars and leading celebrity-like lifestyles while their mining employees suffered. One miner, Marius Ferreira, committed suicide after he lost his house and his car. Vavi accused the owners of getting rich off the back of their political connections: 'Hundreds of workers have not been paid for 10 months by their black empowerment bosses in the company called Aurora. Young people in their 20s and 30s have become overnight multimillionaires. We are rewarding laziness, greed and corruption and discouraging hard work, honesty and integrity.'[11]

Malema and the youth league's relationship with Zuma also began to sour. The young firebrand rattled Zuma and the party's leaders with his populist and militant style, advocating for radical economic change through the nationalisation of mines and banks. Malema was a new breed of politician: brash, reckless and offensive. He sang militant freedom songs, pushed for the expropriation of land without compensation, attacked white monopoly capital and warned of a 'leaderless revolution' that would take Sandton, then move on to the Union Buildings.[12] But before Malema became the ANC's problem child, he had been somewhat of a darling, reconnecting the party with an increasingly disaffected youth, energising the moribund ANCYL with new ideas and making the organisation the centre of media attention with its often outrageous statements, swagger and attitude. Zuma even attended the opening of a church that Malema had built in honour of his mother in Seshego, Limpopo, saying Malema was 'a leader in the making ... worthy of inheriting the ANC'.[13]

But things began to change in 2010 when Malema, increasingly influential and easily the most talked-about public figure in the country, ramped up the ANCYL's campaign to nationalise mines ahead of the party's mid-term national general council (NGC) in Durban. Malema, like Vavi, had become frustrated by the lack of fundamental economic change shown by the Zuma government and used his populist message to force the governing party to implement radical policies.

In April 2010 Malema visited Zimbabwe on an 'indigenisation' tour to see how President Robert Mugabe's policies purportedly benefited the poor. (He also went to Venezuela to get a first-hand impression of President Hugo Chavez's nationalisation programme.) The ANCYL issued a statement on his return, praising Mugabe and the manner in which the country's government had managed the 'land question'. During a briefing at Luthuli House a couple of days later, an angry Malema chased a BBC journalist out of the room, calling him a 'bastard' and an 'agent' after the scribe observed that Malema lived in posh Sandton. Malema had earlier criticised Zimbabwe's main opposition party of having offices in the area. The confrontation went viral on social media, with a video showing an aggressive and animated Malema flailing at the hapless journalist. The ANC – who had hitherto defended and protected the ANCYL president – this time reacted firmly, saying 'the behaviour in question is not in keeping with the culture and traditions [or] conduct of a cadre and leader of the ANC'.[14] Zuma also weighed in, lambasting Malema for singing the struggle song *'Dubul' iBhunu'* ('shoot the boer'), which had been banned by the Equality Court, saying Malema's rants were 'totally alien' to the ANC.[15] Two days later, *Pretoria News* reported Malema as having said that Zuma was 'worse' than Mbeki.[16] On 19 April Malema was formally charged by the ANC for bringing the party into disrepute. He escaped with a fine and had to issue an apology to Zuma, but the damage was done.

Vavi, meanwhile, was fighting his own battles with the ANC and the SACP (the latter had sunk without a trace after Polokwane). Whereas the ANCYL and Cosatu were vocal in their dissatisfaction with government policy, the SACP's most senior leaders, Nzimande and Cronin, along with a host of other senior communists, were appointed to Cabinet as ministers and as chairs of parliamentary portfolio committees. The SACP admitted as much, saying the party was struggling to be part of government while trying to remain critical of it. Cosatu and Vavi felt betrayed. Shortly before the ANC's NGC in 2010, the federation released a 36-page critique of progress by the party after Polokwane, concluding that the country was running the risk of seeing the state 'being auctioned off to the highest bidder'.[17] Vavi, the main author of the document, lashed out at the emergence of a BEE class who used access to state power to grow wealthy. It was also disappointing, the federation added, that the ANC had no plans to deal with it: 'There are no clear measures to actively combat the roots of corruption which has become so endemic ...'[18]

Mantashe, who, earlier in the year, had had to manage the fallout after it emerged that Zuma had impregnated the daughter of Irvin Khoza, one of the organisers of the 2010 FIFA World Cup, hit back at Vavi, questioning why Cosatu under his helm was acting 'like an opposition party'.

Malema's efforts to force the ANC NGC in September that year to take a position on nationalisation also failed. The youth-league delegation got so frustrated that they stormed the stage during a late-night session about the issue, angrily remonstrating with Jeff Radebe, who was chairing the session, after their proposals were voted down. Zuma's patience was now wearing thin. Malema and the ANCYL had been indicating that they would not support Zuma for another term as ANC leader and they were becoming more and more intransigent and uncontrollable. During his closing speech in Durban, Zuma said such behaviour was unacceptable. 'There is no need for intimidation and disruption of meetings simply because you do not agree or want to push a particular position. Not only does such behaviour undermine unity, but it also constitutes ill-discipline. It must not be tolerated,' he said.[19] The ANCYL president then spun out of control. He refused to pay a fine after the Equality Court found against him over a disparaging remark he had made about Zuma's rape accuser; he called the DA's then parliamentary leader, Lindiwe Mazibuko, a 'tea girl'; and referred to the governing party in Botswana as a 'footstool of imperialism'.

Malema reached his zenith as ANCYL leader during the conference in June 2011 where he was comfortably re-elected as president. Almost 5 000 delegates packed the cavernous halls at the Gallagher Estate Convention Centre, where the league's policies of nationalisation and expropriation without compensation were debated. But the occasion was really a crowning event for Malema and his policies. On the final day, he spoke for more than two hours, most of it off the cuff, about the dithering ANC leadership and launched an attack on Zuma, saying the president was using internal party processes to sideline him. Malema had the audience in the palm of his hand. On stage, Deputy President Kgalema Motlanthe and party elder Winnie Madikizela-Mandela were listening intently; behind them Malema's colleagues were hanging onto every word. 'In whose hands is the wealth? It's white monopoly capital. That's who we want to take the wealth from. And we're not going to be apologetic about land. We are asking for leadership, we don't want to remove you. We are asking for radical policy shifts. We want more action from the leadership. We are going to war for radical policy shifts. The Polokwane resolutions must be implemented!' he said to the adoring crowd.

Malema's protracted exit from the party started on 18 August 2011, when the ANC confirmed he would be charged for bringing the party into disrepute and had to face the ANC's National Disciplinary Committee. The following day, Public Protector Thuli Madonsela announced she would be investigating the awarding of provincial-government tenders to a company linked to Malema. The Hawks entered the fray a day later, saying they were investigating Malema for fraud and corruption. It was open season on the embattled ANCYL leader. Some six months later, on 29 February 2012, after numerous arguments and counter-arguments, and less than a year before Zuma was to seek a second term as ANC leader in Mangaung, Malema was expelled from the ANC. 'We have seen under President Zuma democracy being replaced by a dictatorship,' Malema told students at the University of the Witwatersrand shortly afterwards.[20] His appeals were dismissed and he left the ANC on 24 April 2012.

A similar fate befell Vavi, whose campaign to force the ANC to alter its policy ideology alienated him from Zuma and the power brokers in the ANC, just as Malema's had done. Vavi's involvement in the launch of Corruption Watch, a civil-society body combating corruption, irritated many. Mantashe again accused him and Cosatu of acting like an opposition party, while Cronin said that Cosatu had become hostile. But Vavi exposed his flank to his internal enemies after an affair with a junior Cosatu employee came to light. He was also accused of corruption over the sale of Cosatu House, before a new head office in Johannesburg was bought – a charge he denied. He was suspended in August 2013 and charged by Cosatu's disciplinary committee in January the following year. Vavi feared that the internal assault on him, led by S'dumo Dlamini, a Zuma acolyte, would result in the neutering of Cosatu. Vavi had been singled out because he was exposing ANC failures, NUMSA deputy general secretary, Karl Cloete, contended: 'The real intention is to turn Cosatu into a "lame duck", a "labour desk" and a "toy telephone".'[21]

NUMSA became Vavi's staunchest defender, and refused to endorse the ANC in the May 2014 general election – a poll in which Malema's newly formed Economic Freedom Fighters (EFF) garnered 6,35% of the vote, less than a year after it was formed. Irvin Jim, NUMSA's general secretary, led the union out of Cosatu on 8 November 2014. The loss of this key member and the financial consequences of their departure crippled the federation. After numerous court battles and appeals, Vavi was finally expelled on 30 March 2015.

After Vavi's expulsion and NUMSA's exit from Cosatu, and Malema's from the ANC, Motlanthe said that the alliance was dead. 'It only exists in name … the organisations [that made up the alliance] aren't independent any more … they have lost their way.'[22]

Zuma came to power supported by a broad coalition who went to war for him, with Cosatu and the ANCYL being its two most important components. But the ANC president showed exactly why he is such a shrewd operator, cutting both Malema and Vavi loose once they started asking difficult questions and taking contradictory positions. For Zuma, control was everything. With both Cosatu and the ANCYL neutered, it was almost absolute.

CHAPTER 3

The Mangaung whitewash

'Here, there is a different consensus: the ANC has its problems,
but it's not doing badly at all. And, yes, the President may be
building himself a sprawling estate, but what's the problem with
that? It may be yet another symbol of realisable aspiration,
just as Zuma himself is.'

– Ferial Haffajee, Jacob Zuma is going to win Mangaung, News24, 17 December 2012

Just two months after one of the biggest scandals of his political career was laid bare, Zuma was re-elected ANC president with an overwhelming majority of 75% of the votes, defeating his deputy, Motlanthe, at the ANC's 53rd elective conference, in Bloemfontein. Zuma's victory was convincing and, with it, he took complete control of the party, its NEC, provincial leaderships and leagues. What made it even more astounding was that Zuma secured this victory merely a few weeks after it had been revealed that the state had paid over R240 million for upgrades to his private residence at Nkandla. Almost four years later, the same scandal would lead to a finding by the Constitutional Court that Zuma was in breach of his constitutional duties and oath of office by allowing the upgrades to proceed.

However, in December 2012 at the Mangaung conference, there was no talk of Nkandla. It was as if the 'N' word was forbidden from the campus of the University of the Free State, where the conference took place. Only late at night, in the City of Roses' favourite watering holes after a few rounds of Scotland's best, would you hear comrades speaking out against Zuma's blatant abuse of state resources. And they were mostly from Gauteng.

The anti-Zuma camp, led by Motlanthe and former Zuma backers Tokyo Sexwale, Mathews Phosa and Gauteng ANC leader Paul Mashatile, were left licking their wounds. They had been taught a hard lesson in politics: don't come to a gunfight with a knife. The Zuma camp simply bulldozed Motlanthe et al. aside by making sure they had enough votes in the pocket before the conference had even started. Zuma always understood the basic rules of politics: to rule, you need to win. And to win, you need the most votes. Make sure you get the numbers, by hook or by crook. Zuma's slate dominated the election, with Baleka Mbete (chairperson) and Gwede Mantashe (secretary general) retaining their positions. The conference saw two newbies entering the top six: Zweli Mkhize replaced Phosa as treasurer general and Jessie Duarte replaced Thandi Modise as deputy secretary general. Mkhize was the KwaZulu-Natal provincial chair and premier, and Duarte had served as ANC spokesperson, and for a while as chief operations officer in the Presidency. Mkhize would later become a pivotal counterbalance to Zuma's brazen efforts to capture the state, aligning himself with Ramaphosa's campaign to 'save' the ANC. Duarte remained a staunch Zuma sycophant.

Motlanthe never ran a proper campaign. It was only at the last moment that he decided to hedge his bets on the ANC presidency and withdraw as candidate for what would have been his second term as deputy president. Such was the confusion in the anti-Zuma camp that Sexwale and Phosa both ran for deputy president and were both humiliated by the stunning political return of Cyril Ramaphosa.

Afterwards Motlanthe's backers sold the story that he always knew he would lose, but that he wanted to make a 'moral' statement by opposing Zuma for the presidency. It is of course untrue that the wise elder with the trademark goatee didn't want to win. Until the last moment, his supporters still believed he had a chance, particularly in the slipstream of the Nkandla scandal that was reverberating through South Africa's chattering classes. But Zuma had the win sown up months before the conference. Still, it was symbolically important for Motlanthe to oppose Zuma and dispel any myth that he was a unifying president with universal support.

What happened between Polokwane and Mangaung? In a nutshell, it took Zuma less than five years to neutralise the governing alliance and centralise the power in himself. Jacob Zuma became the ANC and the ANC became Jacob Zuma. Whereas Zuma was viewed as a so-called 'Trojan Horse' candidate for Cosatu, the SACP and the ANCYL before Polokwane for whatever agendas they believed he would advance, he was very much his own man coming into Mangaung. Zuma no longer needed rabble-rouser youth leaders, firebrand trade unionists or die-hard communists to hold onto power. He had won over enough block votes from the provinces to secure victory, particularly from his supporters in KwaZulu-Natal, the Free State, Mpumalanga and the North West. Eight months before Mangaung, the ANC had kicked out youth leaders Malema and Floyd Shivambu for sowing division in the party and propagating regime change in Botswana. Malema, and what was left of the ANCYL after their expulsion, attempted to campaign for Motlanthe from outside the ANC, but failed. After five years as ANC president, Zuma was now also firmly in charge of the state. Through several Cabinet reshuffles, he had shown his ministers who was boss. In Hlaudi Motsoeneng he had a strongman at the SABC; he cleaned out the intelligence agencies after they started sniffing too close to home; and he suspended police chief Bheki Cele for a dodgy property transaction. The Gupta family's newspaper, *The New Age*, became the Zuma administration's own Pravda. ANC delegates to Mangaung knew they had to get in on the Zuma list if they wanted to survive and prosper.

The run-up to Mangaung was marred by allegations of vote buying, branch rigging and an assassination attempt. The SACP in Limpopo accused provincial and regional leaders of bribing poor Limpopo delegates with money and food to vote for Motlanthe as ANC president.[1] Then Gauteng ANC deputy secretary Humphrey Mmemezi was accused by former Tshwane mayor and regional party chair Kgosientso Ramokgopa of attempts to bribe Tshwane ANC members to vote for Zuma in Mangaung.[2] Mmemezi denied the claims. Earlier in 2012, Mmemezi had resigned as Gauteng Member of the Executive Council (MEC) for Local Housing after using his government credit card to buy a painting from a McDonald's restaurant for R10 000. The disgraced ANC politician said he thought he could use his official credit card for personal expenses as long as he could pay it back. The previous year Mmemezi's blue-light vehicle had knocked down 18-year-old Thomas Ferreira from his motorbike, resulting in permanent brain damage and lifelong incapacity. Joseph Semitjie, Mmemezi's driver, testified that the MEC had told him to rush to a meeting for which he was late. Semitjie was found guilty of reckless and negligent driving, and sentenced to five years' imprisonment.[3] In December 2012, Mmemezi was elected to the ANC's NEC in position 58 after receiving 1 679 votes and in 2014, he was sworn in as an ANC MP. Despite the public outcry and negative publicity Mmemezi had received over these and other scandals, he made it onto the ANC's highest decision-making body at Mangaung.

Why? Because he was on the Zuma slate. And in Zuma's ANC, revelations like these no longer precluded you from occupying top positions in the party. The ANC had become scandal-resistant: after all, if the president could get away with murder, why couldn't the rest of them?

On 30 November 2011, two weeks before the Mangaung conference was due to start, the ANC's provincial secretary in North West, Kabelo Mataboge, survived an assassination attempt. Mataboge was a vocal supporter of the Forces of Change faction, which supported Motlanthe for president. He was opposed by the North West premier, Supra Mahumapelo, a staunch Zuma ally, who 'delivered' the province for Zuma. Mataboge was attacked outside his house in Mahikeng after attending an audit of branch members who would attend the provincial nomination conference. Unknown gunmen shot at him four times but missed.[4] During the nomination conference, Mataboge was locked in a room and suspended from the party. When he arrived in Mangaung, he was evicted from the conference venue. In the same week, a Bloemfontein house where North West delegates supporting Motlanthe were staying was raided by police searching for 'weapons and heavy weapons'.[5] They found none.

Adding to the pre-conference chaos, the Constitutional Court declared the election of the Free State ANC's provincial executive null and void. The court agreed with an application brought by ANC members that the election of provincial executives was irregular and unlawful. This meant that the 20 members of the Free State provincial executive committee – staunch Zuma supporters under the leadership of Premier Ace Magashule – weren't allowed to vote at the conference.

A few weeks before the conference, reports of ghost members, fraudulent branches and the abuse of government money to pay for ANC membership fees surfaced, particularly from Mpumalanga, the Free State and KwaZulu-Natal. Coincidentally, these were the three provinces that were solidly behind Zuma. Although ANC leaders, including Zuma, spoke out against vote rigging, the party never undertook a serious forensic investigation to establish who exactly re-elected Zuma and his slate in Mangaung.

Zuma's masterful understanding of ANC culture and sentiment was displayed during the opening session of the conference. If there was any chance for Motlanthe's supporters to disrupt the conference and publicly show their disapproval of Zuma, this was it. But, before speaking, Zuma delivered a rousing rendition of the struggle song '*Yinde Lendlela*', whose opening lyrics translate as 'It is a long road still ahead. Mandela told his followers we will meet on Freedom Day'.[6] At the time, Madiba was recovering in hospital after undergoing gallstone surgery. The delegates – almost 4 500 of them – passionately joined Zuma in song and quelled any possibility of a public display of dissidence.

Zuma's crippling charm is legendary; anecdotes of how he disarms his opponents with his warmth and empathy are plentiful. He has a beautiful voice and an incredible ability to connect with people at a personal level.

The Mangaung conference will be remembered for two major developments: the return of Ramaphosa to active ANC politics and the shifting of voting power to KwaZulu-Natal. Delegates from Zuma's home province (974 plus 20 provincial executives) represented 22% of voting delegates at the 2012 conference. Five years earlier, in Polokwane, the province had just 606 voting delegates, or 16% of the vote. According to the ANC constitution, the number of delegates allocated to provinces is decided by the NEC in proportion to the paid-up membership of each province. In a brilliant in-depth study of the ANC's membership numbers, Politicsweb editor James Myburgh tracked provincial membership numbers since the ANC's 1997 Mahikeng conference.[7] Myburgh observed that the Eastern Cape's share of ANC membership increased from 11,6% in 1997 to almost 25% ahead of the Polokwane conference under the presidency of Mbeki, who hails from the Eastern Cape. In 2012, the Eastern Cape was back on 15%, not because it had fewer paid-up members but because of a massive spike in the membership numbers in KwaZulu-Natal. Between 2007 and 2012, this number had tripled from 102 742 to 331 820 members, meaning that Zuma's home province now represented the biggest voting block at Mangaung.

To assess the fairness of the delegate allocations at Mangaung, Myburgh compared the voter composition with the provincial share of the ANC vote in the 2009 national elections and 2011 local-government elections. He concluded that KwaZulu-Natal was 'somewhat advantaged' in its delegate allocations, that the Eastern Cape was not unduly disadvantaged, but that Gauteng was 'severely prejudiced' due to its small party membership number. Gauteng ANC voters represented the biggest share of ANC votes in the 2009 and 2011 elections, but the party was allocated only 12% of provincial delegates in Mangaung. This was bad news for Motlanthe, who was born and bred in Alexandra, Johannesburg. Myburgh noted:

> In 2007 the three provinces where Zuma's support was strongest –
> KwaZulu-Natal, Mpumalanga and the Free State – accounted for
> 34.4% of all provincial nominations. Due to the disproportionate

growth of ANC membership in Mpumalanga and KwaZulu-Natal, these provinces now constitute 43.1% of the provincial delegate allocations. This means that as long as Zuma's support in these three provinces remains secure it will be difficult for the anti-Zuma camp to make up the numbers elsewhere.[8]

This remains true for the ANC's 2017 elective conference in Nasrec, Johannesburg, where Ramaphosa will attempt to dethrone Zuma's anointed candidate.

So why did Ramaphosa decide to leave his lavish life of buffalo farming behind and return to the coalface of dirty party politics? With Motlanthe out, Zuma desperately needed a running partner who connected with the growing black middle class in Gauteng and elsewhere, especially after angering thousands of people with his 'clever blacks' statements to the National House of Traditional Leaders. In November 2012 Zuma slated black people 'who become too clever' and were 'eloquent in criticising themselves about their own traditions and everything. ... Because if you are not an African,' Zuma said, 'you cannot be a white, then what are you? You don't know. You can't explain yourself. How then can you grow children?' the president asked.[9]

Ramaphosa represented the opposite: a successful black businessman who had created a multibillion-rand empire from investments in mining, food and telecommunication. Zuma and his allies knew they had Mangaung wrapped up, but were concerned about the long-term impact of losing middle-class support, particularly with a national election around the corner in 2014. So they lobbied Ramaphosa to return to headline ANC politics for the first time since 1997, when his term as ANC secretary general ended. Ramaphosa had always been a senior member of the party's NEC, serving on its disciplinary and finance committees. But he had withdrawn from public political life after failing to succeed Mandela as ANC president.

When the Zuma camp realised Motlanthe was serious about competing for the top job, they started lobbying Ramaphosa. Senior Zuma lieutenants were delegated to persuade him to join the slate, and he ultimately acquiesced. The KwaZulu-Natal ANC secretary, Sihle Zikalala, said in reaction to Ramaphosa's election: 'He will help the ANC connect and relate better with the business sector, intellectuals and younger voters, especially those born after the unbanning of the ANC in 1990.'[10]

Ramaphosa's return, however, left many, who viewed him as a constitutionalist and Zuma as compromised and corruptible, puzzled. The only explanation forthcoming from those in the know was that Cyril had always wanted to be president – and that is something he cannot buy. Even if he had to remain in Zuma's smelly slipstream for five years (until the next elective conference), he would do so.

For over four years, Ramaphosa remained quiet about his boss's misdemeanours. Then, on 31 March 2017, he spoke out against Zuma for the first time after the president controversially axed Pravin Gordhan, the finance minister. Ramaphosa responded by saying it was 'totally unacceptable that he [Zuma] fired someone like Gordhan, who has served the country excellently, for his own gain and survival'.[11] Five days later, the ANC announced that Ramaphosa and others who had spoken out publicly against Zuma's decision had to apologise.

Towards the end of April 2017, Ramaphosa unofficially launched his campaign for the ANC presidency. Without naming names, he warned ANC supporters that state capture under Zuma by the Guptas had the ability to 'destroy our revolution'.[12] Ramaphosa told supporters that the December 2017 conference was 'make or break, whether we have an ANC going forward that is united, or we have a shell of an ANC'.[13]

PART 2

President of scandals

CHAPTER 4

Pay back the money

—

'*Nkandla stands as a monument to corruption both in scale and in the hubris of power. Add to these the foolishness of its defence. That a chicken run, a swimming pool, amphitheatre, visitors' reception and cattle kraal could conceivably be security features is beyond the human imagination.*'

– Professor Paulus Zulu, University of KwaZulu-Natal, *The Mercury*, 7 April 2016.

When the late journalist Mandy Rossouw decided to visit Nkandla for a feature on the president's home town, she had no idea what she would uncover. It is not an exaggeration to say that Rossouw pushed over the first domino in a series of events that culminated in the Constitutional Court's ruling in 2016 that Zuma had broken his oath of office, substantially weakening his position in the ANC.

The Nkandla scandal, or 'Nkandlagate', as certain media outlets have referred to it, took our democracy to the brink. It tested the independence and strength of our institutions and revealed the stronghold Zuma's ANC had over Parliament, the executive and key state institutions.

Working for the *Mail & Guardian*'s politics desk, in November 2009 Rossouw wanted to gain first-hand knowledge of how Nkandla had changed following the inauguration of its own son, Jacob Zuma, as president of South Africa in May that year. She asked the publication's then digital editor, Chris Roper, who owned an off-road vehicle, to accompany her on a road trip to the village. Writing four years after their trip, Roper detailed their discovery in the *Mail & Guardian*:

> When we drove to the Nkandla residence to take some photos, we noticed there was some lacklustre building going on. Around 12 people were digging away and there was some heavy earth-moving machinery. Mandy's interest was piqued, and she inveigled our way into the site office. ... There was our first evidence of the extent of what Nkandla was destined to become, both as a large complex and as a massive story: architectural drawings taped to a wall, showing extensive development plans.[1]

Mandy's queries raised the ire of the Presidency and the Department of Public Works, who initially lied to her (saying they knew nothing about the development), then changed their tune, accusing the newspaper of attempting to embarrass Zuma and, finally, the Presidency issued a statement to all media before the *Mail & Guardian* went to print:

Construction work at President Zuma's residence

The Presidency has received enquiries from the media relating to construction work at President Jacob Zuma's Nkandla residence, with a mistaken belief that the construction work may be funded by government, or in particular the Department of Public Works.

The Zuma family planned before the elections to extend the Nkandla residence, and this is being done at their own cost. No government funding will be utilized for the construction work. This is a private matter which should be left to the family.

Outside the perimeter of the Zuma household, a few metres from the house, the State is to undertake construction work in line with the security and medical requirements relating to Heads of State in the Republic. The security services have to construct accommodation facilities for their staff that attend to the President, erect a helipad to ensure safe landing for the Presidential helicopter and a clinic as per medical requirements.

The security services have a responsibility to provide suitable care to the President, and to ensure that facilities are in place for that service. At the moment, security and medical staff are accommodated in the Zuma household. The new measures are designed to separate private from State facilities, family from staff, and to afford the Zuma family the privacy that they are entitled to.

The Presidency is fully aware of the need to separate public from private expenditure. The demarcation at Nkandla is very clear, and there can be no reason to confuse the private construction work in the Zuma household and the State facilities that will be constructed outside the perimeter.

We urge the media to leave the family alone to conduct its business, and reject any insinuation that there could be any untoward abuse of State resources by the President or his family.

3 December 2009[2]

Back in the *Mail & Guardian*'s offices in Rosebank, Mandy typed away: 'President Jacob Zuma is expanding his remote family homestead at Nkandla in rural KwaZulu-Natal for a whopping price of R65 million – and the taxpayer is footing the largest chunk of the bill.'[3]

The rest is history. We now know that the Presidency told a barefaced lie when it said that no government funding would be used for the construction work. Seven years later, Zuma himself accepted that the state had funded non-security upgrades to his private home to the tune of at least R7,8 million, which he agreed to pay back. The upgrades included the construction of the now infamous swimming pool, previously known as a 'firepool', at a cost of R2,3 million, a visitors' centre for R2 million, a cattle kraal for R1,3 million, an amphitheatre for R1 million and a chicken run for R250 000. Zuma finally agreed to pay back the money and obtained a R7,8 million loan from the unknown Limpopo-based VBS Mutual Bank, formerly the Venda Building Society.[4] It had been a long and painful road to get to this point, during which Zuma almost broke the country.

On a summer's day in March 2011, Department of Public Works regional manager Kenneth Khanyile arrived at his office in Durban, not knowing that the letter he would pen to his minister that day would rock the foundation of South African politics. On an official letterhead, with the subject 'Discussion of apportionment of costs between state and principal' for what was referred to as 'Prestige Project A', Khanyile informed the then minister, Gwen Mahlangu-Nkabinde, that the cost to the state for the Nkandla upgrades now stood at R203 million and that Zuma would have to pay an additional R10,6 million for non-security upgrades. In no uncertain terms, Khanyile clearly distinguished between security and non-security upgrades, and informed the minister that expenses had already been incurred for Zuma's private benefit. Khanyile listed developments totalling R3 million, including a 'fire pool and parking' and a 'social node', that fell outside the department's mandate. He asked for 'guidance' on 'the way forward' from Mahlangu-Nkabinde and the department's senior management. Earlier, Khanyile had asked his minister to discuss the matter with Zuma 'as the financial implication directly affects him'. Khanyile went further: 'He [Zuma] may want to implement these issues himself without the interference of the department or else he may want to opt to reimburse the department after we complete the same.'[5] Even at this early stage of the saga, there was no uncertainty in the mind of this top public-works official that Zuma had to pay back a portion of the money spent on Nkandla.

Eight months later, in November 2011, the spokesperson for public works told the *Mail & Guardian* that the budget for security upgrades at Zuma's homestead totalled R36 million. Zuma's spokesperson, Mac Maharaj, insisted the president was 'using his own money'.[6] It was clear that a massive cover-up was under way and that the real amount was being hidden from the public.

Another year went past before Khanyile's March 2011 letter was anonymously leaked to *City Press* by a whistle-blower. And on 23 September 2012, the second domino fell when that newspaper published the letter, revealing that the state would not pay R36 million or even R65 million for the upgrades to Zuma's private residence, and that the cost to improve his rural homestead had ballooned to over R200 million. The paper reported:

> The extensive and very hush-hush revamp of President Jacob Zuma's Nkandla homestead is set to cost taxpayers a whopping R203 million. *City Press* can reveal that the public works department approved the budget in March last year, despite earlier claims by the department that Zuma was funding the project from his own pocket. According to official departmental documentation, the president will only pay R10.6 million himself. This is less than 5% of the total cost to revamp his family compound in Nxamalala village.[7]

We now know that Zuma is paying back only about 3% of the final cost.

These revelations led to a public outcry that triggered several complaints to investigative bodies, including the Public Protector, the Auditor-General and the police. On 5 October 2012 then public works minister Thulas Nxesi announced the establishment of an interministerial task team to investigate the Nkandla expenditure. This was met with scepticism: how could the same minister whose department oversaw the project investigate the case? A few days earlier, after the *City Press* story broke, Nxesi issued a bizarre media statement in which he summarily declared that all the work at Nkandla was done in line with the ministerial handbook (which was not the case); that his department was 'not aware' of the amounts mentioned in *City Press* (although the newspaper had quoted from his department's documents); and called for an investigation into how *City Press* 'illegally ended up in the possession of' a top-secret document.

On 15 November 2012, Zuma responded to questions from the DA's Lindiwe Mazibuko and other MPs in Parliament. He was in combat mode, often becoming visibly emotional and angry while talking:

> Honourable Speaker, honourable member, let me make one thing quite clear from the outset. I have noted all sorts of public comments

to the effect that the government built my home in Nkandla. My residence in Nkandla has been paid for by the Zuma family … All the buildings and every room we use in that residence were built by ourselves as a family and not by government. I have never asked government to build a home for me, and it has not done so. The government has not built a home for me.[8]

The Public Protector later found that Zuma misled Parliament when he said this, because the state, through the Department of Public Works, had in fact paid for certain non-security upgrades that formed part of his home. But Madonsela found Zuma could have made a 'bona fide mistake' when he said this, thinking 'home' referred only to his family dwellings.

Zuma tried to separate the state's construction work from what he claimed his family paid for:

A necessary distinction must therefore be made between work which I have mandated and initiated in my home, as opposed to the security enhancement undertaken by government. … We, as the Zuma family, have built our home. … Let me give you the background. What, for example, has been shown on television – which has caused a lot of hullaballoo for many people – are my houses, built by me and my family. They have not been built by government.[9]

What Zuma failed to tell Parliament, however, was:

❑ The architect (Minenhle Makhanya) and builder (the aptly named Moneymine) who were contracted to build new dwellings for the Zuma family were also appointed by the Department of Public Works for the rest of the upgrades without a tender process.
❑ The so-called security enhancement included air conditioning of the president's houses, a swimming pool, a cattle kraal, a visitors' centre, an amphitheatre, a chicken run and a new private medical clinic for the Zuma family's use.
❑ Who had actually paid for the three new houses the Zuma family

built. When Zuma referred to a bond he was still servicing on the 'first phase of my home', he was talking about an earlier loan he had obtained to build rondavels at his property. The furthest Zuma would go was to say that the 'family' paid for the houses.

Zuma refused to hand Madonsela a copy of the bond documents he was referring to, leading her to an inconclusive finding about how the private part of the development was financed. 'I am not able to establish if costs relating to his private renovations were separated from those of the state in the light of using the same contractors around the same time and the evidence of one invoice that had conflated the costs although with no proof of payment,' Madonsela found, raising the possibility that the state may have cross-subsidised the private work through the same contractors.[10] This would constitute corruption.

Investigative journalists from amaBhungane raised the same question in June 2014, after the release of Madonsela's report:

> Neither the president nor any of his contractors has been willing to say how he paid for the 'private' work done at Nkandla, and the presidency again did not respond to questions about this. The president's lack of candour raises red flags, exacerbated by the obfuscation and evasion proffered by his lawyers and supporters. Ultimately, the evidence suggests, Zuma can only have paid for his private houses in two ways – either by cross-subsidisation or through a benefactor. Both are problematic.[11]

Since the scandal broke in 2009, Zuma has not taken South Africans into his confidence and openly declared how the private part of the development was funded. We know he couldn't fund it from his own pocket. Instead, he chose to play the victim – a card he plays so well. After being grilled in Parliament in November 2012 by opposition MPs, the president resorted to the tactic he knows best: 'I have been convicted, painted black, called the first-class corrupt man on facts that have not been tested. I take exception!' he said.

Despite vehemently denying that he was not aware of or responsible for the 'security' upgrades by the state, Zuma's version was challenged a week later when the *Mail & Guardian* and *City Press* published a letter from Mahlangu-Nkabinde to Zuma dated 5 November 2010, four days after she had replaced Geoff Doidge as Minister of Public Works. The letter updated the president in detail on the 'security' upgrades to his property. 'I have taken the view that it is prudent to update you on the progress of the above prestige project,' wrote Mahlangu-Nkabinde, adding that the 'fast-track nature of the project' necessitated daily updating of the project plan to meet a target date of 30 November 2010.[12] The minister attached a project plan and listed 17 outstanding areas, including the cattle culvert, sewage-treatment plant, the relocation of families whose houses had to be demolished for the project and a 'safe haven' and tunnel. Zuma could no longer use ignorance as a defence.

The obscene expenditure on Zuma's private property, which will not be available to future presidents to use, was only one part of the Nkandla scandal. The cover-up was the other.

For about three years, various ANC politicians loyal to Zuma defended the Nkandla expenditure against all reason and logic. Let's call them the sweat brigade: Thulas Nxesi, Jeff Radebe, Nkosinathi Nhleko, Mathole Motshekga, Nathi Mthethwa, Siyabonga Cwele and Cedric Frolick, to mention but a few cheerleaders who led the anti-Madonsela lobby against the former public protector's findings that Zuma was culpable and had to pay back the money. We call them this because frantic perspiration was often the order of the day when these gentlemen had to defend the indefensible in public or Parliament. Although they were exposed as naked emperors alongside Zuma in the Constitutional Court in 2016, they caused enormous damage to the Office of the Public Protector, an institution Madonsela had successfully shaped into a beacon of hope and trust for all South Africans during her tenure. Ironically a number of them were removed from their portfolios by Zuma after they had outlived their usefulness – or, as Malema would say, 'they were thrown out like used condoms'.

In October 2012, shortly after *City Press* had revealed the true cost of Nkandla, Nxesi and his erstwhile colleagues Cwele (state security) and Mthethwa (police) set up an inter-ministerial task team to investigate the upgrade. The task team was made up of employees from public works and state security, and focused on the scope and procurement of the project. In January 2013 Nxesi, together with Radebe (then justice minister), Cwele and Mthethwa announced that Zuma had done nothing wrong and that no state money had been used to fund upgrades to his private residence. They did not interview Zuma and their 'investigation' made no mention of Mahlangu-Nkabinde's letter to Zuma informing him of all the upgrades. Nor did they interrogate the president about who had paid for his houses or the possibility that his own builder and architect, who was appointed by public works without a tender process, could have been cross-subsidised by the state. 'President Zuma is not involved in this process whatsoever. ... He could be informed about the upgrades, but not about the details,' Nxesi said, thereby confirming their unwillingness to investigate their political overlord.[13]

The ministers did a sterling job of protecting Zuma and found a useful scapegoat in officials from his department. 'It's clear there were a number of irregularities with regards to appointment of service providers,' they said, confirming where the focus of their investigation would be.[14] Four year later, disciplinary hearings against a number of public-works officials were yet to get under way after numerous postponements.

It later turned out, thanks to Madonsela's probe, that officials like Khanyile and his colleagues from public works were under enormous pressure to deliver the Nkandla project in record time. All the normal procurement rules were broken; they reported directly to Pretoria on the project; and ministers and consecutive directors general personally issued instructions. There was no budget due to the urgency of the project and no tenders were issued. Zuma's personal architect, Makhanya, also became the principal agent for the state's project (without being vetted). Naturally, civil servants under such intense pressure to deliver for the president would take short cuts. To blame and go after them was an easy way out.

Nxesi and co. declined to release their full report because it was 'secret'. It was only 11 months later, in December 2013, that the task team's report was released after being declassified by Parliament's Joint Standing Committee on Intelligence. Nxesi told Parliament he was releasing the report after a decision by Cabinet that it should be made public. The timing was curious: also towards the end of 2013, Nxesi and his Cabinet colleagues were locked in a fierce battle with Madonsela about the release of her provisional report to the complainants. All indications were that her conclusions were different from those of the sweat brigade. Things got so messy that on 8 November 2013 Mthethwa, Nxesi, Nosiviwe Mapisa-Nqakula (defence) and Cwele applied to the North Gauteng High Court for an interdict to stop Madonsela from disseminating her provisional report.

Unsurprisingly, the ministers argued that the release of Madonsela's report would compromise Zuma's security and that they needed more time to respond in detail to her findings. This was after Madonsela had already given the ministers prior access to her provisional report for them to comment on. Madonsela filed an opposing affidavit in which she detailed how she and her officials were 'frustrated, and in many instances obstructed' in their efforts to investigate the Nkandla case. 'These include only being given sight of certain documents for short periods and in the presence of government officials and key members of the investigation team being excluded from important meetings.'[15] Madonsela also explained how pressure had been put on her by specifically Mthethwa, Nxesi and Cwele to drop the investigation pending the outcome of investigations by the Auditor-General and the Special Investigating Unit (SIU). She refused.

The interdict application was withdrawn by the ministers shortly before the case was due to be heard in court. 'The decision by the Ministers not to pursue the application is welcomed both in the interests of co-operative governance and in recognising the autonomy and independence of the Public Protector,' Madonsela said.[16]

During her term, Madonsela was at pains to emphasise the independence of the Public Protector's office from the state. So she pushed forward with her probe, even against brazen efforts by the executive to stymie her through the courts. Zuma did one last thing before Christmas 2013: he signed a proclamation for the SIU to investigate irregular expenditure and unlawful conduct by civil servants and companies in the Nkandla upgrade, following a recommendation by Nxesi's report that the matter be referred to the SIU. This suited Zuma well: the SIU did not have the powers to conduct criminal investigations and the proclamation was tightly worded to focus on the misdemeanours of public-works officials and contractors. Zuma could prepare for a relaxing Christmas in Nkandla.

Despite a barrage of insults, attempts to quash her investigation and general hostility from government officials and ANC politicians, Madonsela released her report on Nkandla, titled Secure in Comfort, to the public on 19 March 2014. She started her 447-page report with two significant quotes. The first was a comment from a senior public-works official to the acting director general in August 2010: 'Given the very humble beginnings of this project, nothing short of a full township establishment is now required ...' With this, Madonsela wanted to convey how the Nkandla project had ballooned extravagantly over years.

The second was a quote from a former US Supreme Court Justice, Louis Brandeis: 'Our government is the potent, the omnipresent teacher. For good or for ill, it teaches people by example. ... If the government becomes a law breaker, it breeds contempt for law; it invites every man to become a law unto himself ...' This was Madonsela's message to Zuma and every minister and civil servant who broke the rules to ensure the president and his family were 'secure in comfort'.

In her calm, Zen-like way, Madonsela painstakingly read out her main findings and recommendations:[17]

❏ Zuma benefited unduly from the upgrades to his Nkandla homestead and should repay a reasonable portion of the costs to the state.

- ❏ Zuma contravened the Constitution and the Executive Ethics Code by not taking reasonable steps to stop the irregular expenditure at his private residence.
- ❏ The initial cost was R27 million but escalated exponentially when Zuma's private architect was appointed as principal agent by the state.
- ❏ The visitors' centre, amphitheatre, swimming pool, cattle kraal, chicken run and extensive paving were not security upgrades and their cost had to be repaid.
- ❏ There was no previous precedent of former heads of state receiving similar benefits. Former president Nelson Mandela paid for his own kraal and didn't require a 'fire pool'.
- ❏ No tender processes were followed, contrary to Treasury regulations.
- ❏ There was massive 'scope creep', meaning 'runaway' costs occurred due to a lack of oversight, leading to a 'license to loot'.

It was a damning report and the extreme antithesis of Nxesi and his fellow ministers' attempts to clear Zuma, themselves and their colleagues. On the evening it was published, government's fightback plan to protect Zuma and undermine Madonsela's report kicked into action when Radebe addressed a press conference to rubbish her findings. 'The private house of the president was built by the president and his family. The retaining wall, cattle kraal and culvert, fire pool and water reservoir, accommodation for security personnel and visitors' waiting area are all essential security features which ensure physical security and effective operation of security equipment,' Radebe insisted, directly contradicting the Public Protector's findings and clearly signalling government's intent to subvert the authority of her office. He also repeated the falsehood that Zuma was paying a bond on his new houses.

A few days later, on 1 April 2014, Zuma wrote to the speaker, Max Sisulu, saying that there were 'stark differences both in respect of the findings as well as the remedial action proposed in the two reports [by

Madonsela and the ministers]. This much is clear from the reports as well as very public pronouncements made by the respective parties. In my experience in government I have not encountered such an anomaly.'[18] Zuma then shifted the goalposts again. He would wait for the SIU to finalise its final report on expenditure at Nkandla before he provided Parliament with a 'further final report on the decisive executive interventions which I consider would be appropriate'. This was an extraordinary letter by Zuma, in which he elevated himself to the position of judge over various government reports on a matter that implicated himself, his family and their private property. In one fell swoop, Zuma effectively gave the three reports equal weight, notwithstanding the fact that the Public Protector was an independent entity created by the Constitution whose sole purpose was to protect the public from state abuse. And he told Sisulu he would be king on the matter.

On 14 August 2014, 148 days after Madonsela had asked Zuma to respond to her report (he had been given 14 days by her to do so), Zuma submitted a 20-page report to Parliament, reflecting on the 'concerns expressed by government and certain sectors of society concerning the procurement, management and expenditure of the security upgrades at the private presidential residence at Nkandla'.[19] Zuma told Parliament he took 'exception to the continued conflation of the security upgrades with the construction of buildings for the benefit of security personnel. Whilst neither were at my behest, the latter is directly attributable to the fact of my residence being located in a rural area with all the attendant challenges.' Zuma proceeded to summarise each of the reports before him – Nxesi's, Madonsela's and the SIU report – and concluded that his newly appointed police minister, Nhleko, had to decide whether he was liable for any contribution to the Nkandla costs, 'having regard to the legislation, past practices, culture and findings contained in the respective reports'.

With this, Zuma completely undermined Madonsela's authority and effectively asked a member of his executive – Nhleko – to establish whether he was liable for a portion of the Nkandla costs. This angered opposition parties and set in motion the EFF's 'Pay back the money'

49

campaign against Zuma, which saw the party's MPs being violently ejected from Parliament every time they interjected, asking Zuma when he would repay the Nkandla costs. 'Pay back the money' became more than just a political slogan: it captured the frustration of South African citizens with the Zuma administration's disregard for good governance and unwillingness to stop the tide of corruption engulfing the state. Madonsela wrote to Zuma, warning him that his failure to comply with her report could lead to impunity at various levels of state. Zuma wrote back, saying Madonsela was not a judge.

In September 2014, the SIU tabled its final report on Nkandla in Parliament. The report accepted that the Zuma family had benefited from the upgrades, but didn't make any adverse findings against the president. Instead, the unit (whose primary goal is to recover money for the state through civil litigation) fingered the president's architect for wasting R155 million in excessive expenditure. The SIU found that Makhanya should be held liable for wasting millions of rands on unnecessary and excessive upgrades at Nkandla. The unit ruled that his appointment was invalid and that he didn't have the necessary security clearance for the job, but didn't interrogate Zuma's role in recommending his architect and builder to become the principal contractors for the state. The SIU also failed to determine whether Zuma's houses were counter-subsidised by the state through Makhanya and Moneymine; neither did they interview Zuma about this.

Parliament appointed an ad hoc committee, chaired by ANC MP Frolick, to consider Zuma's response to the different reports, but opposition parties soon withdrew from the inquiry when they couldn't agree on the process to be followed. Therefore, a committee composed solely of ANC MPs ended up clearing Zuma of any wrongdoing and criticising Madonsela. They slammed her for making findings about security when she wasn't a security expert and said only the Constitutional Court had the authority to decide whether Zuma had contravened sections of the Constitution. It was clear that ANC MPs were more interested in protecting Zuma from any scrutiny than holding him and the executive to account.

In December 2014, the director of projects for the Department of

Public Works, Itumeleng Molosi, became the first Nkandla fall guy when he pleaded guilty to irregularly appointing contractors and flouting procurement procedures.[20] Molosi received a two-month suspension without pay and a final written warning.

One of the lowest points of the Nkandla scandal (and Zuma's presidency) was when the police minister, Nhleko, presented to Parliament the findings of his investigation into whether Zuma should pay back the money. For three hours, he huffed and puffed his way through his report as he defended the existence of every feature of Zuma's estate that had been identified by Madonsela as non-security upgrades. Nhleko sweated buckets as he explained that the swimming pool at Nkandla was really a fire pool for firefighting and thus a security feature; that the cattle kraal and chicken run kept livestock away from security features and thus enhanced security at the compound; that the amphitheatre served as an assembly point for briefings and debriefings; and that the visitors' centre had to cater for Zuma's guests and meetings, and because privacy and confidentiality were necessary, this, too, constituted a security feature. Nhleko's presentation was interrupted by videos to the soundtrack of Luciano Pavarotti singing 'O sole mio', showing how water from the swimming pool could be used to extinguish fires at the complex. It was desperately bizarre. And as if Nhleko hadn't enraged the nation enough by then, he portrayed Zuma as the real victim of the upgrades, saying his privacy was grossly infringed upon. He also announced that further upgrades were still needed to fully safeguard Nkandla.

On 18 August 2015 Parliament adopted the report by its ad hoc committee, which had considered Nhleko's report. The report exonerated Zuma from paying anything. During the committee's deliberations, then ANC chief whip Mathole Motshekga proclaimed that Madonsela had misled South Africa about Nkandla. 'We should not, and cannot, apologise when we say the report of the public protector is misleading and has misled the nation,' he said.[21] ANC MP Mmamoloko Kubayi, who was appointed by Zuma as energy minister in 2017, said: 'The fundamental issues in the public protector's report were incoherent with what we have seen. We can come to the conclusion that the report was not sound.' With the adoption of the report by Parliament, the ANC thought they had buried Nkandla. But, then, the EFF, members of which had been beaten up by security officers inside Parliament for insisting Zuma tell the nation when he intended to pay back the money, filed a direct application to the Constitutional Court for Zuma to do just that.

The EFF relied on Section 167(4)(e) of the Constitution: that the Constitutional Court may decide that Parliament or the president has failed to fulfil a constitutional obligation. That obligation, the party argued, was to give effect to Madonsela's findings that he should pay back (a portion of) the money. In a surprise to many legal eagles, the court granted the EFF access. The DA was subsequently also admitted as an applicant and Madonsela as co-respondent with Zuma and Speaker Baleka Mbete. Then something extraordinary happened.

A week before the matter was scheduled before the Constitutional Court, Zuma capitulated. The State Attorney, on his behalf, sent a letter to the lawyers of the EFF, Madonsela and the DA, suggesting that the Auditor-General be appointed, assisted by the Treasury, to determine what Zuma should pay back for the non-security-related upgrades.[22] This was a massive turnabout for Zuma, who had been fighting tooth and nail for at least four years to avoid liability for the Nkandla upgrades. After all the sweat and tears that had been shed by Zuma's most loyal backers, the president threw them under the bus and agreed to pay. 'They are pissed off – all of them, including members who were in that Nkandla committee. People are feeling used and abused,' a senior ANC member told *City Press*.[23]

On 9 February 2016, seasoned senior advocate Jeremy Gauntlett, on behalf of Zuma, told the Constitutional Court that his client wanted to bring an end to a 'protracted and difficult issue which has traumatised the nation'. Zuma now accepted that he must carry out the remedial action of the Public Protector and that Madonsela's findings were binding. Zuma followed wrong legal advice, his advocate argued. 'This is a delicate time in a dangerous year,' Gauntlett said, asking the court not to make a 'wide, condemnatory order' against Zuma that could be used to impeach the president in Parliament.[24] Gauntlett also told the court to place no reliance on the reports by Nhleko and the ad hoc committee, and that the upgrades were a 'rip-off operation'. Interestingly, Gauntlett, who had previously represented Zuma's former financial advisor Schabir Shaik during his appeal hearing, was spotted at an ANC NEC meeting the weekend before the Nkandla case.

Wim Trengove SC, on behalf of the EFF, had less sympathy for Zuma. He argued that the president had violated his ethical duty by 'firstly benefiting improperly and secondly by defying the Public Protector … in order to protect his ill-gotten gains'.[25] Parliament had failed by not holding Zuma and his Cabinet to account, Trengove argued. The DA's legal representative, Anton Katz SC, said the case went deeper than the Public Protector's powers. 'It goes to the failure by government to hold to account that which is ultimately a homestead for one family.'

On 31 March 2016, Chief Justice Mogoeng Mogoeng read out the unanimous judgment of the Constitutional Court:

> One of the crucial elements of our constitutional vision is to make a decisive break from the unchecked abuse of State power and resources that was virtually institutionalised during the apartheid era. To achieve this goal, we adopted accountability, the rule of law and the supremacy of the Constitution as values of our constitutional democracy. For this reason, public office-bearers ignore their constitutional obligations at their peril. This is so because constitutionalism, accountability and the rule of law constitute the sharp and mighty sword that stands ready to chop the ugly head of impunity off its stiffened neck.[26]

You could hear a pin drop in the impressive court building in Braamfontein, as Mogoeng berated Zuma over his failure to uphold the Constitution and scolded Parliament for failing to hold Zuma and his executive to account. Mogoeng, on behalf of the court, further ruled:

❏ Zuma had to be alive to the reality that government functionaries may have been inclined to do more than is reasonably required to please higher authority.

❏ Madonsela was the 'embodiment of a biblical David, that the public is, who fights the most powerful and very well-resourced Goliath, that impropriety and corruption by government officials are. The Public Protector is one of the true crusaders and champions of anti-corruption and clean governance.'

❏ The end results of the two streams of investigative processes were 'mutually destructive'. Zuma should have decided whether to comply with Madonsela's report or not. If not, he should have done much more than merely be 'content' with Nhleko's report; he should have approached the court to set aside Madonsela's.

❏ Zuma failed to uphold, defend and respect the Constitution as the supreme law of the land. 'This failure is manifest from the substantial disregard for the remedial action taken against him by the Public Protector in terms of her constitutional powers. ... He was duty-bound to, but did not, assist and protect the Public Protector so as to ensure her independence, impartiality, dignity and effectiveness by complying with her remedial action. He might have been following wrong legal advice and therefore acting in good faith. But that does not detract from the illegality of his conduct.'

❏ The National Assembly flouted its obligations. Neither the National Assembly nor Zuma could have treated Madonsela's report as if it had been set aside. 'The ineluctable conclusion is, therefore, that the National Assembly's resolution based on the minister's (Nhleko's) findings exonerating the president from liability is inconsistent with the Constitution and unlawful.'

The next day, on 1 April 2016, Zuma apologised to the nation for the 'frustration and confusion' caused by the Nkandla matter. 'The judgment has helped me and my colleagues to reflect deeply on the entire matter,' he said. 'With hindsight, there are many matters that could have been handled differently and which should never have been allowed to drag on this long, which we deeply regret. The matter has caused a lot of frustration and confusion, for which I apologise on my behalf and on behalf of government.' He said he would abide by the matter and had never refused to pay an amount towards the non-security upgrades. He never 'knowingly or deliberately' set out to violate the Constitution, Zuma said. He did what he did because of a 'different approach and different legal advice'.

Zuma didn't elaborate on this 'different approach' and didn't fire his legal advisor, Michael Hulley. He didn't apologise to Madonsela and her colleagues for defying and undermining her and her office for years. He didn't apologise to Molosi and other public-works officials for causing them to transgress by rushing through the project without a tender process. He didn't apologise to Parliament for misleading them about his family benefiting from the upgrades. He didn't apologise to his comrades in the ANC, who had lied and made up stories for him. And he didn't apologise to South Africans, who would have benefited from the Inner City Regeneration project, the Dolomite Risk Management programme and an effective Border Control Agency, from which funding was taken away to pay for a cattle kraal, air conditioning, a chicken run and underground bunkers at Nkandla.

Because of our broken criminal-justice system, we will probably never know the true extent of the skulduggery that lay behind the millions of rands wasted at Nkandla. But, despite the brokenness of the Zuma administration and the hangers-on it exposed, the scandal also showcased the power of a resilient and functioning media, and constitutional institutions, opposition and judiciary. When the first layer of checks and balances failed, journalists, like Mandy Rossouw, constitutional servants, like Thuli Madonsela, politicians, like Julius Malema and judges, like Mogoeng Mogoeng, stepped in to correct the wrong. This proved that our democracy was functioning, that we were nowhere close to being a failed state.

CHAPTER 5

Meet the Guptas

—

'This is not the place where you will find A-list celebrities.
Here you find those who pull their strings.'
– Journalist Mandy Rossouw after attending the launch of *The New Age* newspaper,
Mail & Guardian, 23 July 2010

In another life, books would have been written about the busi-ness successes and life story of Atul Kumar Gupta, born in 1969 in Saharanpur, India. Moving to South Africa in 1993 at the age of 23, Atul started making a living selling shoes from the back of his car at Bruma Lake flea market in Johannesburg. Five years later he was running a R100-million-a-year business called Sahara Computers, selling locally assembled computers to businesses and state entities.

But there is a reason why books by Gupta competing with aspirational business titles like *How to Get Rich*, *Rich Dad, Poor Dad* or *Screw it, Let's Do it* won't be appearing next to those by Donald Trump, Robert Kiyosaki or Richard Branson any time soon. And it has nothing to do with the Guptas' Indian origin, as was claimed by Wiseman Ntombela, secretary general of the uMkhonto we Sizwe Military Veterans' Association (MKMVA), in June 2017, when he said South Africans had an issue with the Guptas because they are from India.[1] No, the reason the Guptas' business successes won't be readily celebrated in printed form in South Africa is that the market for books titled *How to Capture a President* just isn't that big locally (it may be in America, but that is a story for a different book). Put differently, the Guptas' business model of buying South Africa's first family for the benefit of their personal empire was just never going to fly in a young, teething and at the best of times fragile democracy that is still recovering from 46 years of corrupt and racist apartheid rule. We've been the skunk of the world before; we don't want to go there again. In South Africa we have a Constitution and the rule of law reigns supreme. And these are obstacles in the way for Atul Gupta and his family to consummate their 'silent coup' of the country.

Despite Atul Gupta's humble beginnings, the family's business turned into a multibillion-rand empire after they started expanding outside of IT into other industries, particularly those that involved state-owned enterprises (SOEs), such as Transnet and Eskom, in the value chain. In 1997 Atul's younger brother, Rajesh 'Tony' Gupta, had joined him in South Africa and in 2003 the eldest brother, Ajay, also moved here from India. News24 investigative journalist Pieter-Louis Myburgh's book *The Republic of Gupta* provides an insider account of how the Indian brothers worked their way into the country's political elite circles – first by cosying up to Mbeki and his confidant, Essop Pahad, shortly after the ANC had taken over control of the government in 1994, then more aggressively to Zuma and his family as it became clear that Zuma would win the day at Polokwane in 2007.[2] Pahad told Myburgh that Ajay Gupta had served on a secret 'consultative council', convened by Pahad, to provide Mbeki with political advice. After the publication of Myburgh's book, Mbeki took umbrage at the suggestion that he was 'close' to the Guptas and denied the existence of a consultative council.[3] He referred to an informal focus group that provided him with political updates, but denied that Ajay Gupta served on this body. There was never any suggestion that Mbeki or his family had benefited from his relationship with the Guptas. With the Zumas, it was a whole different kettle of fish.

It takes two to tango, as the saying goes, and the Guptas needed a willing partner to perfect their decade-long state-capture dance. Despite having worked behind the scenes to establish a network of business and political connections, the Guptas and their businesses were still relatively obscure to most South Africans by 2010. And yet, unbeknown to the public, they had by then already co-opted Duduzane Zuma, one of Zuma's five children with his third wife, Kate Mantsho, into their business empire. In July 2008, less than seven months after his father had been elected ANC president, Duduzane's investment vehicle, Mabengela Investments, was registered, with him and Tony Gupta as directors. Duduzane paid R45 for his shares, which would be worth millions a few years later. Duduzane's sister, Duduzile, was also appointed as a director of Sahara Computers for 15 months.

Over the next two years, Duduzane was appointed as a director in 11 more Gupta companies, including Westdawn Investments, Islandsite Investments 255 and Shiva Uranium.[4] Through Mabengela and Islandsite, the young Zuma became a beneficiary of the Guptas' mining, media, labour-brokering and steel companies. He's become extremely wealthy through the Guptas, who took him in as an IT intern in about 2001 when, according to his father, he couldn't find a job. 'I was introduced to the Gupta family by my father in late 2001, just like I met many people,' Duduzane told *City Press* in 2011.[5] 'At that time, my father said, I've got an interest in taking an IT direction in my life, and at that point they were doing the Sahara thing. It just made sense. Part of my first work experience was at Sahara, I didn't come onto the books recently. They showed me the ropes.'

Duduzane must have been the most useful intern hire of all time because, through him, the Guptas gained direct access to the president. Evidence, including thousands of leaked emails sent from the Gupta empire to the media in mid-2017 (the #GuptaLeaks), shows how the young Zuma became increasingly involved in state matters, including the appointment of Cabinet ministers and applying for residency for his family in Dubai. Various business matters that involved the state or required government intervention were forwarded to Duduzane. The Gupta machine absorbed him – he was their ticket to ride. And, in exchange, they made him very, very rich. The young Zuma scored an R18 million luxury apartment in Dubai's Burj Khalifa; they paid for his five-star wedding at Zimbali Lodge in KwaZulu-Natal; they paid for first-class travel for him and his wife. They had direct access to his most intimate communication with former girlfriends and groupies; and former Oakbay CEO Nazeem Howa even wrote a letter to the *Sunday Times* in Duduzane's name. Zuma's son had been thoroughly captured by the Guptas.[6]

If Jacob Zuma learnt one thing from the corruption and fraud trial of Schabir Shaik, it was that he shouldn't receive financial remittances directly into his own bank account. Shaik was convicted and jailed in 2005 for bribing Zuma to protect and promote his companies, and for facilitating a bribe for Zuma from French weapons company Thales. In exchange, Shaik financed Zuma's lifestyle through a myriad of payments made directly to Zuma's bank account. With the Guptas, Zuma probably didn't receive deposits directly into his own bank accounts (we won't know until a proper forensic investigation has been done), because he didn't have to. His favourite son was now part and parcel of the Gupta empire and became the proxy for the *pater familias* and the family. If Duduzane was Jacob Zuma's investment in the Gupta empire, the president has scored a huge return on that investment through dividends that will sustain the Zumas for many years to come. 'We know that the president's son is just that by name only. His real parents are the Guptas,' *City Press* editor Mondli Makhanya wrote in the wake of the leaked Gupta emails.[7]

There is no clear consensus on a date or event that brought the Guptas and the Zumas together, but there are some clues. In his book, Myburgh interviews a former Gupta business partner, who claims Atul Gupta had told him back in 1998 about the rising star in the ANC: Jacob Zuma. 'It is actually crazy how frank he was about this, but he bragged about having an ANC guy in his pocket. Atul said that when this guy eventually becomes president, their ship was going to come in big time.' Prophetic words indeed. 'Would the Guptas be as wealthy as they are without Zuma?' asks the business partner. 'Not at all. They targeted him right from the start, and they chose to go into that type of business path way back then.'[8]

With Duduzane employed as an intern at Sahara in 2001, thanks to his father, the business relationship was established when Zuma was deputy president of the country. From 2002 until 2007 the focus was very much on Zuma's corrupt relationship with Shaik and the arms-deal bribe. While that trial had the limelight, the Gupta name never surfaced. What did become clear, however, was that Zuma did not have just one benefactor. KwaZulu-Natal property and resources mogul Vivian Reddy, Mpumalanga businesswoman Nora Fakude-Nkuna and Namibian-born stockbroker Jurgen Kögl all made payments to and on behalf of Zuma. After he was fired as deputy president, businesswoman turned ANC MP Sizani Dubazana bought Zuma a house in Forest Town, Johannesburg. And in 2014, shortly after Zuma attended the birthday party of Durban security tycoon Roy Moodley, Julius Malema claimed that Moodley had bankrolled Zuma after he was fired as deputy president in 2005. Zuma's eldest son, Edward, was driving one of Moodley's luxury vehicles.[9]

Above all, the Shaik trial showed that Zuma needed additional cash to fund his lifestyle, including a family of four wives and at least 22 known children. Essentially, he was a politician for sale. If indeed Atul Gupta was already betting back in 1998 on Zuma becoming president, the co-option of Duduzane into their empire was a masterstroke. While the rest of the country was fixated on Shaik's chicanery, the Guptas were setting up a much larger looting scheme in the background. At the same time, they remained close to the Mbeki administration and appointed Pahad onto the board of Sahara after he resigned from the Cabinet in 2008 in the wake of Mbeki's recalling by the ANC.

It was only in 2010, however, that the South African media began to take proper notice of the Guptas. The *Mail & Guardian* published a series titled 'Zuma Inc.' in March that year, which referred to the Guptas as part of the Zuma family's large business network. The newspaper noted Duduzane and Duduzile's directorships in Gupta companies, and the fact that President Zuma acknowledged Atul Gupta during his closing speech at the Indian Premier League Twenty20 series, which was hosted that year in South Africa.[10]

In June 2010 the *Mail & Guardian* reported on the 'growing concern' in the ANC about Zuma's relationship with the Guptas after his state visit to India in May that year, where Zuma was seen 'spending a disproportionate amount of time on meetings with the Guptas'.[11] The newspaper's sources said it was clear that meetings and deals had been set up beforehand. Interestingly, Indian officials questioned South African delegates about Zuma's relationship with the Guptas. The family was not well known in India and didn't have a great reputation there.[12] The newspaper's sources said that the family wanted to leverage their South African status to gain business in India. Only the Guptas and their then business partner Lazarus Zim were given full access to the president.

Three years later, insurance entrepreneur Kalim Rajab wrote in the *Daily Maverick* about a banquet during the same state visit to India: 'In a public forum, the president made clear his love for samoosas, the strong bond the two countries shared ... and, not so subtly, that for the multitude of heavyweight Indian titans in the room who were thinking of investing in South Africa, the suitable way of channelling it would be through the Gupta family.'[13] Top Indian industrialists left in disgust, Rajab wrote. Few of them had heard of the Guptas, and now Zuma was telling them to go through the Guptas if they wanted to invest in South Africa:

> Before arriving in South Africa, they had been a middleweight family in the power stakes on the subcontinent. Those in the know used to scoff at them for having embellished their credentials through a clever sleight of hand, by naming their companies outside India 'Sahara' – thereby trading off the powerful (and unconnected) brand name of the famous billionaire Subrata Roy's Sahara Group. Rumours, never proven (but then few such things ever are in Indian courts) swirled around of them providing money-laundering facilities in Dubai. Good stuff, as far as dodginess goes, but relatively small potatoes in India's high-octane world of corruption. Yet now, it seemed, they were about to be seriously made. Having the direct imprimatur of a President of a G-20 country was an impressive – and lucrative – thing indeed.[14]

In July 2010 the Guptas launched their own daily newspaper, *The New Age*, named after an anti-apartheid leftist publication that had been shut down in 1962. The launch was a glitzy affair, with all the Gupta brothers, Duduzane (a shareholder in the paper), Pahad and even a former Miss South Africa, Claudia Henkel, who would become the paper's lifestyle editor, in attendance. Scantily clad models walked around holding up pages from the paper. Atul Gupta said the paper would focus on good news, 'seeing the glass half full and not just half empty'.[15]

The paper, together with the Guptas' ANN7 news channel, which was launched on DStv in August 2013, would become the official mouthpiece of the Guptas, taking an unashamedly pro-Zuma stance in its selection of editorial content. It had reporters in all nine provinces, but the content was often a rewrite of government press releases or poorly penned stories. In 2015 the DA asked former communications minister Faith Muthambi about government's advertising spend in the news media and found it was disproportionately skewed in favour of *The New Age*. Between 2013 and 2014, the Guptas' newspaper, with a readership of merely 153 000, received R10,2 million in government advertising, compared to the R7,9 million received by the *Daily Sun*, which has a readership of 5,3 million. The only newspaper that received more advertising money than *The New Age* was the *Sowetan*, which has a substantially higher readership of 1,7 million. But this was small change compared with the money the Guptas made from their *The New Age* business breakfasts – to which we will come back later.

In March 2016 the former head of the Government Communication and Information System (GCIS), Themba Maseko, spilled the beans on how Zuma had pressurised him to help with the Guptas' advertising accounts. When Maseko refused, he was sacked. Before the launch of *The New Age*, Maseko told Sunday newspapers, he had received 'numerous requests' from the Guptas for a meeting at their Saxonwold mansion. When he finally agreed, he received a call from Zuma before the meeting: 'As I [was] driving out of the GCIS building [in Pretoria], I got a call from a PA from Mahlamba Ndlopfu [Zuma's official residence in Pretoria], saying: "*Ubaba ufuna ukukhuluma nawe*" [the president wants to talk to you],' Maseko told the *Sunday Times*. (He repeated this evidence to Madonsela during her State of Capture investigation.) Zuma came on the line. 'He greeted me [and] said: "*Kuna labafana bakwaGupta badinga uncedo lwakho. Ngicela ubancede.*" [The Gupta brothers need your help. Please help them].'[16] During the meeting with the Guptas, Ajay allegedly told Maseko they wanted him to channel government advertising money to *The New Age*. 'Tell us where the money is and tell departments to give you money; if they refuse we will deal with them. If you have a problem with any department, we will summon ministers here,' the oldest Gupta brother is alleged to have told Maseko.[17] The Guptas have denied this claim. Maseko refused to give the Guptas preferential treatment and when he was summoned to a meeting at the offices of *The New Age*, he declined to attend. This was followed up with a phone call from Ajay Gupta, who told Maseko, 'I will talk to your seniors in government and you will be sorted out.'[18] In January 2011 Maseko was called to a meeting by the late former minister in the Presidency, Collins Chabane. 'He advised me that he had been instructed by the president to redeploy me or terminate my contract,' Maseko said.[19] Shortly thereafter, Maseko was redeployed to the Department of Public Service and Administration. Zuma's spokesperson responded by saying the president had 'no knowledge' of Maseko's claims.[20]

In 2016 ANN7 fired 13 journalists for their refusal to participate in the company's 'fightback' against the closure of the Gupta businesses' bank accounts by all South Africa's major banks. The journalists objected to being named as parties in a company letter to the banks and resisted being addressed by ANCYL president Collen Maine, a known Gupta ally, over the matter.[21] The Guptas, through their attorney, Abdul Jaffer, who had often acted for the family in property transactions, were linked to Maine's purchase of a R5,4 million house in the luxury Woodhill Golf Estate in Pretoria in 2015.[22]

In September 2010 Atul Gupta was arrested after allegedly refusing to be searched by policemen who had stopped his bodyguard-driven car.

It was reported that Duduzane Zuma went to the police station after Gupta's arrest.[23] A few days later, the case was withdrawn by the NPA. The policemen claimed that Gupta had threatened to have them fired because he knew 'all the top commissioners'. Gupta denied resisting being searched and threatening the cops. Showing off his political contacts, however, he told reporters outside the Randburg Magistrate's Court that he would contact the then police chief, Bheki Cele, to complain.

On 27 February 2011, the *Sunday Times* reported that an internal 'revolt' was brewing inside the ANC against the Gupta family's influence over Zuma and his government. The ANC's top brass had raised concerns about the Guptas' role in the appointment of CEOs and chairs of SOEs (Brian Molefe's appointment at Transnet was specifically mentioned), about how the Gupta family had called ministers and deputy ministers to inform them of their appointments before Zuma, and the pressure put on government officials to advertise in *The New Age*.[24]

On the same day, Malema (at the time president of the ANCYL) set the cat among the pigeons during a speech at the launch of the ANC's local-government elections manifesto at the Royal Bafokeng Stadium in Rustenburg. Without naming individuals, and as Zuma sat right behind him on stage, Malema said: 'When families are exploiting the resources of this country and are enriching themselves in the name of freedom, when those in political office abuse their power to benefit friends, the youth must rise in defence of the ANC.'[25] Malema went on to say that South Africa was 'not a democracy of families; this is a democracy of the people of the country'. One of Zuma's most vocal backers in the ANC, MKMVA chairperson Kebby Maphatsoe (who was appointed Deputy Minister of Defence and Military Veterans by Zuma in 2014) criticised Malema a few days later for his 'populist outburst' against Zuma, saying they had met with the Guptas for five hours and were satisfied 'that there was nothing wrong with what they had done'.[26] Six years later, the Gupta leaks would reveal that the Gupta family's British spin doctors, Bell Pottinger, wrote press statements for the MKMVA defending the Guptas and their companies.

Between 2011 and 2012, all three of South Africa's top spy bosses mysteriously resigned. Jeff Maqetuka, director general of the State Security Agency (SSA), and his deputies, Moe Shaik (foreign intelligence) and Gibson Njenje (domestic intelligence), all left the intelligence services in a couple of months. It was speculated at the time that they had had a fallout with their political head, then state security minister Siyabonga Cwele, over the abuse of intelligence resources to protect Cwele's former wife, Sheryl, during her drug-trafficking case. It was also rumoured at the time that they were asked by Cwele to spy on ANC politicians and were uncomfortable with the request. But the real reason for their departure would only emerge later: their investigation of the Guptas.

City Press reported on 18 September 2011 that the domestic branch of the SSA, formerly known as the National Intelligence Agency, had placed the Guptas under high-level surveillance:

> *City Press* has learnt from a highly placed intelligence source that Njenje ordered that the Gupta family, which is closely linked to President Jacob Zuma and his family, be investigated for, among other things, alleged influence on top government officials and politicians. Cwele ordered Njenje to stop the investigation. This, according to the source, fuelled the bad relationship between Cwele and Njenje, which ultimately resulted in the minister asking him to leave.[27]

This explanation for their exodus was confirmed six years later with the publication of Myburgh's *The Republic of Gupta*. Myburgh interviewed former spies, who confirmed that the SSA had started looking into the Guptas back in 2009 after receiving queries from the US Central Intelligence Agency (CIA) and Britain's MI6 about the family's purchase of the Dominion uranium mine. The foreign agents apparently feared that the Guptas might sell uranium to a country like Pakistan and asked the SSA to keep an eye on them. The Guptas were already on the SSA's radar, but a formal investigation into them was then registered. The SSA investigated their links to government officials and politicians, and their influence over Zuma. 'It is like they built a wall around the president. They controlled who had access to him,' a source of Myburgh's told him. After Zuma heard about the SSA's probe into his friends, all hell broke loose. Cwele summoned the three spy bosses to Cape Town and told them to drop the investigation. 'Both sources I spoke to said it was very clear to them that Cwele was under tremendous pressure to halt the investigation, and that such pressure had to have emanated from Zuma's office,' wrote Myburgh.[28]

Eventually, all three resigned and, in 2014, after the national election, Zuma moved Cwele to the much less glamorous telecommunications and postal services portfolio, and replaced him with a young party hard-liner from Mpumalanga, David Mahlobo. This episode illustrates the high level at which the Guptas were protected from any form of state censure. You had to be kind of a big deal to get the country's three spy bosses fired.

But the one scandal that gripped the imagination of the entire country and catapulted the Guptas onto the front pages of the yellowest of tabloids and into the headlines of every TV and radio bulletin was 'Guptagate' – the landing of Jet Airways flight JAI 9900 at the Waterkloof Air Force Base in Pretoria on 30 April 2013. It was a grotesque display of state capture: a private, commercial aircraft carrying more than 200 guests to a private wedding landing at an air force base. The flight was chartered by the Guptas for the wedding of Vega Gupta, the 23-year-old niece of the three Gupta brothers, and Aakash Jahajgarhia. Vega is the daughter of Achla Gupta, the brothers' sister.

After landing at Waterkloof, the Indian guests were transferred to Sun City's Palace of the Lost City by aircraft, helicopter and police-escorted vehicles for an extravaganza that lasted for days and featured Indian chefs flown in specially for the event, neon lights, fake elephants and thousands of flowers. Even the ANC was outraged by the blatant abuse of state resources by a family who obviously knew some ANC members who would open doors, and runways, for them. A seething Gwede

Mantashe, ANC secretary general, released the following statement on the day of the landing:

The landing at Waterkloof

30 April 2013

The African National Congress has learnt that guests of a family hosting some wedding at Sun City landed at the Waterkloof Airforce Base today. Waterkloof is one of our country's National Key Points ...

The African National Congress waited patiently for the South African National Defence Force (SANDF), the body delegated with authority over the Waterkloof Airforce Base, to explain to the nation how these private individuals managed to land [an] aircraft at Waterkloof. Up until now, no explanation has been forthcoming. The African National Congress, driven by the concern for the safety and sovereignty of South Africa, shall never allow a situation where our ports of entry and National Key Points are penetrated with impunity.

We demand that those who are responsible for granting access to land aircraft in our country also explain the basis upon which such permission was granted, particularly to land at Waterkloof Airforce Base. Those who cannot account must be brought to book. The African National Congress will never rest where there is any indication that all and sundry may be permitted to undermine the Republic, its citizens and its borders ...

Unfortunately, Mantashe's anger didn't convert into action, and four years after the incident, nobody had been punished for this gross breach of national security. The main culprit – the former head of state protocol at the Department of International Relations and Cooperation, Vusi Bruce Koloane – was initially demoted, but later reappointed elsewhere.

A joint investigation by the criminal-justice cluster into Guptagate unsurprisingly cleared Zuma of any wrongdoing and found that his name had been used in vain – chiefly by Koloane – to get the Guptas' jet into a national key point. In communication between air-force officials, they referred to 'Number One', who was putting pressure on them to clear the way for the Guptas to land. Koloane took the fall for this; he testified at his disciplinary that he had lied when he said Zuma, or 'Number One', had pressurised him into action.

Was he summarily fired and prosecuted for this? No. After Koloane was initially demoted to being a liaison officer, Zuma, the man whom Koloane allegedly fraudulently dragged into the Guptagate scandal, awarded him with an ambassadorship in The Hague. It made absolutely no sense and fed into the theory that Koloane took the fall for 'Number One' and that Zuma reciprocated by bestowing upon him an ambassadorship.

But this chapter may not be a closed book yet. Lieutenant Colonel Christine Anderson, who was suspended along with Koloane for Guptagate for more than two years, is suing the Department of Defence after they dropped all charges against her. Pikkie Greeff, her legal representative from the South African National Defence Union, told Netwerk24 in 2015 that Anderson would prove Koloane was acting as Zuma's agent in making Waterkloof Air Force Base available for the Guptas. 'Christine has evidence of conversations between Bruce Koloane and President Zuma,' Greeff boldly claimed.[29]

In the meantime, Koloane has been using his position as ambassador to the Netherlands to advance the business interests of the Guptas – as one does when one is captured. The true extent of Koloane's proximity to the family came to light during the release of the Gupta leaks in mid-2017. The emails show how Koloane met a company in The Hague to negotiate a deal on the Guptas' behalf; how he forwarded confidential information about Waterkloof Air Force Base directly to Gupta lieutenant Ashu Chawla before the event in 2013; that Koloane's friends had been allowed to stay at the Guptas' private game lodge in Limpopo; and how Koloane sent Chawla documents on a prospective mining site around the time of the Waterkloof scandal.[30] Koloane was not immediately recalled or censured and remained in his position as the scandal was unfolding.

CHAPTER 6

Poison ivy and Russian blood

―

'How the alleged attempts to poison the president related to him being terrible at his job is unclear. But Zuma often employs the conspiracy trick to defend himself and to blackmail the ANC into closing ranks around him.'

– Ranjeni Munusamy, *Daily Maverick*, 19 April 2017

On 4 January 2015, Nompumelelo Ntuli-Zuma, the president's fourth wife, was ordered to leave Nkandla by state security minister David Mahlobo because she had allegedly conspired to poison her husband. In one of the most extraordinary and bizarre chapters of the Zuma years – and one that confirmed Zuma's conspiratorial persuasion – Ntuli-Zuma was kicked out of the family home after the president fell ill in mid-2014. In a strange series of events, involving a secretive visit by Zuma to President Vladimir Putin in Moscow, Ntuli-Zuma was effectively excommunicated by her husband and banished to a life outside Nkandla – although no evidence has been produced to prove the first lady's alleged criminal acts.

The sequence of events started with a terse press statement issued by ANC spokesperson Zizi Kodwa on 6 June 2014, announcing that party bosses had asked the 72-year-old Zuma 'to take time off from work following an intense election campaign'. South Africans went to the polls on 7 May 2014. The ANC won with 62,15% of the vote, following a gruelling fight, during which Zuma was the target of campaigns by the DA and EFF that focused on his many scandals, chiefly the Nkandla expenditure. Kodwa's statement came after Zuma had to excuse himself from an NEC meeting following his political overview. *City Press* reported that Zuma stopped speaking ten minutes into his speech and was complaining of neck pain.[1] Shortly afterwards, the Presidency informed the nation that Zuma had been admitted to hospital for exhaustion. 'Doctors are satisfied with his condition,' then spokesperson Mac Maharaj told the media, but Zuma was signed off for ten days.[2]

On 17 June 2014, a frail-looking Zuma delivered his state of the nation address during the opening of Parliament. Zuma had to be driven to the entrance of the National Assembly because he was too ill to walk the red carpet.[3] Radio presenter and political correspondent Stephen Grootes remarked that Zuma looked in poor form: 'Thinner, it seemed, almost not quite filling out his suit. Less bounce in his step. And certainly, the voice was different. It didn't have the power that it normally has.'[4]

On 2 August 2014, Zuma left for the United States to attend a US–Africa Leaders' Summit in Washington. It was apparently during this trip that Zuma self-diagnosed that he had been poisoned. Reports at the time suggested the president couldn't fulfil all his official duties. 'However, he did not trust the Americans and went to Russia for treatment. Russian doctors confirmed the diagnosis,' the *Sunday Times* reported.[5]

Zuma's trip to Russia was shrouded in secrecy and left even ANC insiders perplexed. The Department of International Relations and Cooperation announced on 23 August that Zuma would leave for a 'working visit' to Russia. The statement was filled with general topics that left many unconvinced that these were the real reasons behind Zuma's unscheduled visit:

> The President is scheduled to meet President Putin later in the week, and during the bilateral talks the two Presidents are expected to assess the state of bilateral cooperation, the status and implementation of Intergovernmental Committee on Trade and Economic

Cooperation (ITEC) agreements, key trade and investment issues, and preparations for the 12th ITEC Session to be hosted by South Africa …

Ahead of the bilateral meeting, President Zuma will on 25–27 August hold low-key meetings and use the period to rest.

The two Presidents will also focus on developments on critical international issues of mutual concern, including … the situation in Syria, and the Israel-Palestine matter, as well as developments in Ukraine …[6]

There were several peculiar things about the statement. Firstly, none of the bilateral matters mentioned were urgent enough to justify the visit. Secondly, Putin, with all due respect, didn't have to consult or update the president of South Africa about Russia's foreign policy with regard to Syria, Israel-Palestine and the Ukraine. Thirdly, it was odd for Dirco to mention that Zuma would 'use the period to rest'. Why would an ailing Zuma have to fly to the other side of the world to rest? Finally, Zuma's choice of entourage was very strange. Why did the minister of intelligence and the deputy minister of foreign affairs have to accompany him to discuss trade and investment? By the time of the trip, Mahlobo had been in his portfolio for only three months after Zuma elevated him from a head of department in Mpumalanga to intelligence minister. And, to top it all, when Zuma and Putin finally met, it was at Putin's presidential residence, and not at the Kremlin. Shortly after Zuma's return to South Africa, *City Press* reported on the president's 'mysterious mission' to Russia. As usual, he was accompanied by his doctor and four bodyguards 'but, unusually, no aides, advisers nor wives'.[7]

It didn't take long for the story to get out that Zuma had undergone some kind of medical treatment in Russia. The rumour mill went into overdrive: 'Putin gave Zuma new blood' was one of the versions circulating in Pretoria. The dramatic ousting of Ntuli-Zuma from their home had remained a secret for almost two months, until the *Sunday Times* revealed on 22 February 2015 that Zuma believed his fourth wife was involved in a plan to poison him. The newspaper's sources confirmed that Zuma fell ill in June 2014 (before the opening of Parliament), but that it was diagnosed in the United States only at the beginning of August that he had been poisoned. A few weeks later, Zuma travelled to Russia – not to 'rest' or to carry out bilateral talks, but to receive treatment for his alleged poisoning. The *Sunday Times* reported: 'A source said the president was very angry when he found out about the alleged poison plot, but told close relatives to keep it within the family. They were told that Ntuli-Zuma had done "something terrible that could put her in jail for a long time", a family insider said.'[8]

The specialist newsletter *Africa Confidential* later reported that Zuma believed Putin had saved his life, quoting sources close to the Zuma family. They linked this back to South Africa's planned R1 trillion nuclear plan – a deal that Russia's Rosatom desperately wants to bag. 'Zuma feels "indebted", we hear, for medical treatment he received in Russia when the nuclear deal was agreed in outline,' the publication reported.[9]

Apparently, Zuma believed that he could have been poisoned only by someone with direct access to his food, and therefore suspected Ntuli-Zuma.[10] The president allegedly believed she poisoned him for being pushed out after she was accused of having an affair with her body-guard, Phinda Thomo, in 2009. Although it was later formally denied that Ntuli-Zuma and Thomo were having an affair, Zuma allegedly sent his fourth wife back to her family in Maphumulo, KwaZulu-Natal, for a goat to be slaughtered to cleanse the family.[11] Thomo, who had previously worked as a bodyguard for Malema and Mbalula, commit-ted suicide in December 2009. It was reported that Ntuli-Zuma 'openly sobbed' at his funeral.[12] His family remained sceptical about the cause of his death, saying they had been sidelined during the inquest.

In April 2015 a docket for attempted murder was opened against Ntuli-Zuma at the Nkandla police station. She was required to sub-mit a sworn statement to the Hawks in KwaZulu-Natal by the end of June, which she did. Ntuli-Zuma vehemently denies being involved in a plot to poison or kill her husband. In September 2016, after receiving no further correspondence from the Hawks or Mahlobo, Ntuli-Zuma's lawyer, Ulrich Roux, wrote to Advocate Shaun Abrahams, the NDPP, requesting clarity on the case and whether she was regarded as a suspect or witness. 'This matter has dragged on since January 2015. Despite numerous requests, our offices have not received any feedback and we hereby request that you personally attend to this matter so as to allow our client to continue with her life, free from the burden of a possible criminal charge hanging over her head, alternatively for the matter to proceed against her and finality being reached,' Roux wrote in a letter. A month later, Abrahams wrote back, confirming that Ntuli-Zuma had been 'identified as one of the suspects' in the case.

However, three years after the alleged poisoning, nobody has been charged or brought to book for the crime. Zuma has not spoken to his wife about the case or personally confronted her about what he believed happened. All communication with her has been through Mahlobo.[13] Ntuli-Zuma has moved to Pietermaritzburg as she awaits the outcome of the Hawks' probe.

Meanwhile, Zuma has told the ANC's NEC that there have been three attempts by 'foreign' forces to poison him and that he knows who his enemies are. At an NEC meeting in May 2017, during which he was asked to step down for a second time, Zuma intimated that some NEC members were involved in the plot, but that he'd rather not say who, so as not to harm the party.

This was vintage Zuma: planting seeds of mistrust and doubt, and centralising the 'truth' in himself – or attempting to. The manner in which the entire 'poisoning' saga has been dealt with tells a tale about the Zuma era, one that feeds on paranoia, innuendo and intrigue, and is marred by a complete lack of transparency, mostly by design. It is outrageous to think that there have been three attempts on the life of South Africa's president without a major intervention by the criminal-justice authorities and without a top-level police investigation. And there has been a complete lack of transparency, so that the public have been kept in the dark as to who these 'foreign forces' are who want to kill Zuma. The fact of the matter is, Zuma was ill and if it was because of an attempt to poison him, South Africans are entitled to know about it from the authorities.

It is also outrageous that Ntuli-Zuma has been left in limbo for almost three years after being asked to leave Nkandla in early 2015. Until she is either charged or the investigation against her as a suspect is cancelled, she has been left by the criminal-justice system with a huge cloud over her head. In keeping with the old spy that he is, Zuma's preference is to sort things out in the shadows, hence the involvement of Mahlobo, as opposed to the police. This is the antithesis of what a democracy should be, where strong democratic institutions are supposed to investigate claims and crimes without fear or favour, and guilty parties, irrespective of who they are, are brought to book. It is completely unacceptable for a president to say he knows who his enemies are who want to kill him, but he'd rather stay quiet for the sake of the party.

PART 3

Institutional capture

—

CHAPTER 7

Who will guard the guardians?

'*I am not sure the public fully understand that a dishonest prosecutor is very much worse than a crooked judge.*'
– Retired Judge Johann Kriegler, after charges of perjury against deputy prosecutions head
Nomgcobo Jiba were dropped by the new NDPP, Shaun Abrahams, 21 August 2015

Arguably, Zuma's most destructive legacy is the capture and neutralisation of South Africa's criminal-justice institutions. When Zuma goes, he will leave behind dysfunctional organisations that are not willing or able to counter the scourge of crime that has plagued South Africans for many years. We argue that this was done by design to protect Zuma and his family, friends and comrades against investigation, prosecution and ultimately potential imprisonment. Through a series of bad appointments of compromised, sometimes incompetent, individuals and through political interference, Zuma has succeeded in wearing down the fierceness and independence these institutions need to successfully execute their constitutional mandate. This has rendered them ineffective and open to abuse.

The worst example of this abuse was the Hawks' desperate attempt to bring charges of corruption and fraud against former finance minister Pravin Gordhan in 2016. While other major corruption and racketeering cases were languishing due to lack of will and investigative capacity, the Hawks assigned a senior team from its Crimes Against the State unit to investigate Gordhan for granting early retirement to the former deputy head of SARS, Ivan Pillay. And then they messed it up.

Ironically, it was Zuma himself who complained bitterly about the abuse of state resources when he was investigated for much more serious charges of corruption and fraud by the erstwhile Scorpions before he became ANC president – the so-called 'spy tapes' matter. So successful was Zuma's campaign against his charges that the Scorpions unit was shut down after the ANC's Polokwane conference. The charges against Zuma were dropped and have been the subject of ongoing litigation between the DA and the president since 2009. The Supreme Court of Appeal (SCA) heard arguments in September 2017 on whether the NPA's reasoning for dropping the charges against Zuma was irrational or not. In a surprise move, Zuma's counsel admitted the NPA had acted irrationally.

The abuse of power applies not only to cases like Gordhan's, which were investigated, but also to those that weren't, because it didn't suit Zuma's agenda or the ANC's. The massive looting at the Passenger Rail Agency of South Africa (Prasa) comes to mind. After months of providing the Hawks with detailed forensic reports of the rot their private investigators had uncovered, the unit had still assigned only one overworked detective to work on the case. Prasa laid criminal complaints about tenders worth more than R7 billion, including the infamous Swifambo Rail Leasing contract, where Prasa paid R3,5 billion for 70 locomotives that were too tall for South Africa's railways.[1] But nothing happened. News24 revealed in March 2017 that payments worth at least R80 million from the contract were made to ANC 'fundraiser' and lawyer George Sabelo, and Angolan businesswoman Maria Gomes, who calls herself a friend of Zuma.[2] The situation reached a point where the Prasa board was forced to take the Hawks to court to force them to do their job.

The top leadership structures of the South African Police Service (SAPS), the Directorate for Priority Crime Investigation (the formal name for the Hawks), the NPA, the SIU and the SSA have been in flux since Zuma became state president in 2009. On top of that, the investigative capacity of SARS was effectively destroyed through the purging of the so-called 'rogue unit', which investigated organised-crime syndicates from a tax perspective. Another Zuma loyalist, Tom Moyane, was strategically appointed as SARS boss to oversee operation 'Protect Zuma' at the tax authority. None of these institutions have had a permanent head for longer than five years during Zuma's presidency. The police service has seen five permanent and acting national commissioners since 2009. Similarly, the NPA has had five permanent and acting NDPPs during Zuma's presidency so far. Anwa Dramat was Hawks head for over five years before he was suspended in December 2014. His successor, Berning Ntlemeza, was in the job for less than two years before the court set aside his appointment. The SSA has had three directors general since 2009, and the SIU seven permanent and acting heads in the same period. No wonder South Africa is not winning the war on crime.

Is it a coincidence that the criminal-justice sector has seen such major instability under Zuma? We think not. All along, Zuma's strategy may have been not to allow anyone to become too strong in any of these positions. By chopping and changing and hiring and firing bosses in the criminal-justice institutions, Zuma remained firmly in control of who was investigated, prosecuted and jailed. One could call this the 'J Edgar Hoover fear' that most presidents, not only Zuma, harbour – that their police chiefs would become more powerful than the heads of state themselves. Hoover served just under 50 years as head of the FBI and became a mightily powerful role player in American politics, even more powerful than the presidents he served, some would argue. With his own corruption case dangling over his head like the sword of Damocles, Zuma has had to ensure that he remains in control of the criminal-justice system, particularly the NPA, who have the power to charge him again. At the same time, as the state-capture project, led by the Guptas and Duduzane Zuma, got under way, Zuma had to safeguard his family and friends against investigation and prosecution. So he made sure to appoint weaklings, compromised individuals or people he thought he could control to head these important institutions. Those who stood up to him were swiftly removed with a golden handshake.

In September 2010, Zuma did a very peculiar thing. He expunged the criminal record of a lawyer who was found guilty of stealing a client's money from his trust fund. In the legal profession, this is the lowest you can go. Sikhumbuzo Booker Washington Nhantsi was sentenced to five years' imprisonment for theft by the Eastern Cape High Court in Mthatha in 2005 after stealing R193 000 he held for a client in his law firm's trust account. He was released from prison in 2007. At the time of his conviction, Nhantsi was working as a prosecutor for the Scorpions in the Eastern Cape.

It was a huge embarrassment for the corruption-busting Scorpions, and Nhantsi was dismissed after a disciplinary hearing. Why would Zuma erase the criminal record of a thieving former attorney? Maybe because the thief is married to Nomgcobo Jiba, a very senior prosecutor in the NPA whose career was fast-tracked by her husband's blesser – Zuma. Let's connect the dots: in May 2009 Zuma was appointed president after the ANC won the general election. A few weeks before, corruption charges against Zuma were controversially withdrawn by the NPA after a set of 'spy tapes' surfaced that showed the timing of the charges against Zuma made them politically motivated. In November 2009, Zuma appointed Menzi Simelane as NDPP. The DA initiated two court cases: to have the charges against Zuma reinstated and to have Simelane be declared unfit to lead the NPA. At the same time, Jiba returned to the NPA after a long suspension for assisting the police in arresting ace prosecutor Gerrie Nel on cooked-up charges. In September 2010 Zuma expunged Nhantsi's criminal record and in January 2011 he elevated Jiba to the position of deputy NDPP. At the end of 2011, after the SCA confirmed Simelane's appointment was irregular, Zuma appointed Jiba as acting head of the NPA. He needed a friendly NDPP to protect him against prosecution and found one in Jiba, to whose husband he had given a second lease of life. In 2012 Nhantsi was appointed as a legal advisor for the Department of Cooperative Governance and Traditional Affairs, and formed part of the ministerial task team that had to investigate rampant fraud and corruption at the Madibeng municipality in the North

West.[3] If they were looking for someone with first-hand experience, Nhantsi was suitably qualified for the job.

Jiba acted as NPA boss for almost two years and oversaw the near implosion of the institution during her reign of terror. Topping her list of priorities was protecting crime-intelligence boss and Zuma boot-licker, Richard Mdluli, against prosecution. Mdluli assisted Jiba during her suspension from the NPA by providing her with copies of inter-cepted calls between members of the Scorpions – the same series of spy tapes used by Zuma to get off the hook. After his suspension from the crime intelligence division of the police, Mdluli told Zuma he would help him succeed at the ANC's leadership election in 2012. Mdluli was facing two criminal cases: one for fraud and corruption, the other for the murder and kidnapping of Oupa Ramogibe, a man who was engaged to a woman Mdluli dated. On Jiba's watch, both cases against him were dropped. Jiba and her closest ally, commercial crimes head Lawrence Mrwebi, successfully pushed senior prosecutor Glynnis Breytenbach out of the NPA after they had failed to find her guilty in a disciplinary hear-ing. Breytenbach was vocally opposed to the protection of Mdluli by her bosses and joined the DA as spokesperson for justice after attempts to undermine and discredit her.

The Mdluli saga led to the first major review case brought against the NPA by a non-profit organisation. Freedom Under Law, an organisation that promotes understanding of and respect for the rule of law, led by for-mer Constitutional Court Judge Johann Kriegler, took Jiba and Mrwebi to court for their decisions on Mdluli. Jiba was now in the spotlight for the wrong reasons, and the president was not impressed. In August 2013 Zuma appointed Mxolisi Nxasana, a senior KwaZulu-Natal attorney, as the country's new NDPP. Jiba was furious. At his first media briefing, Nxasana said that he wanted to assure members of society, especially the victims of crime, that it was a new dawn for the NPA. 'I have taken the oath, to prosecute all cases without fear, favour or prejudice,' he said, signalling a breakaway from the politically driven atmosphere that pervaded the NPA.[4] Although he was relatively unknown, Nxasana's appointment brought a sense of calmness and stability to the NPA. The

Black Lawyers Association welcomed Nxasana's appointment, saying they believed he had 'proven leadership capabilities' and an 'in-depth understanding of the South African legal system', and that his 'unblemished track record will bring back the integrity, dignity and respect of the National Prosecuting Authority'.[5]

A month after Nxasana's appointment, Judge John Murphy delivered a scathing judgment against Jiba and Mrwebi in the case brought by Freedom Under Law and ordered the NPA to reinstate corruption and murder charges against Mdluli. He lambasted them for being dishonest and irrational in their decision making. It was Nxasana's first big test: would he set a different tone and go after the man who swore to protect Zuma? Nxasana agreed to appeal the ruling to obtain clarity from the SCA on whether a court could interfere with the decision of an independent prosecutor. 'If I want to reinstate the charges against Mdluli, I can,' Nxasana told the *Mail & Guardian*. 'Nobody should view the decision as a delaying tactic. I owe nothing to Mdluli and I haven't even met him. I owe the NPA and the people of South Africa, and no one else.'[6]

In April 2014 the SCA confirmed Murphy's ruling and Nxasana ordered the reinstatement of charges against Mdluli. In the meanwhile, according to Nxasana, Jiba has been plotting against him, digging up dirt to have him removed as NDPP. As early as October 2013 – two months after his appointment – Nxasana was informed by NPA sources of Jiba's campaign against him. Nxasana was given a voice recording during which a Hawks detective, Colonel Welcome Mhlongo, is heard saying that Jiba had authorised him to collect dirt on Nxasana.[7] According to reports, Jiba was extremely bitter when Zuma didn't appoint her permanently to the position of NDPP. She and Mrwebi told Zuma that Nxasana would reinstate corruption charges against the president, Nxasana later claimed under oath. This would have triggered an immediate, radical reaction from the president whose biggest fear is to face a corruption trial.

The digging yielded results: in late May 2014, then justice minister Jeff Radebe, a staunch Jiba backer, asked Nxasana to resign. Radebe told Nxasana that his top-secret security clearance was turned down by the SSA because of his run-ins with the law as a youngster. This was an astonishing accusation. Nxasana's defence was that he had declared his convictions for assault in 1985 (at the age of 17) and 1986 to the SSA when he had to be vetted. He had also declared the offences to the court when he was admitted as an attorney. Radebe was supposed to make sure the candidate for NDPP was fit and proper for the position before his appointment, particularly in the wake of the court's ruling in the Simelane matter, where Radebe had failed to interrogate Simelane's appropriateness for the position. It looked, tasted and smelled like a hatchet job. Nxasana stood his ground and merely a year after his appointment, interdicted Zuma from suspending him. In a move reminiscent of how the Zuma camp got rid of former NDPP Vusi Pikoli, Zuma announced that a commission of inquiry would be conducted into Nxasana's fitness for the job.

But the legal eagle from Umlazi wasn't taking it lying down. Although he probably knew his time was up, Nxasana and his colleagues set in motion a process to censure Jiba and Mrwebi for protecting Mdluli from prosecution. Firstly, the NPA laid criminal charges of perjury against them for lying to the court. Secondly, it asked the General Council of the Bar to investigate whether they were fit to be advocates. And, thirdly, Nxasana wrote to Zuma, asking him to suspend Jiba and Mrwebi pending an inquiry into their fitness to hold office following Murphy's judgment and the SCA's confirmation thereof.[8] Nxasana further approved charges of fraud and perjury to be brought against Jiba for her decision to prosecute former KwaZulu-Natal Hawks boss Johan Booysen for racketeering, murder and defeating the ends of justice. This after Judge Trevor Gorven had thrown out the charges against Booysen on the basis that none of the information on which Jiba relied linked Booysen to the so-called Cato Manor 'death squad' case. Judge Gorven had ruled that Jiba's decision on the Booysen case did 'not pass muster'.

Zuma ignored Nxasana's request to suspend Jiba and Mrwebi. In secret negotiations between the president and the NDPP, Nxasana allegedly offered to leave if Zuma also got rid of Jiba and Mrwebi. The inquiry into Nxasana's fitness continued and Senior Advocate Nazeer Cassim was appointed as chair. Then, on 11 May 2015, hours before the commission's hearings were due to start at the Law Reform Commission in Pretoria, Zuma and Nxasana reached a settlement: Nxasana would leave office on 1 June 2015 and would be paid out the remainder of his ten-year contract, which came to a cool R17,3 million.

Two years later, Nxasana said he didn't willingly leave office, but settled an 'intractable, undesirable and ongoing dispute' between him, Zuma and Radebe.[9]

After Nxasana's departure, Corruption Watch, the Council for the Advancement of the South African Constitution and Freedom Under Law instituted civil litigation against Zuma, Nxasana and the NPA for what they argue was an 'unlawful and unconstitutional' settlement. Zuma, they argue, was conflicted in paying out Nxasana because his own corruption case was still up for review by the NPA. In April 2017 Nxasana filed his answering papers, in which he stated he would not oppose the court action; would pay back the R17,3 million if the court so ruled, and was ready to reassume his duties as NDPP.

In June 2015 Zuma appointed Shaun Abrahams, a senior state advocate in the NPA's Priority Crimes Litigation Unit, as NDPP. Senior colleagues all agreed that Abrahams was extremely ambitious and politically naive. At his first major media conference, Abrahams announced that the criminal charges against Jiba for her actions in the Booysen case would be dropped. He further announced a reshuffling of portfolios, moving the senior National Prosecutions Service portfolio, which oversees all prosecutions in the country, to Jiba. It was a powerful return of the woman who had tried so many times to become the NPA boss. This time she was overlooked again, but some argued her new elevated portfolio and Abrahams's lack of management experience made her the de facto NDPP.[10]

Abrahams probably thought that having Jiba by his side would give him the political clout and access he lacked. But, although he could protect Jiba from prosecution, he couldn't remove the case brought against her and Mrwebi by the General Council of the Bar. And in 2016, both of them were struck from the roll of advocates for their actions at the NPA – chiefly for having protected Mdluli against prosecution. 'I cannot believe that two officers of the court (advocates) who hold such high positions in the prosecuting authority will stoop so low for the protection and defence of one individual who had been implicated in serious offences,' ruled judges Francis Legodi and Wendy Hughes. Both Jiba and Mrwebi were placed on special leave while appealing the ruling.

The appointment of Major General Mthandazo Berning Ntlemeza as head of the Hawks in September 2015 immediately raised eyebrows and concerns. Ntlemeza is an apartheid-era policeman who started his career in the old Transkei in 1982. After serving as a detective in Gauteng and the Eastern Cape, Ntlemeza was promoted to Deputy Provincial Commissioner for Limpopo in 2003. It was in this position that the unknown Ntlemeza briefly moved onto the national radar in 2012 when it was revealed that he had compiled an intelligence report for none other than Mdluli about an alleged plot to prevent him from becoming head of crime intelligence. Mdluli claimed at the time that Afrika Khumalo, a former high-ranking police officer in Gauteng, was behind a plot to block his promotion. In a poorly-written report, Ntlemeza confirmed Mdluli's suspicions that Khumalo and other police spies were behind the resurfacing of the murder and kidnapping case against him – the same case that was dropped on Jiba's watch and later reinstated by Nxasana.

Former police chief Bheki Cele later confirmed that he knew nothing about Ntlemeza's so-called investigation on behalf of Mdluli and that it had not been sanctioned. So it was no secret that Ntlemeza had done a favour for Mdluli when Nathi Nhleko, then Minister of Police, announced in December 2014 that Ntlemeza would act as head of the Hawks after the dramatic exit of Anwa Dramat. We will return to Ntlemeza's modus operandi and tumultuous tenure in a moment.

After the Scorpions unit was shut down by an ANC majority in Parliament in 2008, Zuma and the ruling party found itself in a pickle. South Africa is a signatory to the United Nations Convention against

Corruption, which obliges member countries to have a dedicated anti-corruption law-enforcement unit (at that point Zuma's ANC still cared about what the international community thought of us; seven years later it would blatantly disregard international law when authorities failed to arrest Sudan's alleged war criminal and dictator, Omar al-Bashir, on a visit to South Africa). To fill the void left by the shutting down of the Scorpions, the Directorate for Priority Crime Investigation was established in the police.

The new unit brought together two existing police units: serious and violent crimes and serious economic offences. No extra corruption-fighting capacity was created and several Scorpions left the state to work in the private sector as lawyers and forensic investigators. The appointment of Dramat, a former uMkhonto we Sizwe operative who had been sentenced to 12 years on Robben Island, as the first head of the Hawks was met with scepticism. Dramat headed up crime intelligence in the Western Cape and was well versed in spy art. The Hawks was supposed to be evidence-driven – every case had to gather evidence that could be presented in court. As a senior Hawks and former Scorpions member put it: 'We moved from a prosecutions-driven operation to an intelligence-driven operation.' The success of the Scorpions lay in their structure: a detective, prosecutor and analyst worked together on each case from the start. This system was discarded and South Africa's ability to fight complicated, commercial crimes weakened with the establishment of the Hawks.

But Dramat gave it his best shot. He soon realised the value of a multi-disciplinary approach to corruption, and the Hawks played a significant role in the establishment of the Anti-Corruption Task Team (ACTT) in 2010. The ACTT effectively replaced the Scorpions and brought together the best minds in the police, NPA, SIU, crime intelligence and SARS in an 'informal' working arrangement. The 'unit' was never branded as such and didn't aim to build a profile like the Scorpions or the Hawks had, which corresponded with Dramat's own style.

The test for the effectiveness and longevity of the Hawks, and by implication the ACTT, was always going to be the first 'politically sensitive' case thrown its way. It turned out to be not one case, but at least three hot-potato dockets: the Mdluli cases, the Nkandla investigation, and the corruption case against Zuma-linked Durban businessman Thoshan Panday. These investigations – all connected to Zuma and his family – would ultimately claim the careers of Dramat, Gauteng Hawks boss, Shadrack Sibiya, and Booysen.

The Hawks, through Sibiya and with Dramat's support, kept the Mdluli murder and corruption investigations alive, despite the best attempts of Mrwebi and Jiba to shut them down. Dramat gave his consent for two senior Hawks detectives from the Western Cape to take over the cases from Gauteng police. They started to unravel a massive corruption scandal in crime intelligence, with the plundering of a secret 'slush fund' at the centre of the allegations. At the same time, the KwaZulu-Natal Hawks, under Booysen, started to investigate allegations of police bribery involving Panday, a business associate of Zuma's son Edward and his cousin Deebo Mzobe.

Booysen and his investigators uncovered evidence of procurement bribery, involving Panday and police supply-chain manager Colonel Navin Madhoe. Panday then allegedly tried to bribe Booysen with R2 million in an effort to scupper his case.[11] 'For 28 years I had a faultless career and won various national and international awards. This was until 2010/11, when I began investigating Thoshan Panday – a multimillionaire businessman from KwaZulu-Natal, with SA Police Service contracts and Zuma connections. From then on, everything began going off the rails. I was ordered to stop the investigation on various occasions, but Dramat and I decided to go ahead,' Booysen told his disciplinary hearing, which cleared him of wrongdoing, in 2014.[12] In 2016 Booysen published his biography, *Blood on Their Hands*, and detailed his interaction with Edward Zuma, who had invested R900 000 in one of Panday's businesses. The young Zuma once came to Booysen to ask him to release R15 million in payments from the police to Panday, because he [Edward Zuma] wasn't receiving dividends from his shares in Panday's company. 'I told him that I couldn't do that or I'd be guilty of corruption myself ... I told him to demand his R900 000 back from Thoshan Panday. Once he had it he should take it and run and not look back. Months later, a friend phoned me and said someone was with him and wanted to talk to me. It was Edward. I jokingly asked if he had taken my advice. He said he had. I didn't believe him.'[13]

The fightback against Dramat, Sibiya and Booysen was fierce. Dramat and Sibiya were accused of assisting Zimbabwean police with the illegal 'rendition' of suspected Zimbabwean criminals back over the border to be murdered. Booysen was accused of running what became known as the Cato Manor death squad in KwaZulu-Natal, a supposedly elite police unit that killed suspected hijackers, robbers and murderers instead of arresting them. The *Sunday Times* published front-page stories by the paper's investigations team, which would later be disbanded after it was discovered that they were running misleading stories about a so-called 'rogue unit' at SARS. In an affidavit, Colonel Kobus Roelofse, the investigating officer in the Mdluli cases, claimed that the *Sunday Times* was used by crime intelligence to smear Dramat and Sibiya:

> The investigating team have also been informed on 10 October 2011 by the member that on the same evening that he was taken to Major General Lazarus's house he heard them discussing the placement of a newspaper article relating to Lieutenant General Dramat and Major General Sibiya. He stated that the Major General Lazarus wanted to use sources within the media (journalists paid by CI) to write a story in order to take the focus away from them. This according to the member is a strategy employed to cast suspicion on those they perceived to be a threat.
>
> This newspaper article was published in the *Sunday Times* on 23 October 2011. Lieutenant General Mdluli has made representations to the National Prosecuting Authority earlier that month and uses the abovementioned article to cast suspicion on Lieutenant General Dramat and the investigating team.[14]

Lazarus was crime intelligence's chief financial officer; he was also on trial for corruption and fraud. The *Sunday Times* story Roelofse referred to was headlined 'Sent to die: Shocking fate of suspects in alleged rendition deal with Zim cops', in which it was claimed that at least three Zimbabweans were kidnapped by the Hawks and killed by Zimbabwean cops after arriving back in Zimbabwe.[15] The story named both Dramat and Sibiya. Then *Sunday Times* editor Ray Hartley strenuously denied that his reporters were part of a crime-intelligence campaign and said Roelofse's claims were 'made on the flimsiest of grounds' and included 'no supporting evidence'.[16] He said the article wasn't written on the prompting of a single source, but was the product of 'a lengthy investigation which included information supplied by several police officers, evidence of police entry ledgers, death certificates and the sworn affidavit of several witnesses'.[17]

Two months later, under the headline 'Shoot to kill: Inside a South African police death squad', the *Sunday Times* reported that an alleged 'hit squad' was operating in KwaZulu-Natal 'under the ultimate command of [Booysen]'.[18] Booysen challenged the case against him every step of the way. In 2014 Judge Trevor Gorven set aside the criminal charges against Booysen and in the same year Nazeer Cassim, who chaired his disciplinary hearing, cleared him of all charges, finding that he had been a victim of political battles.[19]

In a 2016 interview with the *Daily Maverick*, Booysen claimed that Mdluli was behind the *Sunday Times* stories. In the interview, he said he believed that the *Sunday Times* investigative reporters were the 'pawns of a faction within the police's Crime Intelligence unit doing the bidding of suspended head Richard Mdluli'.[20] Booysen went on to say he had

intelligence that Mdluli is still pulling the strings at Crime Intelligence today despite being on paid leave. I can refer specifically to two, or at least three sagas that I believe are interwoven and that's the so-called rendition matter against Dramat and Sibiya. Now I told General Dramat more than three years ago when the so-called exposé appeared in the *Sunday Times* [that] the person behind the story is Richard Mdluli. And I don't think he believed me at the time. It's now become clear after reading the statement of Innocent

Khuba from IPID that Mdluli and [Ntlemeza], the [then] current head of the Hawks, orchestrated the demise of Dramat. ... I know that when we started the investigation against [Panday], members of the so-called rogue SARS team also investigated Panday. So I don't think you need to be a rocket scientist to figure that one out.[21]

Khuba is the former head of the police watchdog, the Independent Police Investigative Directorate (IPID), in Limpopo. He produced an affidavit in March 2016 in which he implicated crime intelligence in the illegal Zimbabwean renditions and the cover-up. He claimed under oath that Ntlemeza had told him Mdluli was 'looking out' for his interests and that he shouldn't be afraid – confirming the suspicion that Mdluli was still pulling the strings behind the scenes, even though he was on suspension.

The IPID ultimately cleared Dramat and Sibiya of wrongdoing in the rendition case, but not before considerable pressure was put on them to leave. On 23 December 2014, Nhleko unlawfully suspended Dramat and replaced him with Ntlemeza, who was heading the Hawks in Limpopo. A few days later, Ntlemeza suspended Sibiya. And in March 2015, Nhleko suspended IPID head Robert McBride for allegedly changing an IPID report to clear Dramat and Sibiya of wrongdoing.

In a bombshell letter to the minister, Dramat accused Nhleko of using the Zimbabwean rendition case as a 'smokescreen'. His suspension, Dramat wrote, had nothing to do with the rendition, but was 'pregnant with ulterior motives':

My appointment as the Head of the DPCI [Directorate for Priority Crime Investigation], I perceived at the time, was based on my credentials, my level of expertise and the fact that I respectfully believe that I have always acted with integrity in the manner in which I deal with people and investigations.

No doubt you are aware that I have recently called for certain case dockets involving very influential persons to be brought or alternatively centralised under one investigating arm and this has clearly caused massive resentment against me.

I can unequivocally point out that I am not willing to compromise the principles that I have always believed in. I am not willing to be 'agreeable', or 'compliant' insofar as I would then be acting contrary to my own moral principles and, also, contrary to the position in which I was appointed.[22]

The case dockets Dramat refers to were the Nkandla matter and the Panday case, both involving Zuma and his family. Dramat wanted the Nkandla docket, as nothing was happening with the case while it was with the newly formed National Investigation Unit, curiously placed in the SAPS head office under the supervision of Lieutenant General Vinesh Moonoo, the head of detectives. The Hawks found it suspicious that then police chief Riah Phiyega and Moonoo felt it necessary to start a parallel investigations unit outside of the Hawks' control. It was also a sign that they no longer trusted Dramat to oversee 'politically sensitive' cases. As Dramat put it in his no-nonsense letter to Nhleko, he was not agreeable or compliant: he would rather resign, he said, than be part of a cover-up machine masquerading as an anti-graft unit.

Shortly after being accused by private investigator Paul O'Sullivan of having corrupt relationships with underworld figures, Moonoo retired from the police. He has denied any wrongdoing. The Nkandla docket never made it to the Hawks and there is no proof that the cops, under Moonoo, conducted even one interview or subpoenaed the bank statements of the contractors to determine if and how Zuma paid for his houses, or whether kickbacks were paid.

In January 2015 the North Gauteng High Court overturned Dramat's suspension. Nhleko immediately appealed the matter and made it clear that Dramat was not about to return to his job. The state would spend any amount of money to block Dramat from resuming his duties. In April 2015 Dramat and the police reached a settlement whereby he would receive a R3 million severance package in addition to his R60 000 per month salary until retirement age of 60. Dramat was 46 at the time, meaning he would receive over R13 million to sit at home.

In February 2015, Sibiya's suspension was also overturned by Judge

Elias Matojane of the North Gauteng High Court. Matojane described Sibiya's suspension by Ntlemeza – then acting head of the Hawks – as unconstitutional, invalid and unlawful. Ntlemeza applied for leave to appeal and then did something that would ruin his own career – he lied to the court. In his application for leave to appeal, Ntlemeza told the court a key witness in the rendition case had died under mysterious circumstances, when the man had in fact died of natural causes.[23] Ntlemeza further failed to disclose to the court an IPID investigation into the rendition claims that exonerated Sibiya. Matojane slammed Ntlemeza in his judgment, calling him 'biased and dishonest', and said he lacked 'integrity and honour'.

Despite this, Ntlemeza was appointed permanently as Hawks head in September 2015. Sibiya was found guilty in a disciplinary hearing and dismissed from the police. The chair of his hearing found he could not be placed on the scene of the 'kidnappings', but that his cellphone records and presence at the Hawks' office when Zimbabwean police met with their counterparts showed he would have known about the case.[24] Sibiya was replaced by Prince Mokotedi, a former NPA director of integrity management who had resigned from the prosecuting authority before he could be charged for leaking information on Breytenbach to the media. At the time of his appointment, Mokotedi had no security clearance and default judgments against him in excess of R1,1 million. Mokotedi famously said the NPA was split between a 'Zuma camp and a Zille camp'. He clearly identified with the former.

Sibiya blamed Mdluli for ending his career and was challenging his dismissal in court. In November 2016, the DA-led City of Johannesburg administration appointed Sibiya as head of its anti-corruption unit.

In September 2016 the Constitutional Court ruled in McBride's favour that Nhleko had no powers to suspend him. The court ordered Parliament to reconsider the law giving the minister of police powers over the IPID, which is supposed to function independently.[25] In February 2017 Booysen took early retirement from the SAPS, although he still faced charges relating to the 'Cato Manor hit squad', which were reinstated by Abrahams after his appointment in June 2015.

Ntlemeza loved the power of the job. During visits to provincial Hawks offices, he would often ask his subordinates only one question: which politicians were they investigating? Who knows what Ntlemeza did with this information. Was he building up a docket against politicians to use as a bargaining tool? One thing is sure – he didn't use the information to institute criminal proceedings. Under Ntlemeza, Zuma and his Cabinet were safe from prosecution.

But his arrogance got the better of him in the Sibiya case, and in March 2017 the North Gauteng High Court set aside his appointment as Hawks boss on the strength of Judge Matojane's findings about his dishonesty in the Sibiya application. A full bench of the court ruled:

> The judgments [of Matojane] are replete with the findings of dishonesty and *mala fides* against Major General Ntlemeza. These were judicial pronouncements. They therefore constitute direct evidence that Major General Ntlemcza lacks the requisite honesty, integrity and conscientiousness to occupy the position of any public office, not to mention an office as important as that of the National Head of the DPCI, where independence, honesty and integrity are paramount to qualities.[26]

At the same time his immediate political protector, Nhleko, was shifted to the Department of Public Works during the 'night of the long knives' Cabinet reshuffle, which saw Zuma sacking Pravin Gordhan as finance minister.

Ntlemeza had overplayed his hand, and with Fikile Mbalula as new police minister, he had lost his assumed political support. Mbalula withdrew his support for Ntlemeza's appeal against the ruling that he was unfit for his job and when he lost his appeal Mbalula immediately replaced him with Lieutenant General Yolisa Matakata, Ntlemeza's deputy. In defiance of the court order, Ntlemeza pitched for work and even signed out an official vehicle in which he was 'roaming around Pretoria' while Mbalula addressed a press conference.[27] It is safe to assume that Zuma was not opposed to seeing the back of Ntlemeza from the Hawks.

This was classic Zuma: he showed absolutely no loyalty to those who had helped him with his project to capture the state and kicked them out when they became liabilities. Zuma had learnt hard lessons from defending Simelane against a ruling that he was unfit for his job, and wasn't going to do the same for Ntlemeza. So he let him go.

Six years after being suspended, Mdluli remains at home on full pay. In June 2017, the DA revealed that Mdluli had earned R8,3 million since his suspension, including a salary bonus of R413 957.[28] Mbalula said internal processes against him were under way, but police and security insiders were convinced that Mdluli was still abetting the president from outside, making him untouchable.

Instability in the upper echelons of the SAPS continued unabated during the Zuma years, with no police chief serving for more than three years before being suspended. When Bheki Cele, a KwaZulu-Natal politician and former Zuma ally took over as police commissioner in 2009, the police service was reeling from the prosecution of Jackie Selebi on charges of corruption. Cele brought a 'shoot to kill' ethos to the police, which his supporters believe led to a decrease in the murder rate between 2009 and 2012, but also drew massive criticism when trigger-happy police started killing innocent bystanders. Cele was suspended in October 2011 for entering into a dodgy R1,5 billion leasing contract for new police headquarters with property mogul Roux Shabangu. (Shabangu was rumoured to be a friend of Zuma's – he was a VIP guest at Zuma's inauguration[29] – but the president later said he 'barely knew' him.) A judicial commission of inquiry set up by Zuma found Cele guilty of maladministration and misconduct. Zuma fired Cele in 2012 and the firebrand politician took the president to court. In 2014 Zuma appointed Cele deputy minister of agriculture.

Cele was replaced by Riah Phiyega, a former Absa and Transnet executive who was appointed by Zuma to lead a presidential review committee into SOEs. A couple of months after Phiyega took office in June 2012, the Marikana massacre at Lonmin's platinum mine, in which 34 miners were killed by police officers, happened on her watch. The remainder of Phiyega's term was clouded by her involvement in the tragedy. The Farlam Commission of Inquiry into the massacre blamed the police's lack of preparedness and found that Phiyega had misled the inquiry about decisions the police made in the week leading up to the tragedy.[30] The commission recommended an inquiry into her fitness for office, the Claassen Board of Inquiry, in which Judge Neels Claassen found Phiyega was unfit to hold office, had lied to the Farlam Commission and should be dismissed.[31] After her five-year term expired while she was on suspension, Phiyega challenged Claassen's findings in court.

In October 2015 Zuma appointed Lieutenant General Khomotso Phahlane, head of the forensic laboratories at the police, as acting police chief. Merely four months had passed before allegations of wrongdoing against Phahlane surfaced, when O'Sullivan opened a case of corruption, money laundering and racketeering against him. The charges related to Phahlane's lifestyle and sources of cash used to build a luxury house and buy vehicles. The IPID opened a case against Phahlane and allegations that the top cop received benefits from service providers to the police made their way into the media. Mbalula asked Phahlane for reasons why he shouldn't be suspended while he was handling the allegations against him. In June 2017 Phahlane's term was over and Zuma replaced him with Lieutenant General Lesetja Mothiba as acting police chief – the fifth person to head the SAPS since the beginning of the Zuma years in 2009.

It will take South Africa's criminal-justice sector years to recover from the destructive impact of the Zuma era, during which good men were booted from their jobs for doing the right thing. The chilling impact this had on prosecutors and police officers is immeasurable. Those who were willing to bend the rules and to apply two sets of rules, one for Zuma and his cronies and another for the rest of us, thrived.

CHAPTER 8

Zupta-owned enterprises

—

'*When the going gets weird, the weird turns pro.*'
– Hunter S Thompson, Fear and loathing at the Super Bowl,
Rolling Stone, 28 February 1974

Before and after being fired as finance minister, Pravin Gordhan urged South Africans to 'connect the dots' when it came to state capture. In the case of SOEs, a clear pattern was unfolding: President Jacob Zuma fires a minister. He appoints a new minister. The new minister appoints a new board of directors, who open the doors of opportunity for the Gupta/Zuma empire. And so it continues.

The capture of the SOEs by the Gupta family and their associates (including Duduzane Zuma) happened with Zuma Snr as the ultimate enabler. Between them, South African Airways (SAA), Transnet, Denel and Eskom have spent hundreds of billions of rands over the past decade to upgrade South Africa's core infrastructure and services. The state-owned sector was the place to be if you wanted to become very, very rich. We will attempt to connect the dots, Mr Gordhan.

Dot 1: In June 2010, Zuma went on a state visit to India. He was accompanied by a number of ministers, including then public enterprises minister Barbara Hogan, a struggle-era veteran and former minister of health. Also in Zuma's delegation were various businesspeople, including Ajay and Rajesh Gupta, and their business partner Duduzane Zuma. The Department of Public Enterprises oversees the country's SOEs and appoints the boards of these entities. The boards appoint the CEOs, who, in turn, appoint senior staff and oversee the awarding of tenders and contracts worth billions of rands, often with the involvement of board members. For those with ambitions to capture the state, gaining control over the Department of Public Enterprises is essential.

In an interview with Thuli Madonsela in August 2016, Hogan recalled what had happened on the June 2010 trip to India. She noticed that the Guptas had 'taken control' of the president's programme. Hogan found it peculiar that the CEO of the Indian airline Jet Airways wanted to meet with her on several occasions. When she asked then SAA board chairperson Cheryl Carolus about rumours that SAA would drop its Mumbai route, Carolus confirmed to her that Jet Airways had been lobbying SAA unsuccessfully to let go of the profitable Mumbai route. In August 2010, during a joint South Africa/India meeting, rumours were circulating that Hogan would be sacked. On 31 October 2010, during a meeting with Zuma, the president dismissed her as minister.[1]

Shortly before the India trip, Jet Airways introduced its first direct flight between Mumbai and Johannesburg – a route already covered by SAA.

Dot 2: In October 2010, colourful ANC MP Mabel Petronella 'Vytjie' Mentor went to Johannesburg to see Zuma after she had asked for a meeting with him to express her unhappiness with the closure of the Pebble Bed Modular Reactor company. Mentor was the chair of Parliament's Portfolio Committee on Public Enterprises. (She had organised the meeting through Zuma's chief advisor, Lakela Kaunda, who would later admit having received money from a Gupta-linked company while working for the ANC.[2])

In a statement to the police, Mentor told how she had been fetched from the airport by two men dressed in black wearing dark glasses and ear-pieces. She had expected to be driven to the Union Buildings for her meeting with Zuma, but was instead taken to the Gupta businesses' office park in Midrand. The bodyguards asked her to step inside to greet someone. Inside was Ajay Gupta. He asked her about her family and offered Mentor access to his suite at Newlands cricket ground, adding that she could take her son there, who happened to play cricket for Western Province. Gupta told Mentor that it was a 'privilege for him' to meet her, she said. 'He knew what my position was and also knew that I had an appointment with the President.'[3] Mentor said she became 'agitated and irritated' by Ajay Gupta, who told her Zuma wasn't yet available to meet her because he had to attend an appointment at Luthuli House. She found it 'very strange' that Gupta knew about her meeting with Zuma and the president's whereabouts.

Mentor was then escorted to the Gupta mansion in Saxonwold. 'I was served with chai tea with naan bread and curry. By then I was upset and not feeling well, therefore I didn't enjoy the food.' Ajay Gupta, she claims, later arrived and told her he was very close to the Indian government and could help Denel with its legal problems in that country. He asked if she would leverage her position of influence to get SAA to stop flying the Johannesburg to Mumbai route.[4] 'You could be a Minister of Public Enterprises in a week's time when the President [...] reshuffles cabinet and removes the current minister of public enterprises [Barbara Hogan],' Gupta told her.

Mentor asked Gupta how he could do that. He responded to the effect that he would put in a word with the president to have her appointed. 'I was doubtful and he could see it,' said Mentor. 'So he said that they have done it previously, I must just play along, meaning I must agree to influence SAA to stop the route.' According to her statement, Mentor then got 'very angry' and in a 'loud voice' asked to be taken back to the airport. Then, like something out of a movie scene, Zuma entered the room.

Mentor stood up and angrily explained to the president the exchange that had just taken place, telling Zuma how Gupta said that he would 'put in a word with the president', so that she would become minister. Zuma, she said, told her to 'calm down and not to worry'; she said that he 'never reprimanded' Gupta.

In her interview with Madonsela, Mentor said Zuma wasn't angry that she declined the offer. 'He apparently said to her in Zulu, something like "it's okay Ntombazane (girl) … take care of yourself".'[5] In her police statement, Mentor said that Zuma didn't seem surprised by what Ajay Gupta had told her but that she had been made to look like 'the mad one'. 'The President didn't even have a meeting with me,' said Mentor. 'He walked me out of the house to the vehicle. … I asked the President why he meets with these people and in that house. He said that his son is staying next door. He also said that he was sorry.'

Shortly after being offered the position of minister in exchange for culling SAA's Mumbai route, Mentor made an appointment with then SAA CEO, Siza Mzimela. She asked her how long it would take to cultivate an international airline route. In her statement she continued:

> She said that the first four years capital [is] invested … from the fifth year up till the ninth/tenth year you break even, and only making profit thereafter. Then I told her that someone approached me to influence SAA to close the route between India and SA. She said it was [SAA's] main and most profitable route and that it would not make economic sense to close that route. Then it made sense to me.[6]

After turning down their offer, Mentor never heard from Zuma or the Guptas again.

Dot 3: Later that week, Zuma fired Hogan and replaced her with Malusi Gigaba as Minister of Public Enterprises.

On 8 May 2012, SAA announced it would be adding additional flights to its Johannesburg–Mumbai route following 'increased demand' on this popular route: 'The airline hopes to be adding even further flights on this route in the near future as travel between South Africa and India has recently shown noticeable growth.'[7]

Five months later, Carolus and seven SAA board members stepped down after a breakdown in their relationship with government, represented by Gigaba and the Department of Public Enterprises. Two weeks later, they were followed by Mzimela and two general managers.[8]

Dot 4: In January 2013, the chair of the Jacob G Zuma Foundation and very close personal friend of the president, Dudu Myeni, was appointed chair of the SAA board.

Dot 5: In April 2013, SAA and Jet Airways announced a code-sharing agreement whereby SAA passengers would code share on Jet Airways' operations between Mumbai and Delhi, Bangalore, Hyderabad, Chennai and Thiruvananthapuram. In turn, Jet Airways would code share on SAA's flights between Johannesburg, Cape Town and Durban.[9] In the same media statement, SAA confirmed the steady increase in tourists from India to South Africa. 'In essence, we are truly bringing the world to Africa,' Manoj Papa, SAA's acting general manager for commercial, was quoted as saying.

Dot 6: Two weeks later, a Jet Airways chartered Airbus A330 didn't bring the whole world to Africa, but landed with 200 Indian guests who had come to South Africa at Waterkloof Air Force Base to attend the Gupta family wedding at Sun City. After the scandal broke, Jet Airways was fined $8 800 for landing at a military airbase without permission.[10] By now, the close link between Jet Airways and the Guptas was there for all to see.

Dot 7: In early 2015, SAA announced that after 20 years it would cut the Johannesburg–Mumbai route owing to financial losses. From being the 'most profitable' flight for SAA five years before and adding more flights to the route in 2012, the airline, now under the management of Myeni and her confidant, acting CEO Nico Bezuidenhout, started reporting from 2014 that the Indian route was making a loss. At the time that SAA shut down the route, a travel industry official was quoted as saying flights on this route were between 82% and 88% full.[11] In a statement announcing the end of its direct flights to India, SAA praised the fact that passengers would now be able to travel to more cities on the sub-continent through code-sharing agreements with Jet Airways and Etihad (which owned 24% of Jet Airways).

Whether the true reason behind the closure of SAA's Johannesburg to Mumbai route was financial losses or not, the fact remains that less than five years after Ajay Gupta allegedly offered Vytjie Mentor a ministerial post in exchange for dropping SAA's Indian route – while Jacob Zuma was in the house – his wishes came true. The Guptas have denied ever meeting Mentor or offering her a ministerial position.[12]

After Mentor took to Facebook in 2016 to reveal her story, Zuma's office responded that the president had 'no recollection of Ms Mentor'.[13] This, despite the fact that Mentor served as ANC caucus chair between 2004 and 2008 while Zuma was deputy president. Mentor wrote in her statement to the police: 'I am of the conclusion that the Gupta family, the son of the President and some ministers whom I have named in this statement, as well as the President to a certain extent, all have a corrupt relationship that gives unfair advantage to the Gupta family and their associates at the expense of the state using state resources and agencies … for their own benefit.'[14]

In 2017 Mentor published a book, *No Holy Cows*, in which she accuses Zuma of sexual harassment.[15]

During her interview with Madonsela for the State of Capture investigation, Hogan, the former public enterprises minister, revealed that Zuma and ANC secretary general Mantashe took an interest in the appointment of board members to SOEs. Zuma was particularly interested in the boards of Eskom and Transnet – coincidentally the two SOEs from which the Guptas and their associates (including Duduzane Zuma) would benefit most handsomely in years to come. In her report, Madonsela said that Zuma, 'made it very difficult for [Hogan] to perform her job, at a certain point he would not even allow her to appoint a director-general in her department'.[16]

In December 2010, two instructive things happened: the Gupta-owned newspaper, *The New Age*, reported that former Public Investment Corporation CEO Brian Molefe would become the CEO of Transnet, and Gigaba appointed former trade and industry official Iqbal Sharma to the parastatal's board. This was two months after Zuma had replaced Hogan with Gigaba as public enterprises minister – the position that Vytjie Mentor claims was offered to her by Ajay Gupta.

The fact that *The New Age* first reported on Molefe's impending appointment two months before it was announced by Gigaba deepened the suspicion that the Guptas had a role to play in his elevation to Transnet CEO. This was interesting, as Molefe was widely perceived to be an Mbeki man during his tenure as head of the Public Investment Corporation. A former Treasury official, Molefe was involved in empowerment deals that benefited businesspeople close to Mbeki. When his term as chief executive of the Public Investment Corporation came to an end in March 2010, the *Pretoria News* opined as such: 'The announcement by Brian Molefe at the weekend that he will not be seeking another term as PIC chief executive brings the curtain down on the fairytale story of the Molefe husband-and-wife team who played important roles in driving the vision of former president Thabo Mbeki.'[17] But it took less than a year for Molefe to 'rehabilitate' himself into an acceptable candidate for the Zuma administration to oversee the massive infrastructure spend the government was about to embark on through Transnet.

At the same time, senior ANC members expressed their unhappiness about the growing influence of the Guptas in state affairs. This was evident in Gigaba's failed attempt to have Sharma appointed as Transnet board chairperson in June 2011. It was reported that the Cabinet vetoed Sharma's appointment because he was perceived as being too close to the Guptas.[18] Sharma, it later turned out, wasn't only close to the Guptas, but was also directly linked to their steel-manufacturing business, VR Laser. When Gigaba couldn't have him appointed as board chair, Sharma was appointed chair of the Transnet board's acquisitions and disposals committee, which oversaw big tenders.

In February 2012, Zuma announced a 'massive infrastructure development drive' during his state of the nation address. One of the five pillars of the drive was Transnet's market demand strategy, which entailed an investment, over the next seven years, of R300 billion in capital infrastructure projects, of which the bulk would be spent on rail projects This was followed by the issuing of a tender for the supply of 599 electric and 465 diesel locomotives to Transnet in July 2012 at a cost of R50 billion – about the same as the cost of the infamous 'arms deal'. In March 2014, Transnet announced that it had awarded the tender to four companies. For the electric locomotives, the tender was split between China South Rail Zhuzhou Electric Locomotive (359 locomotives) and Bombardier Transportation (240 locomotives). For the diesel trains, the contract was split between General Electric Transportation (233 locomotives) and China North Rail Rolling Stock (232 locomotives).

In July 2014 the *Mail & Guardian* revealed Sharma's conflict: while he was chairing the Transnet board tender committee, Sharma entered into negotiations to buy VR Laser Services, a steel-manufacturing company partly owned by Duduzane Zuma and Rajesh Gupta.[19] During this process, the four successful bidders all visited VR Laser's premises 'to assess the possibility of subcontracting work to VR Laser'. In plain language, the guy in charge of awarding the locomotives tender had an interest in providing steel to the winning bidders. Coincidentally, the president's son also stood to benefit from the steel deal.

At this point, it is important to introduce Salim Essa. The Guptas have always surrounded themselves with a coterie of wheelers and dealers to source business opportunities and share in the spoils. As the spotlight of public scrutiny increasingly shone on the Guptas, it was also strategically important for the family to have associates at arm's length doing their bidding. Enter Salim Aziz Essa, the son of a Polokwane-based industrialist, whose family used to own Chancellor House, the downtown Johannesburg building where Nelson Mandela and Oliver Tambo used to run their legal practice in the 1950s. Essa reportedly befriended Rajesh Gupta in 2011 and they soon started exploring business opportunities together.[20] Essa's name has become particularly prominent in the Guptas' dealings with SOEs. He is linked to the family empire, which includes Duduzane Zuma, through at least four entities: VR Laser Services, Tegeta Exploration and Resources, Trillian Capital Partners and Shiva Uranium.[21]

His company, Elgasolve, is the majority shareholder (75%) in VR Laser Services, which stands to benefit handsomely from infrastructure spend at Transnet and Denel. The remaining shares in VR Laser are owned by a company that belongs to Rajesh Gupta and Duduzane Zuma. Elgasolve has a 22% stake in Tegeta Exploration and Resources, the Guptas' mining company that bought the struggling Optimum Coal Mine from Glencore. Essa's wife, Zeenat Osmany, holds a 5% stake in the Gupta-owned Shiva Uranium mine, and Trillian Capital Partners, a boutique investment firm, is majority-owned by Essa. Essa is a Gupta business partner in the truest sense of the word: if he scores, the Guptas win, and vice versa.

Back to Transnet: when articles critical of the Guptas' relationship with Zuma, his family and state officials started to appear, the Saxonwold spin machine retorted that they make very little of their money from government tenders. This was also evident in communication with their PR company, Bell Pottinger, who advised the family to place emphasis on the small amount of direct government work they have received. The leaked Gupta emails released in June 2017 show that the Guptas were right. And wrong. Although they may not have received many tenders directly, they benefited richly from government spend through intricate consultancy relationships, strategic shareholdings and hidden arrangements. That's where the real money was going to be made. They were smarter than the rest, but not smart enough not to be caught out. The brazenness with which they embarked on their mission to capture the state was bound to have major repercussions eventually.

The Gupta leaks confirmed our suspicions: that palms were greased through fancy service agreements to syphon off to offshore bank accounts some of the R200 billion Zuma gave Transnet to spend in 2012 for the upgrade of the rail network. In their first exposé following the Gupta leaks, amaBhungane and Scorpio revealed in detail how the Guptas and Essa scored R5,3 billion in kickbacks from the Transnet locomotives deal.[22] Let's join the dots in ten easy steps:

1. In October 2010 Zuma fires Hogan and appoints Gigaba, a friend of the Guptas, as Minister of Public Enterprises. (Gigaba's former lover, Buhle Mkhize, alleged on Twitter in 2017 that the minister made use of the family's private aircraft.)

2. In December 2010 Gigaba appoints Sharma to the Transnet board. He fails to have him appointed as board chairperson, but puts Sharma in charge of the committee overseeing acquisitions and disposals.

3. In February 2011 Gigaba announces the appointment of Molefe as Transnet CEO. Molefe, it was later revealed, benefited the Guptas at Eskom and was in regular contact with Ajay Gupta. In her report on state capture, Madonsela wrote: 'Mr Brian Molefe is friends with members of the Gupta family. Mr A Gupta admitted during my interview with him on 4 October 2016 that Mr Molefe is his "very good friend" and often visits his home in Saxonwold.'[23]

4. In July 2012 Transnet appoints Anoj Singh as chief financial officer. The Gupta leaks later showed how the family paid for multiple visits by Singh to Dubai – the Guptas' second home.

5. In July 2012 Transnet issues a R50 billion tender for the acquisition of 1 064 locomotives.

6. In December 2012 Transnet appoints global advisory firm McKinsey as transaction advisor for the locomotives tender at a capped amount of R35 million. McKinsey subcontracted large parts of the contract to Regiments Capital, and Regiments subcontracted Trillian Capital Partners. Ultimately, the two companies received over R600 million.[24]

7. Regiments was represented by director and 32% shareholder Eric Wood. The Guptas made an offer to buy Regiments in 2014, but this was rejected by Wood's business partners. Wood, who motivated for Regiments to sell out to the Guptas, proceeded to leave Regiments and form Trillian with Essa – the Guptas' business partner – as a 60% shareholder.

8. Singh tells Molefe it was Regiments' idea to split the contract

between four service providers.[25] In March 2014 Molefe announces the winning bidders.

9. In May 2015 Essa travels to China to sign a 'business development services agreement' with China South Rail, the firm that won the contract to deliver 359 electric locomotives. In terms of the deal, Essa's Hong Kong-registered Tequesta would receive an 'advisory fee' of 21% of the contract value, or R3,8 billion, from the locomotives deal.[26] 'The amounts alone elevate the fees beyond consultancy to where only one explanation is possible: that these are the proceeds of corruption,' amaBhungane concluded.[27]

10. Among the Gupta email leaks, journalists found financial statements on the Guptas' computers detailing 'receivables' from China South Rail to offshore Gupta front companies, which proved they benefited from two more Transnet tenders to China South Rail.[28] The total amount due? R5,3 billion.

As if this weren't bad enough, the Chinese locomotives didn't work when they arrived in South Africa. News24 reported in January 2017 that technical problems have 'plagued' the first batch of locomotives to arrive. Their alternators 'vibrate excessively' and Transnet refused to accept any more trains before the problem was fixed.[29]

After the national election in May 2014, Zuma moved Gigaba to the Department of Home Affairs and replaced him with Lynne Brown as Minister of Public Enterprises. It was rumoured at the time that Gigaba clashed with Myeni, who had defied him at SAA, and hence his transfer to home affairs. Zuma denied this, but didn't explain why he had moved Gigaba to a much less glamorous portfolio.

As well as chairing Zuma's foundation, Myeni has for many years been romantically linked to the president, despite strong denials by both parties. As far as the president's influencers go, she is right up there. She cooked for Zuma at Mahlamba Ndlopfu, his official residence, and has made payments to his children in the past.[30] Myeni's son, Thalente, lived at Zuma's Johannesburg home and once told an embassy that he was Zuma's son.[31] Myeni was even photographed tying Zuma's shoelaces during a function in Richards Bay.[32]

It didn't take long for Brown and Myeni to clash over SAA's affairs as well, and in December 2014 oversight for the national airline was moved to the National Treasury, then headed by Nhlanhla Nene. Myeni was reportedly instrumental in Zuma's cataclysmic removal of Nene as finance minister in December 2015. Days before his sacking, Nene shot down a proposal by Myeni to purchase Airbus aircraft and enter into a sale and leaseback deal with a local partner, instead opting for a leasing agreement directly with Airbus.[33]

Shortly after the ratings downgrade to junk status in April 2017, Myeni, who is part of a pro-Zuma WhatsApp chat group called Black Empowerment Foundation, wrote: 'Let the rand fall and rise and emerge with the masses.'[34] Civil-action NGO OUTA (Organisation Undoing Tax Abuse) has applied to the High Court to have Myeni declared a delinquent director.

Although Brown has consistently denied being captured by the Guptas, a series of events in 2015 at the state's aerospace and defence technology company, Denel, calls into question her motives. Denel was formed in the dying days of apartheid to commercialise the state's weaponry-manufacturing capacity. Because of international sanctions against the country, South Africa was forced to manufacture its own armaments.

In July 2015 Brown 'rotated' the Denel board, with Cabinet approval, and replaced all but one non-executive director. She rejected a proposal by her department to retain experienced board members who had not served the maximum two terms and replaced them with an inexperienced crew, which did not include a single engineer.[35] Brown appointed lawyer Daniel Mantsha as chair of the board. Mantsha had been struck off as an attorney in 2007 and readmitted in 2011, and served as legal advisor to then communications minister Faith Muthambi.[36]

What Brown didn't say – or perhaps didn't know – at the time, was

that Mantsha had been captured by the Guptas. As the Gupta leaks
would later reveal:[37]

❏ Shortly after his appointment, Mantsha started sending his
   municipal bills to the Guptas.
❏ Mantsha accompanied the Guptas on their private jet on a flight
   to India the month following his appointment.
❏ The Guptas organised and paid for Mantsha to visit Dubai at
   least twice.
❏ Mantsha sent confidential documents from Brown's office to the
   Guptas.

What did the Guptas want from Mantsha and Denel in exchange?
In January 2016, the arms company's acting CEO, Zwelakhe Ntshepe,
announced the establishment of Denel Asia, a joint venture between
Denel (51%) and VR Laser Asia (49%) to enter the lucrative Asian military market. Salim Essa, the Guptas' trusted partner and proxy, is the
sole shareholder of VR Laser Asia. The board of Denel Asia would have
included Ajay Gupta's son, Kamal Singhala, a Gupta lawyer, Pieter van
der Merwe, and Denel's Ntshepe and Stephan Burger.[38]

The Gupta leaks revealed that, at the same time, the Guptas were
plotting to establish Denel India, effectively hijacking the ownership and
intellectual property from the South African Government.[39] In Pravin
Gordhan and Lungisa Fuzile, the Guptas met their match though. For a
foreign-based joint venture to be approved, government institutions had
to seek Treasury approval, which Denel didn't do in the case of Denel
Asia. When Gordhan and Fuzile, who were then finance minister and
Treasury director general, found out about this, they were livid and
blocked the deal from going ahead. Denel instituted court proceedings
to overturn their decision. 'VR Laser SA runs its business operations
and capital commitments through loan-financing raised from its shareholders. The shareholders have been identified as politically exposed
persons,' said Fuzile in his answering affidavit in court.[40]

But, before the court case could be concluded, Zuma fired Gordhan

and replaced him with Gigaba, whose every move has been scrutinised since he took over the reins at the Treasury. Gigaba has pursued
Gordhan's approach in the matter, however, and in May 2017 told
Mantsha to drop both the deal with VR Laser and the court case against
the Treasury.[41]

This ain't good news for the Guptas or Mantsha, who must now be
wondering where the payment for next month's municipal bill will be
coming from.

CHAPTER 9

How to hijack a mine

—

'What is clear is that state capture by shadowy elites has profound
implications for state institutions. It destroys public trust in
the state and its organs; it weakens key economic agencies that
are tasked with delivering development outcomes; and it erodes
confidence in the economy.'

– State Capacity Research Project, Betrayal of the promise: How South Africa is
being stolen, May 2017

There is a massive irony in the fact that it was Glencore, the Swiss-based commodities trader with an asset book of about $130 billion, that was the biggest corporate victim of the Gupta family's attempts to capture the state of Jacob Zuma. Glencore made most of its money by busting oil sanctions for the apartheid regime in the 1970s and 1980s, when it was illegal for foreign companies to ship oil to South Africa. The late Marc Rich, who founded Glencore, apparently claimed that his firm made $2 billion in pure profit from its underhand deals with Pretoria.[1] Rich, who saw no issue with bribing his way to the top, was infamous for making deals with a variety of clients, including the Ayatollah of Iran, the Soviet Union and apartheid South Africa.[2]

Rich, who died in 2013, would probably therefore not have been shocked by the skulduggery exercised by the likes of Mosebenzi Zwane, Rajesh Gupta, Salim Essa, Brian Molefe and Ben Ngubane to effectively hijack the Optimum coal mine in Mpumalanga from Glencore. To others in the ANC, who regarded the struggle against apartheid as a just cause for human rights and equality before the law, the behaviour of Zuma, his best friends and their beneficiaries was proof that the ANC had lost its way. This battle, to cleanse the ANC's soul of the cancerous and pervasive corruption that had captured the party from inside, was at the heart of attempts to unseat Zuma and his cronies at the party's elective conference in December 2017.

When Tegeta Exploration and Resources, the Guptas' mining company, set their sights on Optimum, the company already had a coal mine in Mpumalanga called Brakfontein, which supplied coal to Eskom's Majuba power station. This deal was estimated to be worth R3,8 billion over ten years.[3]

The story of how Glencore became strong-armed into selling Optimum to the Guptas started in 1993, a year before the ANC came into power, when Glencore signed a contract to supply Eskom with 5,5 million tons of coal a year for its Hendrina power station at around R150 per ton.[4] The contract was due to expire in 2018, with Optimum losing money for over a decade on every ton of coal it sold to Eskom. The company needed to earn at least R400 per ton to break even.[5] By 2015 the mine was running at a loss of R3,7 million a day and had 500 permanent employees and 1 500 contractors who risked losing their jobs.[6] In 2013 Optimum/Glencore had triggered the 'hardship' clause in its 1993 contract with Eskom and the two parties were negotiating an agreement to keep Optimum afloat.[7] Eskom and Optimum had agreed on a new deal that would last until December 2018, but then Eskom got a new boss – Brian Molefe.

In mid-2015, Lynne Brown moved Molefe from Transnet to Eskom after the suspension of Tshediso Matona. In December 2014, before Molefe's move, Cabinet had almost completely overhauled the Eskom board, with the appointment of nine new directors. Of these, five (including chairperson Ben Ngubane) were directly linked to Salim Essa through family, friends or business connections, and nine of Eskom's 13 directors were part of the Gupta network.[8] This all meant bad news for Optimum's owners, Glencore, and in May 2015 Molefe informed Optimum the new deal was off the table.[9]

In July 2015 four significant things happened:

- ❑ Glencore made a counter-offer to Eskom, proposing that it should receive R300 per ton of coal until the end of 2018 and then R570 per ton between 2019 and 2023.
- ❑ Eskom rejected the offer and imposed an extraordinary fine of R2,1 billion on Glencore for having supplied substandard coal to the power utility since 2012.
- ❑ Glencore announced it would have to retrench 380 workers because of financial constraints.
- ❑ Audit firm KPMG approached Glencore with an 'anonymous' offer (from the Guptas) to buy Optimum for R2 billion.[10]

On 31 July 2015, the board of Optimum placed the company in business rescue, effectively handing over authority to run the company to business-rescue practitioners.

During her investigation into state capture, Madonsela analysed cellphone records to establish relationships between individuals involved in the Optimum transaction. She found that Molefe had called Ajay Gupta 44 times between August 2015 and March 2016, the period during which the transaction was negotiated. Ajay Gupta called Molefe 14 times. Another 20 calls were made between Molefe and the other Gupta brothers, Atul and Tony, and their senior business executives, Nazeem Howa and Ronica Ragavan. By using cellphone-tower tracking technology, Madonsela was also able to place Molefe in the vicinity of Saxonwold, where the Guptas live, 19 times between August and November 2015. It was in reaction to this finding that Molefe memorably said at a press conference, during which he broke down in tears, 'There is a shebeen there, I think it's two streets away from the Gupta house. Now I will not admit nor deny that I was going to the shebeen.'[11]

At the same time, a process was under way to replace Ngoako Ramatlhodi as mining minister. Two years later, after being fired by

Zuma from his Cabinet, Ramatlhodi told amaBhungane that he was kicked out of his job because he wouldn't blackmail Glencore on the instruction of Molefe and Ngubane. 'They insisted that I must suspend all the Glencore mining licences pending the payment of the R2 billion [the fine for supplying 'substandard coal'] ... You must remember that the country was undergoing load-shedding at that time. I said to them: how many mines do these people have supplying Eskom? How many more outages are we going to have? I said I'm not going to shut the mines,' Ramatlhodi said.[12]

Ramatlhodi was clearly a stumbling block for the Guptas in their bid to buy Optimum. He had to be removed, and the only person who could do that was Zuma. The headhunting for an amenable mining minister started in earnest and the Gupta email leaks give us an insight into how Zuma found a very unlikely candidate to head the mining ministry in South Africa.

On 1 August 2015, a man called France Oupa Mokoena from Koena Consulting and Property Developers in the tiny Free State town of Vrede (which, ironically, means 'peace' in Afrikaans) emailed the curriculum vitae of teacher and local politician Mosebenzi Joseph Zwane to Tony Gupta. It remains a mystery how Mokoena got involved in headhunting for Cabinet or how he got hold of Tony Gupta's email address. Zwane's CV shows that he is a qualified teacher who had taught for 11 years before becoming a full-time member of the mayoral committee of the Thabo Mofutsanyana District Municipality in 2000. From 2006 to 2008, Zwane was the executive mayor of the municipality, and between 2009 and 2015 he served as an MEC under the Free State premier, Ace Magashule.

Magashule had long been linked to the Guptas. His son Tshepiso is a Gupta employee who is close to the family and Duduzane Zuma; Magashule's office had helped the Guptas with invitations to local Indian politicians around the time of the lavish Gupta wedding at Sun City in April 2013, so that they could pretend the flight was part of an official state visit. Zwane did the same. Under Magashule, the Free State had become a major advertiser in the Guptas' *The New Age*. In May 2014, shortly before the national election, Tshepiso Magashule emailed Tony Gupta a list of 362 cellphone numbers for Free State ANC party agents in need of R120 of airtime each.[13]

It is safe to conclude that Zwane was introduced to the Guptas by Magashule, who, his critics would argue, had long perfected the art of state capture in the Free State. Magashule is the longest-serving provincial chairperson in the ANC and had serious ambitions to be promoted to Luthuli House. He had always flown below the radar, but his star shone under Zuma, who appointed him as premier in 2009, after he had been overlooked by Nelson Mandela and Thabo Mbeki several times.

Magashule is part of the so-called Premier League, who are trying to use their bloc voting numbers to determine the future of the ANC. One of the biggest scandals laid bare through the Gupta leaks was that of the Estina dairy-farm scandal, through which the Guptas pocketed at least R50 million of the R184 million the farm received from the Free State agricultural department. Zwane previously oversaw this department, which approved the farming project near his home town of Vrede.[14] Magashule would have identified Zwane as the perfect candidate for a portfolio that needed a Gupta-friendly minister. And so, a few hours after receiving Zwane's CV from Mokoena, Tony Gupta emailed the document to Duduzane Zuma.

A month later, on 2 September 2015, the ANC's deputy secretary general, Jessie Duarte, sent a letter to Parliament, informing them that Zwane had been nominated to fill the vacancy left by the resignation of an ANC MP. To become a minister, you must first be an MP. On the same day, Duarte's letter was in Tony Gupta's inbox (it is unclear how he obtained the letter).

Ramatlhodi told amaBhungane that Ngubane called him to a meeting with Molefe around 1 September 2015, during which he was told to suspend all Glencore's mining licences. Ramatlhodi refused.[15] Three weeks later, Duduzane Zuma's father moved Ramatlhodi out of mining to the vacant portfolio of public service and administration, and appointed

Zwane, until then an unknown (outside of the Gupta and Magashule circles), as Minister of Mineral Resources. The dots were big, red and flashing for all to join.

With Zwane in place, the ground was fertile for Glencore to be pushed out of Optimum. The company was now under the control of business-rescue practitioners Piers Marsden and Peter van der Steen, who had to find a solution for the company's woes, primarily driven by charging 1993 rates for coal and a R2 billion fine for 'substandard coal'. As the Guptas were putting together Tegeta Exploration and Resources' pitch to take over the Optimum mines, another prospective bidder was interested in buying Glencore's struggling assets.

Pembani, an investment holding company, led by former MTN CEO Phuthuma Nhleko, which bought out Ramaphosa's stake in Shanduka, was Glencore's BEE partner in Optimum and owned 12% of the company's shares. Pembani geared up to invest in Optimum and had sufficient financing to do so.

In November 2015, as the company was preparing to take over Optimum, Tegeta's shareholding changed from Gupta-owned to a joint ownership comprising the Guptas' Oakbay Investments (29%), Duduzane Zuma's Mabengela Investments (28,5%), Salim Essa's Elgasolve (21,5%) and two unknown Dubai-based companies – this partly to satisfy BEE requirements.

At the same time, Eskom's group executive for generation, Matshela Koko, turned the heat up on Glencore and told the business-rescue practitioners he had an 'offer on the table' from the Guptas.[16]

Zwane boarded a flight to Zurich via Dubai on 29 November 2015. He arrived the following day and checked into the five-star Dolder Grand Hotel, a luxury establishment dating back to 1899 with views of the Alps and Lake Zurich. According to Madonsela's report, Zwane met with none other than Glencore CEO, Ivan Glasenberg, Tony Gupta and Essa at the hotel between 30 November and 2 December 2015. Zwane later admitted that he persuaded Glasenberg to sell his company's shares to the Guptas, but said there was nothing wrong with this and that he was only trying to save jobs.[17] This meeting, which culminated in Glencore selling its mines to the Guptas, illustrates the extraordinary influence the family had over the state. Although his department had booked tickets for Zwane to fly back to South Africa, he never used them and accompanied Tony Gupta and Essa on their private jet back to Johannesburg via Dubai.

Back in South Africa, Pembani had desperately wanted to get in on the deal, but was allegedly told by Molefe in no uncertain terms that the company would not get a supplier contract from Eskom (as was required for the Optimum transaction).[18] Molefe denied stymieing Pembani's chances.

On 11 December 2015 – two days after Zuma fired Nene – it was announced that Tegeta had purchased the two Optimum coal mines and an export allocation at Richards Bay coal terminal from Glencore for R2,15 billion.

To recap: the Guptas wanted a coal mine. Molefe and Ngubane used their power to squeeze Optimum, under Glencore, into business rescue. Ramatlhodi refused to shut down all Glencore's mines. Tony Gupta sent Zwane's CV to Duduzane Zuma. Jacob Zuma appointed Zwane as mining minister. Zwane travelled to Zurich with the Guptas to persuade Glencore to sell them their coal mine. Zwane flew back with the Guptas on their private jet. The Guptas got a coal mine.

In her final report on state capture, Madonsela found that if Zwane travelled to Zurich in his official capacity to support Tegeta's bid – as he did – his conduct would give Tegeta an unfair advantage over other interested buyers (like Pembani). 'Further, it is potentially unlawful for the Minister to use his official position of authority to unfairly and unduly influence a contract for a friend, or in this instance his boss's son, at the expense of the State. This scenario would be further complicated if his actions were sanctioned by the President,' Madonsela concluded.[19]

Only one outstanding matter remained for the Guptas: they had to find R2,1 billion to pay for their mine. And guess who they turned to? Eskom. When Tegeta (jointly owned by the Guptas, Duduzane Zuma and

Essa) took over the Optimum mines, they were running at a loss of R3 million a day.[20] The Gupta leaks revealed that on 9 December 2015, two days before the Optimum sale was announced, Tegeta's chief executive, Ravindra Nath, sent an email to Eskom's Koko (who would later become acting CEO), referring to a meeting where a prepayment from Eskom to Tegeta for R1,68 billion was agreed upon.[21] Although the payment never actually materialised, Eskom's chief financial officer, Anoj Singh, admitted in July 2017 that he had signed a R1,6 billion guarantee to Absa for Tegeta to buy Optimum. This convinced the business-rescue practitioners that Tegeta had the financial backing to purchase Optimum. Singh was previously the chief financial officer of Transnet and moved over with Molefe to Eskom in 2015.

Experts said it was highly irregular of Singh to have agreed to the guarantee, and the DA filed criminal charges against him for contravening the Public Finance Management Act and the Companies Act.[22] Singh was implicated in the deal – he made multiple visits to Dubai, courtesy of the Guptas.

The Guptas didn't get the R1,6 billion Singh signed for, but soon after the Optimum purchase, money started flowing to the company from Eskom.

❏ In April 2016, Tegeta urgently needed R600 million to meet the 14 April deadline for payment of the R2,1 billion purchase price for Optimum. Eskom came to the rescue: Madonsela's report reveals how the Eskom tender committee during a late-night meeting over telecon approved a R659 million prepayment for coal to Tegeta to deliver emergency stock at a cost of R580 per ton.[23] Koko famously lied to *Carte Blanche* presenter Devi Sankaree Govender when she challenged him about the prepayment. After denying the payment, Koko said, 'Let's say I made a mistake' when Govender showed him his signature on the contract. Eskom also argued that the coal was for load shedding, even though government had announced that load shedding was a thing of the past.[24] Koko, it later emerged from the Gupta leaks, went on a Gupta-sponsored junket to Dubai early in January 2016, shortly after the Optimum deal was clinched.

❏ Trillian, the advisory firm of which Essa owns 60%, invoiced Eskom for about R420 million between April and December 2016 for consultancy work, even though the company was only subcontracted by Eskom via McKinsey in March 2016.[25]

❏ Madonsela found that Trillian had contributed R235 million towards the purchase of Optimum by Tegeta.

Madonsela's report eventually claimed Molefe's career at Eskom and on 11 November 2016 he resigned. In a statement, Molefe said his name would be cleared: 'I am confident that, when the time comes, I will be able to show that I have done nothing wrong ... I shall dedicate myself to showing that an injustice has been done by the precipitate delivery of "observations" ... which the former Public Protector has drawn back from calling "findings". The truth will out,' Molefe said.[26]

In February 2017 Molefe was sworn in as an ANC MP amid speculation that Zuma would appoint him as finance minister in Gordhan's place. But Zuma was apparently convinced by senior ANC leaders that Molefe was too big a risk due to his proximity to the Guptas, and instead appointed Gigaba to take over Treasury. After less than three months as an MP, Molefe resigned and, bizarrely, returned to Eskom as CEO after he didn't succeed in securing a R30 million payout. There was a public outcry over his return and after a few days the board rescinded his reappointment. Molefe instituted legal action in the Labour Court to get his job back.

Koko was suspended in June 2017 after it was revealed that a company in which his stepdaughter was a director netted contracts worth at least R1 billion from Eskom over 11 months.[27] In the same month, Ngubane resigned after Brown refused to appoint his choice of Eskom board member Zethembe Khoza as new CEO. Instead Brown made Khoza the acting board chairperson.[28]

Remember the R2,1 billion fine that Molefe and Koko slapped on Glencore, which forced them to put Optimum into business rescue? That was lowered to R255 million for Tegeta after arbitration in March 2017. Singh told a shocked media in July 2017 during the release of the entity's financial results that a faulty coal crusher had actually caused the quality of the coal to be lowered, when in fact it wasn't that bad.[29]

Despite a tumultuous year, during which Eskom's dodgy dealings with the Guptas were laid bare, Molefe still received a handsome bonus of R8,1 million, Singh a bonus of R1,8 million and the suspended Koko a R1,4 million reward, as part of the utility in decline's R4,2 billion bonus bonanza in 2017.[30] After a series of revelations about his role in the capture of Eskom, Singh was suspended in late July 2017 following pressure from the Development Bank of South Africa and other commercial banks that they would withdraw their loans to the utility if it didn't clean up its act.[31]

CHAPTER 10

'I am Hlaudi Motsoeneng, baby!'

——

'But baba loves Hlaudi, he loves him so much,
we must support him.'
– Former communications minister Faith Muthambi to the late SABC board member
Hope Zinde after the latter expressed concerns about Hlaudi Motsoeneng's appointment,
9 March 2015

Of all the state institutions captured by Zuma loyalists during his disastrous presidency, the public broadcaster probably came closest to complete collapse following its plunder and destruction by a megalomaniac called Hlaudi Motsoeneng. When Motsoeneng was finally fired in mid-2017, he left the broadcaster reeling, financially ruined and directionless.

The SABC, with its four television channels, 18 radio stations and a combined audience of over 30 million people, is the largest media platform in the country and as the ANC's support slipped away from the metropolitan municipalities, it was crucial for the Zuma administration to have a clear line to rural South Africa. Although the popularity of the broadcaster's platforms has been challenged by private companies in the cities, the SABC's influence in rural South Africa remains unparalleled.

Zuma cannot be criticised for having wanted a sympathiser at the head of the SABC during his term. It's not unusual for presidents and prime ministers to appoint someone 'safe', even pliable, to head up the

120

public broadcaster. It's something all presidents do: the public broad-caster is as much a service to the people as it is a conveyer of news. So it was no surprise that Zuma would bring in someone who sympathised with his cause – in other words, being the victim – and who would pro-tect the president when times were tough. Little did we know, however, the nightmare that Zuma would bestow on the SABC, and the country, through a madman nicknamed 'Cloudy'.

Mbeki had Snuki Zikalala as 'his master's voice' at the SABC. Despite his faults, of which there were many, Zikalala, the head of news, at least didn't view the SABC as his personal fiefdom. Being loyal to the president is one thing, but treating the corporation, which is run with public funds, like your personal spaza shop is something quite different. Ironically, Zikalala would lose his job in 2009 after refusing to take Motsoeneng back into the SABC. This after Motsoeneng, who was described in a 2006 Deloitte forensic report for the SABC as a 'semi-literate journal-ist, inexperienced and not able to communicate in English', was sacked by the public broadcaster in 2007 as executive producer at Lesedi FM for dishonesty and abuse of power, including lying about have a matric certificate.[1]

He managed to lobby his way back into the SABC and by the time he was reappointed to the corporation in 2008, Zuma was ANC presi-dent and firmly on his way to take over as state president the next year. Dali Mpofu, the former SABC CEO who reappointed Motsoeneng, later became national chairperson of the EFF and a fierce critic of Zuma. Mpofu suspended Zikalala for gross insubordination after he refused to reinstate Motsoeneng. The following day, the SABC board suspended Mpofu.[2]

Motsoeneng's story is one of extreme opportunism, good fortune and his ability to push through crazy ideas against any logic or reason. The origins of his relationship with Zuma are unclear, but some of his former colleagues at the SABC in Bloemfontein recall that Motsoeneng knew Zuma from before 1994 when he came to speak in the Free State.[3]

A story that has become almost an urban legend is that Motsoeneng's mother is Zuma's sangoma. When News24 visited Phuthaditjhaba in 2016, previously known as Qwaqwa, locals were nervous to talk about 'Ma Motsoeneng', but confirmed that she was a sangoma. 'Is she Zuma's sangoma? They did not know,' they said'.[4] The urban legend will remain just that.

Zuma's fondness of Motsoeneng is strange, as the latter has no struggle record and was effectively working for a former Bantustan leader, Qwaqwa's Kenneth Mopeli, while the ANC was fighting apartheid. (ANC leaders have found it strange that Zuma associated closely with figures like Motsoeneng, Mdluli and Ntlemeza, who were servants of the apartheid state.) Locals told News24 how Motsoeneng used to file positive stories about Mopeli and his Dikwankwetla Party for Radio Sesotho (which became Lesedi FM).[5]

Motsoeneng pushed hard to be moved to the SABC's Bloemfontein office, which happened in 1992. There he started forging relationships with ANC politicians, like Magashule and Ivy Matsepe-Casaburri, and met SABC staffers Sebolelo Ditlhakanyane and Sophie Mokoena, who would both play a role in his reign of terror at the broadcaster.[6]

In 1995 Motsoeneng lied on his application form for a permanent position at the SABC, claiming he had matriculated from Metsi-Matsho High School. On his application form, Motsoeneng indicated that his matric subjects were English, Sesotho, Afrikaans, 'bibs' (a possible reference to Bible studies) and history.[7] He claimed to have achieved grade E for his subjects, apart from an F for History. This falsehood would haunt Motsoeneng for the rest of his career at the SABC. In her report into a litany of allegations of mismanagement and corporate-governance breaches at the SABC, Madonsela found that Motsoeneng had committed fraud. In fact, Motsoeneng admitted to Madonsela that he had made up the subjects and grades on the application form, but blamed a human resources official who 'gave him the application form to fill in anything to get the job'.[8] Madonsela was perturbed by Motsoeneng's explanation. 'If anything, this defence exacerbates his situation as it shows lack of remorse and ethical conduct. The conduct is improper and constitutes a dishonest act,' she concluded.[9]

Motsoeneng ingratiated himself with the new ANC political elite in the province and cosied up to the provincial chairperson, Magashule. 'The only person I ever saw Motsoeneng defer to was Ace Magashule. Everyone else he treated like crap. That group pushed Ace all the way. We all saw it,' a former colleague in Bloemfontein told News24, referring to Motsoeneng, Mokoena and Ditlhakanyane. Another claimed that Magashule would decide what the story of the day would be.[10]

Motsoeneng quickly rose through the ranks, and in 2003 repeated the lie of his matric qualification to be promoted to executive producer for Lesedi FM. He butted heads with regional editor James Barkhuizen and was accused of undermining Barkhuizen by dishing out jobs and salary increases.[11] A forensic investigation into the Bloemfontein office led to Motsoeneng's first disciplinary hearing at the SABC for racism, dishonesty, disruption of relations, intimidation and violation of SABC policies in 2006. In 2007 he was fired but later made a spectacular return in 2008, which cost both Mpofu and Zikalala their jobs.

By then Zuma was ANC president and had risen to power by casting himself as the victim of Mbeki and what Zuma saw as a political campaign driven by the Scorpions. This would have appealed to Motsoeneng, who himself was on the wrong side of a forensic investigation. His main political backer – Magashule – was also a 'victim' of the Mbeki era and overlooked twice as premier. 'Zikalala was an Mbeki man. He saw that Motsoeneng was using resources to push Ace and so Motsoeneng fell out of favour. When he was fired it was at the time that the fight to make Zuma the current president started,' an SABC employee told News24.[12] It was reported that Motsoeneng became a 'regular visitor' to Zuma's homestead at Nkandla, 'where a goat or sheep would be slaughtered on his weekend pilgrimages'.[13]

In December 2009, former Inkatha Freedom Party politician turned ANC ambassador Ben Ngubane was appointed chairperson of the SABC board. Ngubane was a Zuma man. He was premier of KwaZulu-Natal when Zuma served as MEC for economic development and the two had forged a close bond during the peace negotiations in the province. Ngubane's daughter, Nokuthula, is the chief executive of the Jacob

Zuma RDP Education Trust. Ngubane, who would later be appointed chair of the Eskom board, became Motsoeneng's chief cheerleader at the SABC and hailed his legacy even after his destructive reign was laid bare for all to see.

In February 2011 Motsoeneng was appointed general manager for board and stakeholder relations in the CEO's office – a position widely seen as the personal political advisor to the chief executive.[14] 'Everyone was told that the board needed Motsoeneng to open doors to Zuma. Their relationship had already been long established. So, he sat in board meetings even though he was not a member of the board,' an employee who witnessed events told News24.[15]

In December 2011 Motsoeneng was irregularly appointed as the acting COO (chief operations officer) without the necessary board resolution. He became the de facto CEO, having private meetings with Ngubane without involving the then group CEO, Lulama Mokhobo.[16] Financially, Motsoeneng hit the jackpot in Auckland Park. Madonsela's investigation found that his salary increased from R1,5 million to R2,4 million a year after he moved to Johannesburg. As acting COO, he was earning R211 172 a month – almost double what he had earned the year before, thanks to his blesser, Ngubane.

At the end of 2011, Charlotte Mampane and Phumelele Ntombela-Nzimande, two former senior SABC executives who were paid out by Motsoeneng to leave, lodged a detailed complaint with Madonsela's office against Motsoeneng. The charges against him included lying about his matric certificate; irregularly receiving massive pay rises; purging senior officials at the SABC whom he didn't like and paying them huge settlements, and increasing the salaries of his allies.

His meteoric rise perturbed SABC staffers, who saw him as an obvious Luthuli House deployee who had to look out for Zuma and the ANC's interests. The criticism and investigation didn't perturb Motsoeneng, however. He continued to act like the editor-in-chief of the SABC, and in December 2012 ordered a political discussion on Metro FM to be canned because the ANC wasn't invited. Presenter Sakina Kamwendo hosted a political panel of senior journalists about the ANC's elective conference, which was due to start in Mangaung a few days later. Minutes before the show was due to be broadcast, Kamwendo was told to pull the plug.[17] When confronted with his interference in editorial decisions, Motsoeneng responded by saying people were trying their luck with the SABC and that he would not allow anyone to influence his decisions. 'We mean business here at the SABC. This is leadership at its best,' he famously said.[18]

Late in 2012, the SABC banned a commercial advertising fish and chips that satirised Zuma and his extended family. With the ad line 'Dinner time at Nkandla', the Fish and Chips Company advertised its R25 combo deal showing several women and children dishing up fish and chips around a large table. 'There are many of you in this house – at only R25 even Pravin will approve this,' the ad quipped.[19] Motsoeneng said the SABC decided not to flight the commercial because 'freedom of expression came with responsibility'.[20]

By this time, the SABC board had become concerned about Motsoeneng's editorial interference and blatant disregard for good corporate governance. He cynically tried to lobby board members to push for his permanent appointment as COO, threatening that an SIU probe would implicate them in wrongdoing and offering them legal assistance if they voted for his permanent appointment.[21] On 26 February 2013, the SABC board, without Ngubane being present, removed Motsoeneng from his acting position at a board meeting and appointed veteran journalist Mike Siluma in his place.

Chaired by deputy chairperson Thami ka Plaatjie, the board ordered Motsoeneng to return to his position as general manager. Motsoeneng was furious. He refused to vacate the COO office and told board members he would deal with them. Siluma stepped down from the acting position almost immediately. Ngubane, who was supposed to be Motsoeneng's protector, desperately tried to overturn the board's decision, but failed. The only option he had left was to resign, which he did. Ngubane was followed by Ka Plaatjie and the other board members appointed by the ANC. Soon the entire board collapsed, but Hlaudi remained. To those who hold freedom of expression and good corporate governance dear, this was a sad realisation that political expediency had won the day and that Motsoeneng had the protection of the highest office in the land.

Zandile Ellen Tshabalala, a Transnet director and advisor to Zuma, was appointed as interim chair. Soon afterwards Motsoeneng formally returned as acting COO. He was back with a vengeance and in 2013 announced that the SABC's news bulletins should be made up of 70% positive news stories and 30% negative news stories:

> We want to concentrate more on positive stories, rather than to put everything in a negative way. ... You should love this country. When you love this country, you will do what is right for it, which is what we are doing now at the SABC. The message I put out very strongly at the SABC is to think about the positive when people go out and do stories. The difference is our own citizens are tired of crime and tired of people talking about negative things.[22]

This came at the time the country was fervently debating whether Zuma should pay back the money spent by the state on his Nkandla residence.

Journalists inside and outside the SABC were outraged by Motsoeneng's decree that violated the sacrosanct 'Chinese wall' that exists between commercial and editorial departments in media houses. Effectively, Motsoeneng was prescribing to SABC journalists how to do their jobs, thereby undermining their ability to cover the news without fear or favour. Unfortunately, this wasn't the last time he would interfere in the editorial affairs of the public broadcaster.

In July 2013, Motsoeneng 'sold' the SABC to MultiChoice, the paid-for video content company owned by Naspers.[23] *City Press* revealed that Motsoeneng received a R30 million bonus for negotiating a deal that saw the SABC handing over control of its archive to a private company. In exchange, the SABC was paid R553 million over five years to set up two new channels on DStv.[24] A parliamentary investigation recommended in 2017 that an independent forensic investigation be undertaken into the deal. At the same time, the Competition

Commission scrutinised the transaction to determine whether it constituted a merger.

On 18 July 2013, an ANC employee nominated Tshabalala for a permanent position on the SABC board.[25] She submitted her CV, which included the following qualifications: a diploma in labour relations and a B.Comm. degree from Unisa. In October 2013 Zuma appointed Tshabalala as SABC chair.

In February 2014, Madonsela released her damning report into the SABC titled When Governance and Ethics Fail. As mentioned, she found that Motsoeneng had faked his matric certificate. She also found that his appointment as acting COO was irregular; that Ngubane irregularly changed the qualification requirements for the position of COO to suit Motsoeneng; that Motsoeneng's massive salary increases were irregular; and that the SABC board failed to exercise its fiduciary obligations when it appointed Motsoeneng as acting COO.[26] Madonsela referred to 'pathological corporate governance deficiencies' at the public broadcaster and directed the board to institute disciplinary action against Motsoeneng. They all but ignored her.

In May 2014, Faith Muthambi, an ANC MP from Limpopo who had defended Zuma during parliamentary hearings on Nkandla, was appointed as Minister of Communications. At parliamentary hearings into the fitness of the SABC board in December 2016, evidence was given of how Muthambi interfered with the work of the board. Two months after her appointment as minister, Muthambi allegedly arrived at a board meeting and, after meeting Tshabalala privately, told the board to appoint Motsoeneng permanently as COO.[27] This despite Madonsela's recommendation that he should be disciplined by the board. Muthambi would later tell the court that she and the SABC had appointed a law firm to look at Madonsela's report and Motsoeneng was 'cleared of all wrongdoing'.[28]

On 8 July 2014 Motsoeneng was permanently appointed as COO. This meant another salary increase for the man who loves to refer to himself in the third person: his annual salary package was now topped up to R3,7 million.[29] The DA immediately challenged Motsoeneng's appointment in court.

Tshabalala's reign as SABC board chair was cut short by the revelation that she had fabricated the qualifications on her CV. Unisa told a parliamentary investigation that Tshabalala never achieved the qualifications she claimed to have.[30] She had originally claimed her qualifications were lost during a burglary. In December 2014 she resigned. Tshabalala reacted furiously to a report in the tabloid newspaper *Sunday Sun* about her alleged affair with Zuma. The newspaper said it had four sources who confirmed the affair was a 'well-known secret'.[31] Tshabalala denied having an intimate relationship with the president. Zuma's then spokesperson, Mac Maharaj, said: 'Did they see them in the bedroom? Do those people have a dress or semen or condoms, like in the Monica Lewinsky saga? Have they seen them smooching?'[32]

Professor Mbulaheni Maguvhe, Tshabalala's deputy, who was also closely linked to Muthambi and Motsoeneng, was appointed by Zuma as the new chair of the SABC.

Between 2014 and 2016, Motsoeneng and the SABC were tied up in legal proceedings brought by the main opposition party, the DA, to prevent Motsoeneng from continuing as a senior SABC executive until Madonsela's recommendations had been effected. The DA picked Motsoeneng as one of the prime targets of their 'lawfare' strategy, which challenged maladministration and poor governance through the courts.

In November 2015 Judge Dennis Davis set aside Motsoeneng's appointment as COO in the Western Cape High Court. Davis ruled that his appointment was irrational and illegal. A month later, Motsoeneng was cleared of all charges after the SABC eventually decided to charge him internally, as recommended by Madonsela. Advocate Willem Edeling, who chaired the disciplinary hearing, was particularly impressed by the evidence of Alwyn Kloppers, an SABC old-guard veteran, who claimed to have recruited Motsoeneng in Qwaqwa in 1993 because he saw talent in him. Kloppers, who was one of Motsoeneng's close confidants at the SABC, testified he had no doubt that Motsoeneng did not possess a matric certificate.[33] The DA immediately filed an application to declare the disciplinary hearing invalid, calling it a 'charade'.

Motsoeneng was back at work and ready to roll. Despite there being several legal cases against him involving Madonsela's findings, he continued ruling the SABC as if it was his kingdom. But, in May 2016 two things happened that would ultimately break the camel's back.

First, Motsoeneng announced that 90% of music played on the SABC's radio stations had to be local. This decision earned him the love of local musicians, but contributed substantially to moving the SABC to the point of financial bankruptcy. He announced that the 90/10 quota would apply to the broadcaster's TV stations too. Without any market research on how this decision would impact the SABC's audiences and finances, Motsoeneng moved ahead like a bulldozer and threatened anyone who dared to disobey his orders. 'I am Hlaudi Motsoeneng, baby! I am in charge. I will make sure that it happens. Nobody will go against what I have put in place – this policy and those responsible for implementing directly report to me,' he told a journalist.[34]

When a new interim board started to mop up after him in 2017, they determined that this decision alone led to a loss in advertising revenue of R183 million for TV and R29 million for radio. This excluded costs of R72 million to produce new local content and losses on foreign contracts that were already signed.[35]

Secondly, Motsoeneng banned the broadcasting of violent protests on the SABC's platforms. This after residents in Tshwane took to the streets to show their dissatisfaction with the ANC's candidates for the local-government elections of August 2016. The broadcaster announced that it would immediately cease to broadcast footage of burning buildings because such publicity was 'destructive and regressive'. Motsoeneng added the SABC would not 'assist these individuals to push their agenda that seeks media attention … As a public broadcaster, we have a mandate to educate the citizens, and we therefore have taken this bold decision to show that violent protests are not necessary.'[36]

This led to a massive outcry from inside and outside the SABC's newsrooms, with many a commentator comparing the SABC's new 'protest policy' to censorship under apartheid. On 31 May 2016 Motsoeneng and Jimi Matthews, then acting chief executive, summoned two seasoned radio journalists, Foeta Krige and Krivani Pillay, to a meeting.

Krige is executive producer for current affairs at Radio Sonder Grense (RSG) and Pillay holds the same position at SAfm. Motsoeneng scolded them for discussing the new protest policy on air and inviting independent analysts, who criticised the decision. Motsoeneng and Matthews wanted no criticism of the decision to be aired on the SABC's platforms. Motsoeneng said: 'If people do not adhere, get rid of them. We cannot have people who question management ... This is the last time we have a meeting of this kind.'[37] Matthews added: 'It is cold outside. If you do not like it you can go. You've got two choices: the door or the window.'[38]

A week later, at a workshop about the SABC's election coverage, Motsoeneng told senior staff to respect Zuma in their reportage: 'I'm in charge, you must adhere to my instruction. President Zuma is the president of the country. I do not regard him as ANC. You cannot treat him the same ... We will give him more time. And you can question everyone except our president. We need to respect him. Especially you, SABC. I expect you all to align with my instruction.'[39]

On the morning of 20 June 2016, advocacy organisation Right2Know organised protests at SABC offices to petition the new protest policy. At the morning news-diary conference – a holy space for journalists – the acting head of news, Simon Tebele, told staff to stop covering the Right2Know marches. SABC economics editor Thandeka Gqubule, Krige and the late RSG producer and presenter Suna Venter recorded their disagreement with the decision.[40] Three days later they were suspended.

Six days later, Pillay, Special Assignment producer, Busisiwe Ntuli, and investigative reporter Jacques Steenkamp sent a letter to senior SABC management, objecting to the suspension of their three colleagues and criticising the protest policy. This led to disciplinary steps being initiated against them. Two more journalists who dared to speak out were punished: SABC parliamentary reporter Lukhanyo Calata wrote an open letter in the media titled 'SABC's decisions fly in the face of what many, like the Cradock 4, sacrificed'.[41] Lukhanyo's father, Fort Calata, was killed by the apartheid security police in 1985. Lukhanyo too was suspended. Contributing editor and anchor Vuyo Mvoko was disciplined after publishing an article in the press titled 'My hell at SABC: In power mongers' grip'.[42]

The journalists, who became known as the SABC 8, filed a direct application to the Constitutional Court for access to challenge the steps initiated against them. A few days after being awarded the Nat Nakasa award for integrity and courage, the SABC fired seven of the journalists and terminated Mvoko's contract. It was the ultimate abuse of power to silence dissent.

A massive public outcry followed their sacking and the SABC eventually capitulated, withdrawing their dismissals. Motsoeneng's empire started to crumble: Matthews resigned due to the 'corrosive atmosphere', which had affected his moral judgement. He admitted compromising his values and beliefs, and apologised to the people he had let down by remaining silent.[43] At the same time, Parliament instituted an ad hoc committee to probe the SABC board's fitness.

But the pressure did not prevent Motsoeneng from blatantly abusing his position to benefit the Zuma family. In July 2016, he personally intervened to extend Uzalo, a TV series produced by a company co-owned by Zuma's daughter Gugulethu Zuma-Ncube. This after the SABC's official review panel had turned down the pitch for a second season of the series. When Motsoeneng found out about the decision, it was reported, he stepped in and made sure a three-year deal, worth R167 million, was signed.[44]

In October 2016, SABC board members Krish Naidoo and Vusi Mavuso resigned in front of Parliament's Portfolio Committee on Communications, saying they had no idea who compiled the board's presentation on the state of affairs at the SABC to Parliament.[45] In early December 2016, the ad hoc committee, chaired by veteran ANC MP Vincent Smith, started its public hearings on the state of the broadcaster. Witness after witness told the committee about the perilous state of the broadcaster, detailing how corporate governance was flouted, how Muthambi interfered in the running of the SABC, and how Motsoeneng ruled by fear and intimidation.

The committee also heard how the SABC helped to fund a rival TV station, the Gupta-owned ANN7, by airing the Guptas' business break-fast events for free on SABC TV. The interim board chair, Khanyisile Kweyama, told Parliament in June 2017 that the SABC had funded the Gupta breakfasts to the tune of at least R20 million.[46] Executives testified how Motsoeneng behaved like the CEO, meeting MultiChoice without the chief executive being present.[47]

Motsoeneng's fatal blow came through a High Court judgment in December 2016, declaring that the disciplinary hearing that had cleared him should be set aside and that his appointment of general manager of corporate affairs was unlawful and irrational. This meant Motsoeneng could no longer work at the SABC in any capacity. Judge Owen Rogers of the Western Cape High Court ruled that the Edeling disciplinary was 'wholly inadequate' and that a fresh hearing had to be convened.[48] Rogers confirmed that Madonsela's findings against Motsoeneng would stand until being set aside by a court of law.

Motsoeneng had to vacate his office in Auckland Park.

In March 2017, Zuma appointed an interim board, led by Kweyama, veteran editor Mathatha Tsedu (deputy chairperson), former board member Krish Naidoo, experienced regulator John Matisonn and diplomat Febe Potgieter-Gqubule. The new board immediately invigorated the broadcaster with a sense of hope and they set out to return stability to the SABC.

Motsoeneng, reeling from the court judgment that cost him his job, called a four-hour-long media briefing on 19 April 2017, during which he lashed out at his critics, including Naidoo, and defended decisions made during his tenure. His egotism took a new turn: he told the media that people wanted him to run for president, but that he wouldn't because he supported a woman for the position of ANC leader.[49]

But the new board would have none of his antics and immediately charged him with bringing the SABC into disrepute and causing irreparable harms to his employer. On 12 June 2017 Motsoeneng was found guilty after a disciplinary hearing and sacked. By mid-2017 he was still challenging his dismissal at the Commission for Conciliation, Mediation and Arbitration.

The damage caused to the SABC by Motsoeneng, with the political backing of Muthambi and Zuma, will be calculated for years to come. Because of him, the corporation is technically insolvent and has lost many talented journalists and managers who refused to obey the madman's rules. But the tide turned owing to the courage of people like the SABC 8 and Naidoo, who wouldn't stand by while one man destroyed a nation's voice.

CHAPTER 11

Zuma's Parliament

---

*'Some people who could not pronounce "Nkandla" have now
learnt "Nkandla! Nkandla! Nkandla!" ... Even when we discuss
very serious matters, they will get up and say, "On a point of order
... Nkandla". ... That is part of the problem ... It emphasises the
poverty of politics in our opposition parties.'*

– President Jacob Zuma, National Assembly, 27 May 2015 (Hansard)

When Parliament reconvened early in 2008, after Zuma's clean
sweep at Polokwane in December 2007, there was an air of optimism in the corridors of the parliamentary complex – a mix of Victorian
and Edwardian architecture, rounded off by apartheid cubism. During
the latter years of Mbeki's presidency, the ANC in Parliament fulfilled
one role: that of a dutiful rubber stamp. There was no appetite to provide oversight of the executive, no tolerance of the opposition's views or
its role and no willingness to engage in national discourse.

With Zuma's ascension, that changed immediately: ministers were
hauled in front of committees, a spirit of cooperation swept through the
stuffy meeting rooms and ANC MPs demonstrated a newfound commitment to the separation of powers and constitutional democracy. But
the change in attitude was due to political expediency: Mbeki, who was
still head of state, and his executive needed to be kept on a tight ANC
leash. There was to be no funny business.

Zuma has loomed large over the legislature ever since he displaced Mbeki as ANC leader. The institution, a supposed beacon of transparency, accountability and debate, has in the decade since the Polokwane rupture been manipulated, manoeuvred and moulded into a Zuma protection racket. Despite opposition parties' best efforts, a succession of ANC chief whips and committee chairpersons have aided speaker Baleka Mbete in her quest to protect Zuma and his executive from scrutiny. This they have done by shielding him from having to answer direct questions, militarising Parliament to intimidate MPs and cynically abusing process to delay, smother and kill oversight. ANC MPs like Mathole Motshekga, Cedric Frolick and Cecil Burgess have been Zuma's biggest allies in causing interference, attacking institutions or shifting blame. But Mbete – who also serves as the ANC's national chairperson and who has supported him in all his biggest factional conflicts over the years – has surely been Zuma's biggest benefactor. Whenever the heat has been on in the National Assembly, she has contrived to release the pressure by shepherding him out of danger – at least until the vote of no confidence against Zuma in August 2017. During the Nkandla saga – the defining issue for Parliament during the Zuma years – time and again, Mbete helped Zuma escape without having to answer questions coherently and honestly. And Zuma has always been too pleased to accept the speaker's largesse in undermining democracy.

After Polokwane, Parliament sprang into action on Zuma's behalf, appointing a joint committee to dissolve the Scorpions, who were leading the investigation into the ANC president. Even though the Scorpions had achieved notable and demonstrable success with their internationally renowned method of prosecutor-led investigations into big corruption, the ANC insisted the unit had to go.[1] Maggie Sotyu, whom Zuma later appointed as deputy police minister and who served as co-chairperson of the joint committee, said before the committee had even met: 'We are going to dissolve the Scorpions ... we are going to do it. Our job is to implement the Polokwane resolutions.' The parliamentary process, with co-chairpersons Sotyu and Yunus Carrim acting as the Scorpions' pallbearers, resembled a proper consultative process. It had all the hallmarks of inclusivity and probity: public hearings, discussion documents, debates and reports. But there was only ever going to be one outcome. The Scorpions – accused of plotting against Zuma and involving themselves in political campaigns – were killed off and replaced by the pliant Hawks. Parliament had struck its first blow for Zuma.

The legislature (Parliament, led by the speaker), along with the executive (the elected government, led by the president) and the judiciary (the courts, led by the chief justice), forms one of the three arms of state. Its primary function is to craft laws in accordance with the Constitution, as well as to provide oversight of the executive and state institutions. The executive is tasked with proposing and giving effect to laws, while the judiciary interprets laws passed by Parliament. Max Sisulu, scion of the Sisulu family, son of ANC leader Walter and brother of Lindiwe (and a minister in both the Mbeki and Zuma governments), had an acute awareness of the role of Parliament in a constitutional democracy during his tenure as speaker between 2009 and 2014. A dignified man who managed to rise above partisan posturing and bias, Sisulu announced on 9 April 2014 that Parliament would immediately establish an ad hoc committee to consider Secure in Comfort, the Public Protector's explosive report into the upgrades made to Zuma's Nkandla homestead.

Zuma's strategy throughout was to ensure Madonsela's report wasn't the only investigation into or report about the massive spending at Nkandla, thereby swamping it with counter-narratives. If he could bury Madonsela's report among a host of other investigations and reports, he could slither away unharmed. The president used the state to launch his own investigations: by a government task team, by Police Minister Nathi Nhleko as well as by the SIU. In addition, loyal cadres in Parliament ensured that the full statutory weight of the institution was brought to bear in support of their president, with two full parliamentary committees exonerating him of any blame.

Zuma's letter to Sisulu on 2 April 2014 attested to his long game. He told Sisulu he would fully account to Parliament only after the completion

of the SIU investigation, but that he was perplexed by the stark differences between Madonsela's findings and those of the government task
team, led by Thulas Nxesi, his Minister of Public Works. Nxesi found
that no taxpayers' money was used on the private residences and that
Zuma should carry no blame.

Opposition parties immediately submitted names of MPs to serve
on the Nkandla committee to the speaker's office. It had three weeks
to complete its work before the deadline of 30 April, when Parliament
would disband before the general election. Sisulu had given Parliament
an opportunity to scrutinise Madonsela's report and make recommendations but there was no guarantee the new Parliament, under a new
speaker and new whippery, would even want to investigate Nkandla,
which meant speed and urgency were of the essence. But the ANC
stalled. And stalled. Lindiwe Mazibuko, the DA's parliamentary leader,
was livid at the governing party's foot dragging, but the ANC went
about their business unperturbed. Its unflappable caucus spokesperson
Moloto Mothapo casually said the party would submit the names of
its representatives according to parliamentary rules – which stipulates
this must be done within ten days: 'The ANC has to thoroughly apply
its mind with regard to the selection process in terms of the calibre of
people that should serve in this committee.'[2] Almost two weeks after
Sisulu announced the establishment of the committee, ANC Chief Whip
Stone Sizani sent his names to the speaker's office.

The committee's first meeting, on 23 April 2014, set the tone for the
ANC's approach right up until the Constitutional Court's stinging
rebuke two years later. MPs Frolick, Burgess, Muthambi, Doris Dlakude
and Buti Manamela obstructed and obfuscated their way through the
engagement, saying they hadn't had time to read Madonsela's report and
refused to entertain the possibility of calling Zuma to the committee or
getting the Public Protector to explain certain findings. 'We don't want to
be dictated to by the media,'[3] Dlakude said. Burgess added that he hadn't
seen the report 'for whatever reasons' and that he needed time to read
through it.[4] This even though the report had been forensically dissected
in the media since the moment it was publicly released and the fact that

for weeks it was the biggest talking point in the country. Madonsela's Nkandla report was everywhere. Proposals by Mazibuko that the committee should meet the following day, and if necessary over the coming weekend to ensure it could meet the deadline were shot down. Wilmot James's (DA) protests that the committee had constitutional obligations were simply ignored. 'There's no rush,'[5] Dlakude declared.

It all broke down during the second meeting, on 28 April. Proposals by the DA to invite role players to testify before the committee were again rejected by the ANC, who proceeded to table a motion that the committee disband and recommend to the Fifth Parliament – after the election – that it look into the matter. Mazibuko called this 'sheer arrogance'; James said it was 'scandalous'. Manamela said 'we get our mandate from the ANC'. The committee ceased to exist after 30 May.

Nkandla was the biggest crisis Parliament had faced since the arms-deal inquiry in the early years of the 2000s, when parliamentary process was also subverted in favour of executive interests.[6] The whole institution was cynically re-tooled in the defence of one man and his folly, with MPs feverishly attacking Madonsela, undermining the constitutional order and religiously sticking to the party line delivered from Luthuli House.

Then Julius Malema and his red-overall-clad EFF members also disrupted the whole dynamic of Parliament. Whereas the DA stuck to parliamentary rules and procedures, Malema and his band of street fighters had a different tactic: to embarrass Zuma and to find out when he was going to pay back the money. They showed scant regard for convention and protocol, and their brash manner disrupted and derailed National Assembly plenaries whenever Zuma appeared.

On 14 August 2014, Zuma submitted his long-awaited official reply to Madonsela's report to Mbete (who replaced Sisulu as speaker after the election), wherein he confirmed that Nhleko was tasked to determine whether or not he should repay any monies to the fiscus. He made no reference to the Public Protector's remedial actions and indicated he was not bound by them. Madonsela reacted angrily, telling Zuma a week later he was assigning powers to the minister that he constitutionally does not have. Her findings, she explained, are reviewable only in a court of law and not 'by a second-guessing minister or Cabinet'. She asked him to comply with her findings. Zuma, as became his wont, laughed it off and said her office was 'akin to an ombud'. He took three weeks to reply to Madonsela's concerns, and then only by saying Madonsela should wait for the parliamentary process – skilfully stage-managed by Mbete and her minion, Frolick – to conclude. Zuma told the SABC that matters were now 'in the hands of Parliament'.[7]

The affair first blew up in Zuma's face in the National Assembly on 21 August 2014, a week after Zuma had mandated Nhleko to look at Nkandla afresh. Replying to a written question from Malema, Zuma said he had complied with all legal prescripts and furnished Parliament with answers. Malema was not to be swayed:

> We are asking this question precisely because you have not provided the answer. Firstly, you failed to meet the 14 days [deadline] of the Public Protector, and, secondly, when you responded, you told us that the Minister of Police must still decide who must pay. In our view, the report of the Public Protector supersedes any other form of report which you might be expecting somewhere else. So the question we are asking today, and we are not going to leave here before we get an answer … [laughter] … is: When are you paying the money because the Public Protector has instructed you that you must pay the money, and we want the date of when you are paying the money?[8]

All hell broke loose and Mbete lost control over the session. MPs started heckling and hurling insults while the serjeant-at-arms entered the chamber and riot police took up position outside. EFF MPs chanted, 'Pay back the money! Pay back the money!' while some banged their red mining helmets on the tables. Zuma stood at the podium, not knowing what to do. Mbete suspended the sitting for two hours, eventually adjourning it without Zuma completing his oral replies. The ANC were livid; the DA didn't quite know what to make of it; Mbete was shocked. Malema, however, made it clear the EFF were not going to back down:

'Zuma is doing the same he has done with Guptagate, [using] delaying tactics in the hope we will forget. We are not going to forget. For the next five years he will have to answer: where the money is, when he will he pay it back ...'[9]

The multi-party ad hoc committee meanwhile was reconstituted, but lasted for all of four meetings before opposition parties realised they were merely legitimising a fait accompli. Mmamoloko Kubayi, whom Zuma would later appoint as minister of energy, was one of the president's most ardent defenders, telling the committee it could not investigate beyond what the speaker determined. (She was also photographed absent-mindedly painting her fingernails during one of the heated debates, which illustrated with what contempt the ANC approached the process.)

ANC MPs fell in lockstep behind Zuma, saying all reports, including the government task team's, the SIU's and others, needed to be considered in conjunction with the Public Protector's 'recommendations'. They also refused attempts by the opposition to get Zuma to appear in front of the committee or to get legal opinions on the Public Protector's powers. Godrich Gardee (EFF) said the ANC was employing a 'Stalingrad defence',[10] fighting back every attempt to extract accountability from the president. Before he led the opposition out of the committee on 25 September 2014, DA parliamentary leader Mmusi Maimane said: 'What is clear to me and very apparent is that the ANC is not going to agree to a single thing; they don't want a legal opinion, they don't want a legal review, they don't want people to be called here. If it is going to be a read-shop then I think they must sit together and do it.'[11] It didn't take Frolick and his cohorts long to reach the conclusion Zuma wanted. The committee – without any opposition party present – adopted its report on 11 November 2014 and forwarded it to the National Assembly for consideration. Parliament was satisfied with the president's response. There were to be no consequences for him.

The annual opening of Parliament is a grand affair. MPs prance down a red carpet like faux movie stars before they enter the chamber to take up their seats, while photographers and reporters jostle to see what staid, nondescript politicians look like with their hair done up. On Thursday 12 February 2015, there was a different atmosphere, however, on the cobblestoned Parliament Street, which runs past the Marks Building, the old Senate and the National Assembly to Stalplein and Tuynhuys, where the media assembled to watch the spectacle unfold. This time, Mbete was preparing for a confrontation and had recruited security personnel to protect Zuma. To do that she had to circumvent parliamentary rules. And she had no qualms about it. Shortly before proceedings started, an image flashed around social media of a column of burly, barrel chested parliamentary security personnel goose-stepping into the building through a side entrance. In the press gallery in the National Assembly, behind the podium, journalists were all of a sudden struggling to connect to the internet. Scurrying around for answers, Mbete's spokesperson promised the media he would get to the bottom of the issue. 'There's a jamming device in here,' a parliamentary official told a reporter. The spooks had effectively conspired with Parliament to prevent journalists from reporting from the gallery. It was to prove a night like no other. Zuma was visibly tense when he walked to the podium, but Maimane interjected:

> The leader of the opposition: Madam Speaker, I rise on Rule 14(s) to draw your attention to the fact that the cellphone signal in the House has been jammed. A device has been installed in the National Assembly. I would submit to you, Madam Speaker, that this is in direct violation of Section 59(1)(b) of the Constitution [applause]. Madam Speaker, it is also in violation of Section 16(1)(b) of the Constitution and the Bill of Rights – the freedom to receive or impart information or ideas. Madam Speaker, the DA would like to request you to instruct whoever is responsible for this – because it was never discussed in the Chief Whips' Forum at any time – to please turn the device off, and allow us to impart our ideas and our viewpoints which the Constitution – which was hard fought for – provides. I request your ruling [interjections, applause].

The speaker: We will make sure that the Secretary to Parliament follows up on that issue [interjections].[12]

Remarkable scenes followed. Mbete was bombarded from all sides by opposition parties raising objections and demanding answers about the jamming device, while the hacks on the gallery held up their unconnected cellphones, the most important piece in a modern journalist's armoury. Then MPs started chanting, 'Bring back the signal, bring back the signal!' with journalists enthusiastically joining in. Ramaphosa, sitting in the government benches, wrote a note, gave it to a messenger, who took it to David Mahlobo, the Minister of State Security. He read the note and put it away. The signal returned. But the real drama was still to come. When Zuma eventually started to speak, he was almost immediately interrupted by the EFF's Godrich Gardee: 'May we ask the President as to when he is going pay back the money in terms of what the Public Protector has said? That is the question of privilege we would like to ask, and, accordingly, since he has not been answering questions, we hope that today he will answer that question. I thank you.'[13]

Mbete was having none of it and said the order paper stated that the only item on the agenda was the president's state of the nation address. Gardee would have ample opportunity to ask questions during the debate on the speech the following week, she said. But the EFF had been emboldened.

> Mr G A Gardee: Madam Speaker, I rose on a question of privilege, not a point of order. So, you have addressed the issue of a point of order, Madam Speaker. But on the issue of the question of privilege, can that question be answered or can we be told that it is in the speech. Is he still going to tell us when the money is going to be paid? Is it going to be paid by EFT, cash or eWallet? Thank you.[14]

A succession of points of order were raised by EFF MPs as the country watched and as Mbete grew increasingly impatient, her finger itching on the trigger. It was perfectly set up for Malema, who rose to object to

Mbete's dismissal of EFF MP Younis Vawda: 'We want the President to answer a simple question: When is he paying back the money, as directed by the Public Protector? That is all we are asking.'[15]

Mayhem ensued, with points of order being raised, insults traded and swear words shouted across the chamber. Ambassadors in the diplomatic bay were craning their necks to see what was happening, and the public gallery roared with glee. It was more like a rugby test match than the opening of Parliament. And a dirty match at that. The EFF loudly demanded that Zuma answered the question, and Mbete ordered Malema and his fellow agitators out of the house.

> The speaker: I will now ask the serjeant-at-arms to assist hon Malema to leave the Chamber! [applause] [interjections] I now ask that the serjeant-at-arms, the usher of the Black Rod ... [interjections] ... the Parliamentary Protection Services ... [interjections] Hon members, you are not going to block the state of the nation address [interjections]. I am asking the Parliamentary Protection Officers to please come in ... [interjections] ... and take out the hon members [interjections] [Parliamentary Protection Officers enter the chamber]. I also order the security officers to please assist! The security forces must come in, in terms of the Powers and Privileges Act [interjections].[16]

The 'white shirts', as the parliamentary protection staff became known, marched into the chamber, surrounded their prey and proceeded to rough up the EFF MPs, who resisted with all their might, kicking and screaming and attacking their aggressors with their red mining helmets. Desks were overturned and microphones broken in the scuffle.

But it was the country's image that was shattered as the unruly EFF caucus were removed. The aftermath was devastating for Parliament. It was revealed the 'white shirts' were actually highly trained police officers who were seconded to – and eventually joined – the Parliamentary Protection Services. Mbete was challenged in court, and it was found that Parliament had acted outside of its powers when it violently removed the EFF and cut the television broadcast during the fracas. In addition, the SCA found it was unconstitutional and unlawful for Mbete and others to block cellphone signals in the house.

Parliament was broken. Even though committees continued to function, Mbete had finally lost the respect of the opposition and, with it, control of the National Assembly. Zuma was heckled and jeered every time he appeared – but still did not answer Malema's question. Mbete appointed a third ad hoc committee in June 2015 after Nhleko's famous 'O sole mio' report in which he, too, rode to the president's defence and declared Zuma innocent.

On 6 August 2015 Malema again rose in Parliament to ask Zuma when the money would be repaid and, for the umpteenth time, Zuma said Parliament was still dealing with the matter. 'It's very clear we won't get an answer, Mr President. Let's meet in court,' Malema retorted.

And, on the same day, Malema and the EFF lodged papers at the Constitutional Court. Parliament, Mbete and Zuma's day in court was approaching apace. Seven months later the court ruled that Zuma had violated the Constitution and his oath of office and that Mbete and Parliament had failed to hold the president to account.

CHAPTER 12

Dismantling SARS

—

*'SARS is one of the key pillars of our fiscal order, and therefore
our democratic dispensation. It is an institution whose very
foundations are built on the trust and credibility that South
African taxpayers have in it.'*

– Minister of Finance Pravin Gordhan, 12 July 2013

Adrian Lackay, who had been part of the SARS top management team as spokesperson for years, was gradually sidelined after Zuma appointed Tom Moyane as SARS commissioner on 24 September 2014. Moyane shifted most of Lackay's responsibilities elsewhere and excluded him from meetings, and then Moyane moved to another building. As a result, Lackay saw Moyane a total of four times in five months. Under Gordhan, Oupa Magashula and acting commissioner Ivan Pillay, Lackay could walk into the office of the taxman whenever there was a pressing issue the commissioner had to consider. This he was encouraged to do because management understood that public confidence in the tax administration was paramount if a high level of tax morality and tax compliance was to be sustained. SARS, and its leaders and processes, had to be like Caesar's wife: above suspicion. Damaging publicity could not be left to fester in the public's mind.

But under Moyane things had changed. Moyane's appointment coincided with the institution's most tumultuous period ever since it was formed in 1997, when the departments of inland revenue and customs and excise were merged to form SARS. The *Sunday Times* was accused of waging a campaign against SARS, and in particular against a specific group of senior staff in the service. The organisation's integrity, culture and operations were clearly under threat. Where Lackay previously had the authority and support of the commissioner to swiftly and efficiently deal with disinformation campaigns, Moyane simply refused to let him counter a series of sensational reports that were appearing mainly in the *Sunday Times*, which published more than 40 damaging stories between October 2014 and October 2015.

By the time Lackay forced his way into Moyane's office on 22 January 2015 – past strict security and stringent access control – the country had come to believe that a so-called 'rogue unit' operated within SARS. They had been led to believe that this unit was operating outside of the law, that it was beyond the control of the institution's leadership, that it managed a brothel and illegally planted listening devices in Zuma's home, in addition to a host of other unsavoury activities. Furthermore, by the beginning of 2016, 55 senior staff members had left the organisation,[1] including senior managers, executives, group executives, officers who served on the SARS executive committee, the chief operating officer and Pillay, the deputy commissioner.[2]

Lackay was exasperated. SARS's reputation, painstakingly built over many years and maintained by high levels of professionalism and success, was being torn apart Sunday after Sunday, and he wasn't allowed to do anything about it. 'What is your endgame?' he demanded from Moyane. After an argument and some nonsensical platitudes from Moyane, Lackay insisted on an answer. Moyane threw his hands up in the air and said: 'To clear the air!'[3] Lackay left SARS less than a month later, uncertain what air exactly Moyane wanted to clear.

SARS has been hailed as one of South Africa's biggest success stories and one its best-functioning state institutions.[4] It is respected by friend and foe alike, and has enabled government to remain independent from development aid by providing sufficient revenue to finance a developing social democracy. Pravin Gordhan, SARS commissioner between 1999 and 2009, played a pivotal role in the modernisation of the institution. 'If you are able to raise 90 per cent, 95 per cent of resources within your country from your own tax base it gives you a lot of latitude in policy terms,' said Gordhan. 'If you become too indebted to international financial institutions you have to follow their dictates.'[5]

During Gordhan's time in office, SARS managed to increase the number of personal-income taxpayers from 2,6 million to 4,1 million.[6] That number had grown to 6,6 million by 2016.[7] SARS has been 'strikingly successful' in strengthening its tax-collection abilities since its establishment, with government revenue doubling in real terms between 1994/95 and 2010/11.[8] And it has made a habit of not only hitting revenue targets set by the National Treasury, but regularly exceeding them.[9] This has given the state fiscal breathing room to absorb shocks, such as the global financial crisis of 2007/08, and ensured that annual increases in social-welfare grants are affordable.

Johann van Loggerenberg, a former group executive at SARS for tax and customs enforcement and investigations, says SARS's success has been a combination of better enforcement, improved service and public education. Under Gordhan, the institution sharpened its enforcement edge and went big game hunting, targeting tax dodgers and organised-crime bosses, such as Dave King, Metcash, JCI and the Kebbles, Glenn Agliotti, Lolly Jackson and Radovan Krejcir. It also imported world-class technologies into its systems, which helped with one of its most important strategies: to win the hearts and minds of South Africans. Tax administration under apartheid was ineffective and unwieldy, with a small taxpayer base and inherent resistance among the public. Although not quite making the country fall in love with it, SARS did succeed in explaining and illustrating to South Africans how paying tax contributes to the national effort of building a new society. Tax compliance shot up and SARS managed to increase revenue, even though tax rates steadily decreased.[10] 'Its efficiency and excellent service delivery instilled awe in most South Africans, and fear in some. The rise of SARS from a fairly nondescript institution to one of the most trusted state organisations can be ascribed to the strong leadership and vision of individuals such as former Minister of Finance Trevor Manuel and Pravin Gordhan,' Van Loggerenberg, whom the *Sunday Times* identified as the leader of the 'rogue unit', writes in his book, *Rogue*.[11]

Manuel was finance minister during Gordhan's entire term as SARS commissioner. When Zuma shifted Manuel in 2009, Gordhan replaced him, and Gordhan, in turn, was replaced by Magashula, who was internally groomed for the position. A study by the Centre for Policy Studies found 'the political leadership and SARS's senior executive share a common objective in enhancing revenue collection and closing loopholes, based on a shared set of values'.

But despite its leadership excellence, or perhaps because of it, Zuma has never been fond of SARS. The taxman audited Zuma in the run-up to the ANC's Polokwane conference and he paid a 'large amount' to make the issue go away. 'We have been in discussion with SARS for some years now in order to regularise his tax affairs,' Michael Hulley, Zuma's lawyer, said after Zuma became ANC president.[12] More recently, calls were made to SARS to institute an investigation into whether Zuma is liable to pay fringe-benefit tax on the alterations to his Nkandla compound. This after the Public Protector found millions of rands were spent by government on his private homestead. According to independent tax experts[13] and the DA, Zuma must be held liable for tax, which, according to some estimates, could be as high as R63,9 million.[14] Pillay even visited Zuma in person at the Union Buildings to explain his tax obligations.[15] Under Moyane, however, SARS has been unable to confirm whether Zuma's liability has been assessed. During an appearance in Parliament, a senior SARS staffer confirmed the revenue service is looking at the fringe benefits,[16] only for SARS to deny this in a later statement.[17]

Besides Pillay's visit to the Union Buildings, officials have met the president on three other occasions to give guidance to the head of state. Journalist Ferial Haffajee reported on the first of these – when SARS had advised Zuma about the investigation into companies implicated in illegal tobacco smuggling, with which his son Edward was involved. The second time was when SARS officials identified 'a risk in various businesses and trusts in which the president's wives were involved'. A third occasion involved the president's alleged meeting with Cape gangsters arranged by former ANC strongman Marius Fransman. 'On the agenda had been the gangsters' various pains with SARS.'[18]

Many of Zuma's family, friends and benefactors are known to have clashed with SARS, including some of his sons, his nephew, his lawyer and business associates linked to him through family. For example:

❏ Edward Zuma has had a particularly tempestuous relationship with the receiver, being a target of Van Loggerenberg's investigative unit when SARS started to clamp down on the illicit tobacco trade in 2013, issuing a written warning to the whole of the industry that SARS will institute 'the most punitive measures available' to authorities against companies found wanting. In that year alone more than R5 billion in tax and excise was lost to smuggling and fraud in relation to illegal cigarettes. Amalgamated Tobacco Manufacturers was one of the victims of Van Loggerenberg's unit when 'a huge consignment of illicit cigarettes' linked to Zuma Jr's company was seized.[19] Edward Zuma immediately fought back, accusing SARS of 'corruption, racism and a smear campaign' against him.[20] He later said there was a well-orchestrated campaign by 'white monopoly capital' to remove his father from power.[21]

❏ Khulubuse Zuma, the president's rotund nephew, stood accused of money laundering and tax evasion after the Aurora mining scandal, in which he and partner Zondwa Mandela – a grandson of the former president – were held liable for the asset stripping of the mine. Also implicated was Michael Hulley, Zuma's lawyer, whom he eventually employed in his private office in the presidency.

❏ Another of Khulubuse Zuma's partners, Robert Huang, was the target of SARS after an extensive investigation into his massive business empire revealed that he had been dodging tax for years, allegedly owing SARS R1,8 billion in unpaid dues. One of Huang's companies, Mpisi Trading, imported thousands of ANC T-shirts ahead of the 2014 general election, but the shipment was seized by customs officials. Zuma apparently personally intervened to try to broker a deal between SARS and Huang, asking Moyane to find 'a settlement outside a tax audit'.[22]

Moyane was very close to Zuma. Like many others, he had gone into exile during the struggle against apartheid and was welcomed in Mozambique by Zuma when he arrived there to study. He has acknowledged their close relationship and said during a radio interview that he regards Zuma's first wife, Kate Mantsho, as a 'family sister' and Duduzane as his 'nephew'. Sbu Ngalwa, editor of the *Daily Dispatch*, Tweeted on 22 January 2016 that he had seen Moyane and Duduzane 'in seemingly intense discussions in some obscure coffee shop in Midrand'. It is unclear what they spoke about, but when Zuma's close friends and Duduzane's business partners, the Gupta family, needed cash it was Moyane who intervened to ensure a speedy VAT return of R70 million amid criticism that SARS's systems were creaking to a halt.

Moyane has held various government positions since his return from exile, his most senior role being National Commissioner of Correctional Services. His spell overseeing the prison service was not without controversy: Moyane agreed to extend a tender to service providers Bosasa, even though a report by the SIU found there had been corruption with the awarding of the tender in the first place. Moyane was also roped into the team that investigated the Guptas' Waterkloof landing in 2013, which did little other than identify fall guy Bruce Koloane, who was later awarded an ambassadorship for facilitating the landing of the private jet.

SARS had achieved remarkable success over the years with the introduction of specialised units to counter organised crime and the illicit economy, like the illegal tobacco trade, which cost the fiscus billions of rands every year in lost taxes. Some units, like the Large Business Centre, were established to provide big corporates with an access point to SARS to ensure compliance and improve tax collection. The Anti-Smuggling Unit, Criminal Investigations Unit, the Illicit Economy Research Group and the National Enforcement Unit are all examples of entities that made SARS the formidable institution it became.

That was up until October 2014, when it all started to unravel. Two weeks after Moyane took up his new posting, the *Sunday Times* published a front-page story under the headline 'SARS bugged Zuma'.[23] The report gushed about how a top-secret 'rogue unit' operating in SARS had broken into Zuma's home before he became head of state and planted listening devices. This unit appeared to have been illegally established, and Pillay, it was claimed, even paid a bribe of R3 million to a former head of the unit to remain quiet about the whole affair. It was a bombshell story. SARS's squeaky-clean image was soiled instantly. It didn't stop there: a couple of weeks later, the newspaper ran the next instalment in the assault on SARS: 'Taxman's rogue unit ran brothel'. The newspaper claimed that a SARS unit – the National Research Group – had set up a brothel in Durban and provided prostitutes to members, that its agents posed as bodyguards to top ANC leaders and that it 'became a law unto itself and supplied members with aliases and fake IDs'.[24]

Moyane sprang into action immediately, suspending the entire SARS executive team without answering any questions. He told Parliament: 'Under my leadership, things of this nature will not be condoned, [including] rogue activities within the organisation. I will take decisive action if any credible evidence is found where the law has been breached.'[25]

SARS never refuted any of the claims and never denied any of the outlandish reports in the *Sunday Times*.

For an organisation that had been painstakingly constructed over the better part of 17 years, the unravelling of its top management and executive team happened very quickly. In May 2014, four months before the *Sunday Times* ran its first 'rogue unit' story, Belinda Walter, a triple agent who simultaneously was on the payroll of the State Security Agency, British American Tobacco and Carnilinx, a cigarette manufacturer, sent an email to Pillay and other SARS executives, alleging that Van Loggerenberg had shared confidential taxpayers' information with her and that he was unfit for his job. He was in charge of a number of specialised SARS units, including the High-Risk Investigations Unit, the so-called rogue unit. Walter, who acted as chairperson of a trade organisation representing smaller cigarette manufacturers while she was spying on them on behalf of rivals and the SSA, targeted Van Loggerenberg. He started moving in on the lucrative illicit cigarette trade and made powerful enemies, including Edward Zuma.

Walter ensnared Van Loggerenberg, and a romantic relationship ensued, which ended acrimoniously in early 2014. The *Sunday Times* published all the details of their relationship and Walter's allegations in a series of front-page stories – which led to Van Loggerenberg going on special leave while an investigation was launched against him.

Around the same time, assaults on the Hawks and the IPID began, with those institutions' leaders being accused of illegal activities. Anwa Dramat was accused of illegally deporting Zimbabwean citizens and Robert McBride was accused of protecting him. Dramat would later be suspended and he resigned; McBride fought back following a suspension to regain his job.

Van Loggerenberg was the first SARS domino to fall. After the series of allegations by Walter appeared in the *Sunday Times*, culminating in the story on 12 October 2014 ('SARS bugged Zuma'), he was put on leave and eventually suspended by Moyane. Over a period of months in 2014 the narrative around SARS morphed from the Van Loggerenberg–Walter 'affair', to Van Loggerenberg abusing a charity to shake down taxpayers audited by SARS and finally into reports about the 'rogue unit'. It seemed that whoever was behind the assault on SARS was looking for anything and everything on Van Loggerenberg, and when they couldn't find dirt, it was simply made up – with the *Sunday Times* as a willing, albeit perhaps unwitting, co-conspirator.

Even though an initial panel of inquiry found that Walter's allegations against Van Loggerenberg were devoid of any truth or fact, Pillay decided to appoint a respected advocate, Muzi Sikhakhane, to lead a second inquiry to clear SARS for once and for all. But midway through the panel's lifespan, Sikhakhane met with the newly appointed Moyane and the scope was expanded to include the High-Risk Investigations Unit. The final report, handed to Moyane and Finance Minister Nene in

December 2014, found that the unit had been established illegally and engaged in extra-judicial activites.

Moyane disbanded the unit, and Van Loggerenberg was suspended. Shortly after, in the first week of December, Moyane suspended Pillay, as well as Pete Richer, group executive for strategic planning and risk. In the same month, Barry Hore, SARS's chief operations officer, Jerome Frey, head of modernisation and strategy, Jacques Meyer, head of case selection, and Clifford Collings, head of anti-corruption and security, left the taxman. In February 2015 Van Loggerenberg and Lackay resigned, and Pillay and Richer followed in May, as well as Yolisa Pikie, Pillay's special advisor, and Marika Muller, Lackay's deputy. In the course of the year, Gene Ravele, chief officer: tax and customs enforcement, Elizabeth Khumalo, chief officer: human resources, Godfrey Baloyi, group executive: tax and customs enforcement, and Brian Kgomo, group executive: internal audit also departed. SARS's senior management team had been decimated.

Two other probes into the High-Risk Investigations Unit followed: one by the Kroon advisory board and another, a documentary review, by auditor KPMG. Both relied heavily on Sikhakhane and found that the unit was a rogue entity. Neither Van Loggerenberg nor Pillay was called on to testify. Evidence that showed the unit had been formed under the watch of Gordhan and signed off by Manuel was ignored. In reaction, Lackay forwarded a 25-page memorandum to the Parliamentary Standing Committee on Finance and the Joint Standing Committee on Intelligence to try to convince MPs to investigate events at SARS. Nothing happened. Yunus Carrim, ANC chairperson of the finance committee – the same MP who oversaw the destruction of the Scorpions on behalf of Zuma – told Lackay that the issue was to be discussed at an ANC study group. The memorandum, a detailed timeline of events and evidence, sank without trace. Pillay, Van Loggerenberg, Lackay, Richer and the rest of their colleagues were hung out to dry.

The five units that reported to Van Loggerenberg were all closed down, their projects and cases mothballed or scrapped: National Projects, which investigated underworld figures, such as Mark Lifman, Lolly

Jackson and Radovan Krecjir, and the illegal cigarette trade; Central Projects, which investigated Dave King, a billionaire businessman who battled SARS for 13 years over a tax bill of more than R3 billion, Huang and Julius Malema; the Tactical Intervention Unit, which covered border posts; the High-Risk Investigations Unit, which worked on high-risk projects alongside sister units; and the Evidence Management and Technical Support Unit, which consisted of world-class forensic and IT laboratories, as well as tax, customs, audit and other experts. They were all gone, destroyed by Moyane in the aftermath of Walter, the *Sunday Times* and the rogue-unit narrative.

SARS sued Lackay for R10 million and laid charges against Pillay, while Walter sued Van Loggerenberg for R12 million.

In March 2016 journalist Max du Preez wrote a column in which he alleged the reason why the SARS top management team was cleared out is the existence of a top-secret dossier deep inside the taxman's vaults containing all the incriminating information on Zuma, his cronies, friends and associates.[26] It fell to David Mahlobo to engineer the wholesale regime change at SARS and to secure the contents of the dossier – which, according to those who have seen it, isn't so much a folder, but more a case of thousands of files, reports, planning documents, affidavits, spreadsheets, investigation diaries, case notes, memory sticks, dockets, instruction notes, correspondence with other law-enforcement agencies, bank statements, compliance checks, taxpayer records and third-party data. Du Preez has never been challenged in his assertions and he seems to be spot-on. And the dossier allegedly contains information on Zuma, Nkandla and related matters; Edward Zuma, Amalgamated Tobacco Manufacturing and related matters; Thoshan Panday; Khulubuse Zuma, Michael Hulley and Aurora; the Guptas and related matters; Huang and related matters; Lifman and related matters; the ANC and related matters; Prasa; Eskom; SABC; Denel; Transnet and provincial tenders in North West, KwaZulu-Natal and Mpumalanga.

In April 2016 Bongani Siqoko, who took over as editor of the *Sunday Times* after the previous editor, Phylicia Oppelt, was removed by Times Media Group management, acknowledged that the 'rogue unit' stories were false and that failures in editorial systems had led to the publication of untested allegations. This came after the Press Ombudsman ordered the newspaper to retract various reports and editorials about the 'rogue' unit, including reports about KPMG's findings and Gordhan's involvement. In the right of reply that the newspaper offered Van Loggerenberg, he defended his unit's work, saying it was legal and above board. Pillay, in his opinion piece, said the extent of the damage done to SARS by the reports still had to be determined and that the reports were not in the public interest.

Given the sensitive nature of the SARS enforcement units' work, it was inevitable that they would be attacked so viciously. Illegal cigarettes, the Zumas and their associates, and organised crime seemed to have worked hand in glove to neuter one of the last remaining institutions that enforced the law without fear or favour. The long game however became apparent in February 2015, when Gordhan was subtly but consistently pulled into the 'rogue unit' narrative, with references in the *Sunday Times* and images of him increasingly being used along with headlines such as 'Pressure piles on former Finance Minister'.

Capturing SARS may have been a major prize, but holding the keys to the National Treasury was the ultimate goal.

PART 4

9/12

CHAPTER 13

The day everything changed

—

'The axe has fallen.'

– Minister of Finance Nhlanhla Nene, in a text message to Lungisa Fuzile, director general

of the National Treasury, 9 December 2015

It had been a long and stressful day. The Treasury director general, Lungisa Fuzile, was driving through Pretoria in the early evening of Wednesday 9 December 2015. Earlier that day, in the final Cabinet meeting of the year, at the Presidential Guest House, the Treasury team had presented details of the 2016/17 national budget. It was a difficult meeting. University students were demanding that fees be scrapped, while the medium-term budget policy statement, the so-called mini-budget, delivered three months before, had made it clear that fees would at the very least need to increase by 6% the following year. Zuma, however, announced unilaterally that fees would not rise in the coming academic year, leaving Treasury to figure out how to pay for the shortfall.

During Treasury's presentation to ministers and senior officials, Finance Minister Nhlanhla Nene laid out the options to finance the president's promise to students: government either shifts money from other departments and development programmes to the Department of Higher Education, or it will have to borrow. It was vital, Nene argued, that government stuck to the expenditure framework and ceiling set during the mini-budget so as to maintain the country's debt rating. Luckily

– for the fiscus, Nene and Fuzile – a decision was taken against borrowing and it was agreed that money would be found within the existing budgetary framework. But Fuzile, along with colleagues Michael Sachs (head of the Treasury's Budget Office) and Dondo Mogajane (head of Public Finance), returned to their headquarters at 40 Church Square worried. Ever since Trevor Manuel's tenure as finance minister, the national expenditure allocations – how much money each department would be getting – has always been finalised before Christmas. Fuzile, Sachs and Mogajane talked about the implications before agreeing that they would come back straight after Christmas to start looking for the money. It was a precarious situation to be in and unknown territory for these experienced Treasury professionals.

Fuzile, director general since May 2011, got a text message from Nene while he was weaving his way through the capital's traffic. It simply said: 'The axe has fallen.' Nene had been fired – in the middle of a budgeting crisis. Fuzile knew there was a large degree of unhappiness with his minister, who was comfortable telling his colleagues no when they asked for money. He was also aware of the sniping attacks on him during Cabinet meetings, often led by the president, when the minister preached austerity and fiscal responsibility. 'It isn't Treasury's place to tell us there isn't money, Treasury should simply go and find it,' one minister had said during a previous heated Cabinet exchange.[1]

Fuzile phoned Nene, who confirmed he had been removed, and drove to Monument Park, the suburb where the ministerial residence is. On his way there, Mogajane called Fuzile: the Presidency had called earlier, looking for Nene's phone number. His colleague wanted to know what it was about. Fuzile's phone rang again. A member of the ANC's NEC said: 'Have you seen the news? I suppose you're going to get a Gupta minister now.' Fuzile was dumbstruck and told the NEC member so. 'Don't you know the modus operandi? Look at what happened at the Department of Mineral Resources. The Guptas decide who they want as minister. They then send along advisors,' he said. Fuzile didn't know what to make of it.[2]

Nene had left the Cabinet meeting at Bryntirion just after 5 pm to go to the gym, but on his way there he got a message from the president's office: could he come to the Union Buildings, the head of state wants to see him. His driver turned the car around. Arriving at the presidential suite, he saw staff typing furiously on their computers and spotted just enough to confirm his worst fears: the curriculum vitae of Minister David Des van Rooyen.

'The ANC has decided to deploy you to the Africa division of the BRICS Development Bank,' Zuma told Nene, before thanking him for his service and sending him on his way. Fuzile arrived at Nene's home, offered his condolences and shared some thoughts before leaving. He sent a text message to his new political principal, welcoming him to the Treasury and advising the new minister to issue a full statement early in the morning. He received no reply. He didn't tell Nene about the worrying call from the ANC NEC member, but did remark on the fact that a few days before a report had appeared in *Business Day* speculating that Nene might be redeployed to 'an international finance institution, like the planned Brics Development Bank'. It was all very curious.[3]

Just after 8 pm, the Presidency issued a statement saying Zuma had decided to replace Nene with an unknown backbencher, Des van Rooyen, ahead of Nene's redeployment 'to another strategic position'.

At the exact same time as the statement was released, Zuma was delivering a speech at a gathering of business leaders in Johannesburg, convened by ANC benefactor and mining magnate Patrice Motsepe. Zuma told these captains of industry: 'I think there is a bigger struggle to fight, to liberate ourselves economically. Even that definition I'm talking about ... I rebelled against it, that what determines the value of a commodity is the law of supply and demand. No! I define it differently, the value of a commodity. It is the necessary labour time taken in the production of a commodity, that is what determines the value.'[4]

The rand tanked, losing 80 cents against the dollar and threatening to breach R16. The news exploded on social media and reporters were scurrying around: who the hell is Des van Rooyen? Where's he from? If Nene has done so well and is so well respected, why remove him? When the next day had dawned, the South African economy was already being

buffeted by the worst storms since the unmitigated disaster that was PW
Botha's infamous 'Rubicon speech' of 1985. And that's saying something.

Nene was appointed Minister of Finance in May 2014, replacing
Gordhan, when the president shifted him to the local-government
portfolio. He was a respected chair of the Standing Committee on
Finance in Parliament and shepherded the Money Bills Act, which ena-
bles Parliament to change the budget, through the legislature. This bill
ensures that MPs can change departmental allocations without breaching the expenditure ceiling, which prevents populist policies being forced
through with a simple parliamentary majority. While Gordhan navi-
gated the worst of the global financial crisis, Nene had to contend with
a sharp slowdown in economic growth and continued on the path set by
Gordhan to balance public spending with responsible budgeting. This
invariably led to a growing budget deficit and increased foreign debt, but
Nene had room to manoeuvre thanks to the fiscally conservative policies established by Manuel, which enabled the country to withstand and
absorb the shocks of 2007/08. Nevertheless, the country's economy was
extremely volatile going into the Christmas break in 2015.

On 6 December 2015, a few days before Zuma decided to axe Nene,
credit-rating agencies Fitch Ratings and S&P Global Ratings cut South
Africa's rating to within a hair's breadth of junk.[5] On 7 December 2015,
Anglo American announced it would be retrenching almost 4 500 workers at its mines owing to the protracted commodities slump[6] and Rand
Merchant Bank's business-confidence index fell to its lowest levels in five
years.[7] Nene tried to rally his team to look beyond the political scandals
that dominated the environment – Zuma and the ANC's culpability in
the Nkandla debacle, the Gupta family's growing influence, the fallout
of the Waterkloof Air Force Base saga and government's defiance of the
courts when authorities ignored an order to arrest Sudan's president,
Omar al-Bashir. But it was difficult. The world economy was still splut-
tering and local growth forecasts were being further cut; Treasury was
preparing for an unprecedented tax-revenue shortfall; inflation was

rising; debt service cost was increasing; and a growing public-sector wage bill was stretching the budget deficit to its highest levels since 1994.

'There we were,' said Fuzile. 'The economic situation got tougher, and it was harder than what Nene had inherited from Gordhan. One of the amazing things about Nene was his ability to take tough decisions. We started to reduce expenditure during Gordhan's time, but went further under Nene – and we raised taxes. We were adamant that we were not going to give up our fiscal sovereignty and end up at the doors of the IMF or World Bank, because then you can kiss your macroeconomic and social policies goodbye.'[8]

The campaign against the Treasury – which had been built around the notion that it was obstructive, that it resisted government's developmental agenda, that it was a 'state within a state' – kicked into high gear during the latter part of Zuma's term. Where the president used to be content in controlling the security cluster (the armed forces, police and intelligence structures), he became increasingly frustrated with his lack of influence in the 'finance family' (including the Treasury, SARS and the Financial Intelligence Centre) during his second term. 'This is because the Guptas had realised that the Treasury, Eskom, Transnet and the Passenger Rail Agency of South Africa were key to unlocking great wealth,' a public-finance official told *City Press*.[9] 'Nene was doing a good job. His firing was unexpected, but it was becoming obvious that there was a lot of unhappiness with him, about Treasury, because he was not doing what some people wanted him to do,' said Fuzile.

Those 'people' turned out to be the Guptas, who, by the latter half of 2015 appeared to be running two major projects simultaneously: the capture of the Treasury and the subjugation of the Department of Mineral Resources. Both were crucial to what is widely believed to be their larger project of gutting the state: the former because it was an obstacle to unbridled looting, enabled by their deployees in senior positions at crucial state-owned enterprises, and the latter because it gave them preferential access to the mining industry – still a source of great wealth and with the potential to further fleece the state. On 23 September 2015, the Guptas scored big when the president appointed their kept man at the

Free State provincial government, Mosebenzi Zwane, as mines minister (see Chapter 9 for the full story).

The bigger prize, however, would have remained the Treasury. The institution had been a fierce opponent of the Zuma government's plans to embark on a massive nuclear-energy programme to provide the country's energy security, resolutely insisting that 9,6MW of nuclear power is an unaffordable investment for this generation and the next. South Africa had been plagued by electricity blackouts as its creaking electricity grid was giving way under the pressure of growing demand – and introducing nuclear energy into the mix was presented as a way out of the dark. But it was also an opportunity for some to grow rich beyond measure. The Guptas, their eyes always on the prize, invested in a uranium mine in the North West province, awaiting the big payday when it would be a supplier to the eight massively expensive nuclear reactors Zuma wanted to build.

With mineral resources seemingly in the bag – and other ministers like Malusi Gigaba having laid the foundations for further state capture with the reorganisation of various SOE boards – the Guptas were now on the scout for a new minister to take the reins at the Treasury. On 23 October 2015, Mcebisi Jonas, Nene's respected deputy, was lured by Duduzane Zuma to the Guptas' Saxonwold mansion for a meeting with Ajay Gupta. Without wasting time ('there was no exchange of pleasantries'), Gupta allegedly told Jonas they had been gathering intelligence on him and those around him. He then went on to state, matter-of-factly, that they were going to make him finance minister. Shocked and irritated, Jonas rejected the 'offer', saying only the head of state can make such appointments and that he wanted to leave. Duduzane was present, but didn't say a word. Gupta, however, wasn't about to give up. He divulged the names of other 'comrades' they were working with and protecting, and added the family had made R6 billion out of the state and wanted to increase that figure to R8 billion. But, he said, the Treasury was a 'stumbling block', and that Fuzile and other key members of the department's executive team needed to be removed. After Gupta bragged how they had turned Duduzane into a billionaire with property in Dubai, Jonas had had enough and turned for the door. It was then that Gupta made his play: if Jonas would accept the position of finance minister and agree to work with them, he would deposit R600 million into a bank account of his choice and, to show his commitment, he would hand Jonas R600 000 in cash – then and there. Jonas again refused and insisted that Duduzane take him to the airport. He immediately called Nene and told him about the incident.[10]

But the Guptas weren't too worried. Des van Rooyen, an unknown, pliable ANC backbencher who used to serve as mayor of the embattled Merafong Municipality, was already hovering in the wings. Three days after Jonas rebuffed the Guptas' offer, on 26 October 2015, Eric Wood, CEO of Gupta-aligned Trillian Capital Partners, reportedly sent an email to Essa,[11] the majority shareholder in Trillian and partner in various Gupta ventures (and considered 'the fourth Gupta brother'[12]). The email was subject-headed 'National Treasury 26 October': 'Hi Salim, as discussed … I have quickly jotted down a few points for the FM. These are not comprehensive – in time I can develop a more comprehensive list … regards, Eric.' An attached document, under the heading 'National Treasury Discussion Points – Key Initiatives', sets out what appear to be eight key priorities for the Minister of Finance, including plans for municipalities to access credit and the establishment of a 'black bank'. On the same day, Wood told senior staff at Trillian that Zuma was going to fire Nene, a staffer said, adding: 'He subsequently sent me an email outlining National Treasury's new initiatives and his proposed fees for each initiative he had drafted.'[13]

Van Rooyen – who had served on Parliament's Standing Committee on Finance and, according to Fuzile, 'played a constructive role' – started appearing on the Guptas' radar screen during that time. Cellphone records place him in Saxonwold eight days before Ajay Gupta made his offer to Jonas, on 15 October 2015, and five times between 20 and 27 November 2015.[14]

Ajay Gupta has denied that he ever met Jonas.[15] Des van Rooyen has also denied that the Guptas 'hired' him or that he flew to Dubai to consult with them before his short-lived spell as finance minister.[16]

At the same time, Nene and Treasury tried to keep the perpetually delinquent national airline, SAA, on a short leash. On 3 December 2015, less than a week before he was fired, Nene vetoed plans by the SAA chair, Dudu Myeni, to buy five Airbus passenger planes, lease them to a local company and then hire them back from them. In a detailed statement, Nene fired a volley of warning shots across Myeni's bow, saying the Treasury had instructed SAA to stick with the plans approved by it and that if it did not, it would constitute a breach of the Public Finance Management Act. Myeni never said who she wanted to lease the planes to.

The Guptas' two flagship projects – Treasury and mines – were fast approaching maturity. In November 2015, Zwane accompanied Tony Gupta and Essa to Switzerland to negotiate the purchase of Glencore's Optimum coal mine (see Chapter 9),[17] thereby helping engineer one of the family's great coups. Van Rooyen, meanwhile, was gearing up for his new posting, visiting the Gupta family home every day between 2 and 8 December 2015.

On 7 December 2015, Nene briefed the president on the details of the budget presentation to Cabinet to be delivered on 9 December 2015. By all accounts, the meeting at the official presidential residence was cordial and positive. There was full engagement by the president in debates on government's financial constraints and discussions on future plans beyond the tabling of the budget, due nine weeks later. To Treasury officials accompanying the minister, there was no inkling that their political principal would be fired in 48 hours.

On 8 December 2015 Nene and his colleagues again met the president, but this time at an afternoon meeting of the National Nuclear Energy Coordinating Committee at the presidential guest house. This time, the atmosphere was much less cordial. Before the meeting started, Zuma spoke with his confidants, David Mahlobo, Lynne Brown, Tina Joemat-Pettersson (energy) and Maite Nkoana-Mashabane (international relations and cooperation), but avoided Nene. When the meeting started, the finance minister and his team of technocrats were bombarded with reasons why nuclear-energy capacity was needed. Nene agreed to a Cabinet statement announcing that an engagement process around nuclear procurement could start.[18] 'It was a difficult meeting and left me with the clear impression that political considerations superseded the technical, economic considerations,' said Fuzile.[19]

After the meeting, Zuma joked to a Treasury official, saying: 'Your last minister defied me in many ways.'[20]

CHAPTER 14

Gents, finally …

—

'*Look, there's going to be another change at Treasury, this one
hasn't worked, you are getting PG back.*'

– President Jacob Zuma to Lungisa Fuzile, director general of the National Treasury,

13 December 2015

The reaction on Thursday 10 December 2015 to Zuma's removal of
Finance Minister Nhlanhla Nene was immediate and scathing.

The DA said the decision was 'reckless and dangerous', while the EFF
said it indicated that there was 'a serious and pathological crisis in the
country's leadership'.[1]

Analysts were left 'speechless,'[2] decrying the fact that the new Minister
of Finance, Des van Rooyen, was a 'complete outsider with no experience at Treasury',[3] while some were warning that the rand could slide as
far as R20 to the dollar.[4] 'This is a shock, coming so close to the recent
downgrades of our debt. This will be interpreted in the worst possible
light by markets,' said analyst Nic Borain.[5] Academic Mzukisi Qobo
said it was a 'crony appointment' and one that gave a clear indication
of Zuma's mindset as to how he runs the state – 'a patronage system
essentially',[6] while the then *Business Day* editor, Songezo Zibi, said the
choice was based on who to fire – Nene or Dudu Myeni: 'There'd been a
number of instances where Treasury had taken a line that was somewhat
contrary to the president's wishes … and this pattern had become more

urgent recently with the disagreement between the Treasury and the SAA board, led by Myeni.'[7] Bruce Whitfield, 702's business presenter, Tweeted that Genghis Khan had wreaked less havoc on Mongolia than Zuma had on the financial sector, and the South African Chamber of Commerce and Industry demanded answers, saying macroeconomic stability was crucial.[8]

But not everyone was quite as distraught, though. Collen Maine, ANCYL president, said Nene's firing couldn't be held to be the cause of the rand's losses: 'Nene is not so special that the rand can fall because of him, who is he? [...] It's not about Nhlanhla Nene, it's because of the recession we are in that the economy is not growing … and there are problems with the rand. He might be beautiful to others but he's not so beautiful that he can make the rand fall.'[9]

The extent of the carnage wrought on the financial markets, however, was undeniably massive. Besides losing 80 cents against the dollar in the immediate aftermath, the currency lost 90 cents to the euro and 110 cents to the pound, while the country's major banks lost between 3,8% and 7,7% in equity. South African bonds and equities lost more than half a trillion rands in value[10] and the Public Investment Corporation suffered losses of R106,2 billion.[11]

Nene went to the Treasury on Thursday morning to clear out his office, say his farewells and to wait for the new minister, so he could do a formal handover. Trevor Manuel had gone to great lengths to do the same for his successor, Pravin Gordhan, while Gordhan had extended the same courtesy to Nene. Likewise, when the long-serving Lesetja Kganyago became governor of the SARB, he took time to onboard Lungisa Fuzile in the demanding role of Treasury director general. Van Rooyen, however, wasn't interested; he sent word that he would 'come in his own time'.

Fuzile was instructed to attend the swearing-in ceremony of his new boss in the Union Buildings at 1 pm – and that's where the penny dropped, Fuzile explained. 'This guy, Mohamed Bobat, walks up to me and hands me a statement that is supposed to be issued on behalf of the minister. I ask him who he is, and he replies he is the minister's advisor.' Fuzile suddenly understood what the ANC NEC member had meant when he got the mysterious phone call the previous evening on his way to Nene's house. Van Rooyen introduced Fuzile to Bobat, and he could see they didn't know each other. Van Rooyen proceeded to make a short acceptance speech, saying his task was to 'demystify' Treasury and make it more 'accessible'.[12]

Back at Trillian, Eric Wood was seemingly triumphant, telling employees in the immediate aftermath of Van Rooyen's appointment that a former colleague, Mohamed Bobat, would be appointed ministerial advisor. Bobat, he reportedly said, would appoint a 'team of experts' with experience at Trillian. A colleague of Wood claimed that Bobat would 'channel all tenders from Treasury and SOEs to this team'. In addition, the new minister would 'approve requests from SOEs seeking approval for funding initiatives/transactions that Treasury historically did not approve'.[13]

The Gupta takeover of the Treasury became apparent on Friday 11 December, when Van Rooyen rocked up with three hangers-on: Bobat, who was linked to the Guptas through Wood, Malcolm Mabaso, linked to the Guptas through his association with mineral resources minister Zwane and Ian Whitley, son-in-law of ANC deputy secretary general Jessie Duarte. Van Rooyen told Fuzile: 'Appoint Bobat as advisor and Whitley as chief of staff … do it as quick as possible. This guy [pointing at Mabaso], don't worry about him, he's going to be hanging around … just arrange an access card.'[14]

Fuzile was flabbergasted. As the department's accounting officer, he signed off on appointments and he couldn't just ignore protocol and procedure laid out by the ministerial handbook and the Department of Public Service and Administration. He told Van Rooyen as much after finding out that Mabaso was already on the payroll of the Department of Mineral Resources, advising Zwane – a Gupta appointee. 'I had to tell them a few times, "This is not how things work here. He [Mabaso] can't just hang around!" Bobat would not have lasted. I found his rudeness annoying. He started issuing instructions, including to me, this young boy pushing me around … a lightweight. He was making a terrible mistake with me,' said Fuzile.

But it got worse. Bobat and Whitley immediately got to work and started asking around for information on the SAA/Airbus deal, saying they were authorised to act and approve spending on behalf of the minister. They wanted to see all Treasury's files on the carrier. Bobat and Whitley needed a place to work, so they kicked out Nene's former chief of staff, Malcolm Geswint, from his office. 'The bullying was bad,' Fuzile recalled.

Fuzile was badgered with requests for documentation the whole day. Later that evening, he sent a confidential memorandum on the state of the economy and Treasury's plans to avert a further ratings downgrade to Whitley. The document detailed the effect of the recent downgrades by rating agencies on the economy, a breakdown of government expenditure, issues around SOEs, corruption and perceptions thereof, mining and beneficiation as well as input around the government's nine-point plan to revitalise the economy and every department's role in these efforts. Whitley was overjoyed. Not only were they now running the show, they also had direct and unfettered access to Treasury's workings and clear sight of its plans and machinations. After all the stalling and blockages preventing increased state expenditure, they had finally established a beachhead. Whitley sent it to Bobat and Mabaso – whom Fuzile in the end refused to take on – with the simple but sweet message: 'Gents, finally …' Bobat sent it on to Wood.[15]

The Treasury, the institution that blocked spending, canned tenders and almost religiously clung to the Public Finance Management Act, had at long last been captured.

The ANC was at a loss. The leadership did not know of Zuma's plans beforehand and the president had merely informed Zweli Mkhize, the party's treasurer general, shortly before the announcement to dismiss Nene was made. 'We understand it is your right, even though we might not agree with it,' Mkhize told Zuma. The party issued a terse statement, saying it 'respects' the presidential prerogative to appoint a new minister. Jeff Radebe, briefing the media on Friday morning, said the executive had not been not informed and reiterated the president has the final say on ministerial appointments. Zuma was struggling to contain the fallout, and by Saturday the Presidency had issued four statements, including one saying Nene was to be seconded to the planned new BRICS Development Bank and another one denying allegations by the EFF that Myeni was Zuma's 'girlfriend'.

Organised business was also in disarray. Business Leadership South Africa – who represented around 50 of the country's biggest corporates – didn't know how to respond or how to engage the governing party, and Ramaphosa and Mkhize were scrambling for solutions to the unfolding disaster. The private sector's response therefore was by no means a coordinated one, and informal conversations between businesspeople with links to the ANC and its networks proved to be the catalyst in setting up a crucial meeting between representatives of the ANC leadership and heavy hitters in the banking sector on Sunday 13 December 2015.

This high-level crisis meeting was held at auditors Ernst & Young's offices in Sandton in the afternoon, with the participants confirmed only by midday. Some of the banks' research staff were still running around at the last hour trying to get the relevant data points and market reports to their principals before the meeting began.

Mkhize, who was central in all conversations between the ANC's disaffected leadership and business over the course of the previous days, and Jeff Radebe, the ANC's head of policy and Minister in the Presidency, represented the ANC. The banks' delegation was headed by Dave Munro from Standard Bank and included, among others, Colin Coleman from Goldman Sachs and Maria Ramos from Absa. Also in attendance was Jabu Mabuza, president of Business Unity South Africa, and Motsepe. Nine banking executives attended the meeting.

Munro opened discussions by explaining the toxic mix of repercussions should the markets open the following day with Van Rooyen still at the helm of the economy. Mkhize and Radebe were presented with a survey of top international asset managers about their views on the country, research into the market impact of Van Rooyen's continued tenure at Treasury and the impact of the new appointment on the macro- and microeconomic level. The arguments were also framed in such a way so as to speak to the ANC's policy of alleviating the effect of the so-called 'triple challenges' of poverty, unemployment and inequality. The bankers had to speak ANC language in order to get their message across. Munro explained to Mkhize and Radebe that what set South Africa apart in the eyes of international investors was the strength of its institutions, specifically the steadfastness of the Treasury in determining fiscal policy and the SARB in managing monetary policy. It's what made South Africa stand out from its peers in the developing world, like Brazil and Turkey, and what made it a premium investment destination.

They were also warned by the corporates that should the country continue on its current path, it would lock in low GDP growth and struggle to close the yawning wealth gap. The arguments hit home. The meeting concluded at around 5 pm with a consensus: the country faced unmitigated disaster if an immediate course of correction was not effected.

Mkhize and Radebe relayed the outcome of the meeting to Ramaphosa, who earlier had threatened a Cabinet walkout if changes were not made. The deputy president led a delegation of ANC leaders to see Zuma at his official residence, where he gave an account of the afternoon's meeting and explained that the country could not afford the continued upheavals. There was some debate on who Van Rooyen's replacement should be, with Kganyago also being considered to take over from him. In the end, it was decided that although the SARB governor would be a shoo-in in a normal course of events, Zuma's overreach demanded a commensurate response and that Gordhan had the trust of international investors, the markets and rating agencies. Zuma had gone too far when he appointed the unknown and pliable backbencher Van Rooyen; the corrective response needed to be equally drastic. By 6.30 pm that evening, Gordhan had been reappointed as finance minister. Van Rooyen – who was mocked on social media as 'Weekend Special', the title of Brenda Fassie's famous song – was no more. He was finance minister for four days.

At 7 pm Fuzile received a call from Lakela Kaunda, Zuma's chief of staff, who handed him over to the president: 'Look, there's going to be another change at Treasury, this one hasn't worked, you are getting PG back.' Shortly afterwards he received another call, this time from his newest minister, saying it was time to get back to work. They immediately started preparing for the next day, and drafted a statement, which was circulated among senior staff.

By 11 am on Monday 14 December 2015, Gordhan was back in his old office at 40 Church Square, finalising the statement before addressing a lunchtime press conference at the GCIS building in downtown Pretoria. Flanked by his A-team of Jonas, Fuzile and Kganyago, a confident Gordhan set out to re-establish Treasury's authority. He called the appointment of Van Rooyen 'a miscalculation'[16] and said his return to the portfolio indicated that government was responsive to criticism and the reaction of the investor community. The Treasury would stay the course of fiscal consolidation and discipline, the expenditure ceiling remained 'sacrosanct' and state-owned enterprises would be whipped into line, he said. He slammed Myeni in a thinly veiled attack, saying SOEs aren't 'personal toys', adding that the nuclear acquisition programme needed to be affordable. 'There are some who forget, that think state resources are there to enrich them,' Gordhan said.[17] Jonas and Fuzile accompanied Gordhan back to the Treasury, where the minister had a teleconference with investors, who wanted to know if fiscal policies would change and if demands around student fees were going to 'bust the budget'. But Gordhan handled the call with aplomb. 'It was amazing. You could see PG's prowess, he was out of the business for 18 months but he's an old hand. The currency didn't recover as we had hoped, and he was worried about it, but we decided to ensure that things were fixed by February,' said Fuzile.

The ANC's National Working Committee met to discuss the calamitous events of the previous 96 hours. At a media briefing afterwards, Duarte, a loyal Zuma acolyte, tried her best to spin the story that Gordhan's return pointed to Zuma's 'bold' leadership and the ANC as 'responsive'. It was a shameful performance, breathtaking in its dishonesty and obfuscation. Duarte – as was her wont – lauded Zuma and dodged questions about the prudence of firing an established and respected minister, replacing him with someone who had no experience or standing.

On 17 December 2015, the South Gauteng High Court ordered that a memorandum that Myeni wanted to keep secret be made public. In it the SAA's chief executive warned Myeni against going ahead with her plans to defy Treasury with the Airbus deal, saying the airline was 'technically insolvent' and its board 'reckless'.[18] Four days later, the SAA board informed Gordhan it would abide by Nene's earlier directive and lease the aircraft directly from Airbus.[19] The adults were back in charge.

Lindiwe Zulu, known for her aggressive defence of the president, was angry at the turn of events. She had been part of a group of ministers – including Bathabile Dlamini and Nomvula Mokonyane – known to be critical of the Treasury and its position in the constitutional architecture. It may have seemed counter-intuitive when Zulu, the Minister of Small Business Development, told the *Mail & Guardian* on 18 December 2015 that the private sector had written off Zuma. She claimed business had forced Zuma's hand, essentially opposing the head of state instead of supporting him.

Manuel, who saw the true state of South Africa's national accounts when he took over at the Treasury in 1996 and helped construct the fiscal framework within which government now operates, disagreed flatly. In response to Zulu, he said Nene's dismissal without warning or explanation (he didn't buy Zuma's story about the BRICS Bank) had led to a breakdown in trust. It was furthermore worrying that an 'outside hand', which isn't the ruling party, knew more about events than Cabinet. 'Please help us by explaining how we might repair the trust, the legitimacy and, if you must, the obedience of the governed. In my limited view, it is possible for autocrats to rule, but not for democrats to govern without the vital ingredient of trust,' Manuel said.[20]

The removal of Nene was a political event of seismic proportions. It illustrated the extent to which the Treasury had become a target for capture and how determined its enemies were to breach its defences. Zuma was exposed as the Gupta family's principal agent when he showed his willingness to prostitute his constitutional mandate to their advantage.

But it also galvanised a push back by a broad coalition of interest groups and individuals against the captured and compromised president, and ensured that the Treasury, one of the country's outstanding institutions, was not overrun. The president had gambled that there would be no resistance to his manipulation and gerrymandering. He had grown stronger over the previous year and had succeeded to manoeuvre his pawns and surrogates into key positions, including in certain ministries and SOEs. Gordhan's return was a setback to these efforts, but Zuma still commanded the full reach of the state. There would be other opportunities to bring the Treasury to heel. 'We were happy to get PG back,' Fuzile said. 'He was an old hand, a pro, who thrived under these sorts of challenges. But we knew we weren't going to have a moment's peace or stability.'

And the fight started almost immediately.

CHAPTER 15

The State vs Pravin Gordhan

——

*'I have a job to do in a difficult economic environment and
serve South Africa as best I can. Let me do my job.'*
– Pravin Gordhan, 24 August 2016

Pravin Gordhan stepped into a toxic political environment when he
returned to the Herbert Baker-designed headquarters of the National
Treasury at 40 Church Square, Pretoria, in December 2015. The country's premier state institution had been under constant pressure for more
than a year by then, facing frequent attacks from within government and
the governing party while having to steer the economy to calmer waters
amid slowing growth prospects.

So-called rent-seekers – political and criminal parasites that extract
value from the state while investing none of their own capital – had
been waging a low-intensity war against the frugal fiscal policies of the
Treasury, especially after the establishment of the office of the chief procurement officer, which regularised and standardised the awarding of
all government tenders and contracts. State-owned companies were also
running amok: Prasa was issuing multibillion-rand contracts without
consulting properly; Eskom was being turned into the Gupta family's
private development bank; Myeni, Zuma's close friend at SAA, was ruling the national carrier by decree; and Tom Moyane, who took over as
commissioner of SARS in the last quarter of 2014, was busy gutting and

repurposing the taxman. Meanwhile, the rating agencies were eyeing the country, assessing the damage after the dismissal of Nene.

Amid all of this, Zuma had been strengthening his position. He had always been a savvy political operator, keeping his opponents in Cabinet on their toes with regular reshuffles, and Luthuli House just close enough to bat it away. He had complete command of party and state.

In his quest to dodge corruption charges and strong-arm his opponents, the president calculated that even though he couldn't control the judiciary, he could rig the system that leads to the courts and the judges. So he appointed minions and acolytes into the key positions of NDPP (Abrahams), head of the Hawks (Ntlemeza) and Minister of State Security (Mahlobo). Those three, through a combination of sycophancy, ineptitude and skulduggery, formed the Praetorian Guard around the president: impenetrable, unmovable and utterly loyal. They controlled criminal investigations, manipulated prosecutions and gathered covert intelligence. A dream team. And they made inroads, helping remove IPID head Robert McBride, and removing and then charging both Dramat (head of the Hawks) and Booysen (head of the Hawks in KwaZulu-Natal, a favourite hunting ground for connected criminals).

Officials at the Treasury were therefore expecting trouble. Those in senior executive positions tried to grit their teeth and support Gordhan and Jonas even though they privately feared the worst. Middle managers were downright afraid, constantly awaiting the next offensive. This came less than a week before the new(-ish) minister was to deliver his much anticipated budget speech, when a letter arrived from Ntlemeza, demanding answers to a number of questions about the continuing saga of the 'rogue unit' at SARS. Rumours had been circulating that the Hawks' crimes against the state unit and the NPA were investigating Gordhan and two of his former colleagues at SARS, Pillay and Van Loggerenberg, and that their prosecution and arrest were 'imminent'.[1]

To add insult to injury, Zuma, two days before Gordhan tabled the budget initiated by Nene, said the hapless Van Rooyen, finance minister for four days in December, was 'more qualified than any minister I have ever appointed in the finance issue'.[2] The budget speech was downbeat, drawing on Nene's mini-budget from the previous October and staying the course of fiscal conservatism. It was received optimistically, given the political firestorm after Nene's dismissal, but was promptly eclipsed by Gordhan's admission that the Hawks were indeed targeting him.

At a business breakfast on the Friday after the budget, Gordhan said there were attempts at a 'coup' at the Treasury[3] – and it became clear that the Hawks were being used to intimidate the minister. Ntlemeza asked Gordhan very forcefully to provide his office with a hand-delivered copy of his answers by the beginning of March, which would afford him enough time to consult with his legal advisors. In the letter Ntlemeza clearly hedges his bets: the focus is undoubtedly on the National Research Group/High-Risk Investigations Unit but also, for good measure, on a pension arrangement between Pillay and SARS.

Gordhan was furious at what he saw as attempts to destabilise the Treasury and to challenge his authority. It was also clear to him that the modus operandi used to deal with Dramat, Booysen, McBride and SARS was being deployed again: create a diversion, leak documents and undermine the victim's integrity by launching a bogus investigation.

Gordhan said that he and the Treasury were the targets of a group of people who 'are not interested in the economic stability of the country or the welfare of its people'. He said it seemed instead that they were 'interested in disrupting institutions and destroying reputations'.[4] He added he would not hesitate to go to the courts to protect the finance ministry. Gordhan dismissed the allegations about the 'rogue unit' and said that the unit had been established legally and operated within the bounds of the law and SARS procedures. It also made major contributions in fighting the illicit economy and helped the fiscus to recoup millions in lost tax revenue. 'I can categorically state that the Hawks have no reason to "investigate" me,' Gordhan said in a statement.[5]

Gordhan, his deputy, Jonas, and director general, Fuzile, as well as leaders from business and labour, left on an international investors' roadshow during the second week of March 2016, meeting investors in London, New York and Boston. It was a crucial visit, Fuzile said, because international markets were skittish after the Nene debacle. 'Gordhan was nervous before the meeting in New York because we couldn't coordinate our message beforehand. But when we got into a room with business leaders like Christo Wiese and Jabu Mabuza, as well as trade unionists Tyotyo James and Dennis George, we came together as South Africans, and investors, who hold billions in South African stock and government bonds, could see we were working together. Things were beginning to settle.'[6]

But Ntlemeza continued to badger Gordhan for answers, even during the roadshow, delivering an ultimatum saying he would not 'indulge' the minister any longer. Gordhan responded again, comparing the Hawks to the apartheid 'security police' and saying the Hawks' harassment of him and the Treasury had to stop. On 30 March 2016, Gordhan replied in full, after weeks of acrimony, leaks to newspapers and statements by Ntlemeza's office about Gordhan's 'tardiness'[7]. In a four-page statement he said there was nothing for the Hawks to investigate and that there was no basis 'to demand answers, set deadlines and threaten me with retaliation'. Gordhan reiterated that the 'rogue unit', which served as the basis for Tom Moyane's dismantling of SARS's investigative capabilities and led to an exodus of institutional knowledge, had been established during his time as commissioner. It was also done with full ministerial acquiescence and within the ambit of all relevant statutes. 'This unit was part of the broader enforcement division of SARS – similar to the enforcement capabilities required in any tax and customs administration in the world,' Gordhan said. The unit wasn't illegal and it did its job – now leave me alone to do my job, was his message.[8]

Then, on 17 May 2016, Gordhan issued a remarkable statement, unparalleled in democratic South Africa, where he called on 'all South Africans to protect Treasury'.[9] It was the end of the phoney war. In private, Gordhan knew Zuma wanted him out of the way, but the president was still under conventional and constitutional obligations to protect his Minister of Finance. That veneer of respectability and governance had worn off and Gordhan was forced to take the fight into the open. Days before, the *Sunday Times* – the same newspaper that wholly swallowed the rogue unit disinformation – reported that Gordhan, Pillay,

THE STATE VS PRAVIN GORDHAN

Van Loggerenberg and others were going to be prosecuted for 'espionage' related to the unit, saying a docket had been handed to the NPA for a decision.[10] All that was needed was the 'political go-ahead'.[11]

In his statement, Gordhan openly spoke about the distress that reports about his pending arrest were causing his family: 'I cannot believe that I am being investigated for something I am completely innocent of ... it is indeed true that no one is above the law. But no one should be subjected to the manipulation of the law and agencies for ulterior motives ... the malicious rumours and accusations about "espionage" activities are false and manufactured for other motives.'[12] For the umpteenth time, Gordhan defended his management of SARS, saying it had been built up into a world-class institution and if it were harmed there would be less money to spend on the government's social-welfare payments. 'I appeal to all South Africans to protect the National Treasury staff, who have diligently, honestly and skilfully served the national interest to the best of their ability. They are recognised worldwide for their professionalism and competence,' Gordhan said.

Zuma-Gupta aligned praise singers, including the ANC's women's league and military veterans, as well as sponsored groups, like Black First Land First, immediately retaliated, accusing Gordhan of putting himself above the law and trying to hide wrongdoing. Constitutional scholar Pierre de Vos, however, said there exists no such thing as 'espionage' in South African law.[13]

While Gordhan was trying to protect the Treasury from insidious political attacks, the economy was struggling to track the emerging global recovery, and the rating agencies – which suddenly became part of the political lexicon – kept their eye on unfolding events. Chief among their fears about the country were the volatile political environment and Zuma's reluctance to come to the defence of his finance minister.

Analysts warned that the Treasury was the bulwark against unbridled spending and corruption, and, should it fall, the repercussions would be dire. Gordhan, business and unions all made the case for a stay of execution, arguing that a ratings downgrade would play into the hands of those forces that wanted to 'capture' the Treasury. Goolam Ballim, Standard Bank's respected chief economist, warned that Zuma was 'a compromised president at the head of a compromised executive presiding over compromised outcomes' – and that it would be touch and go whether or not the country would slip into junk status.[14] Mercifully, after meeting the minister, unions and the private sector, Standard & Poor's Global Ratings and Fitch Ratings both kept South Africa one notch above junk, but warned that instability was scaring off investors.

If Moyane's disembowelling of SARS's investigative capacity and Ntlemeza's series of attacks on Gordhan represented two fronts of assault on the Treasury, the Guptas emerged as the main thrust of the attack by rent-seekers. In December 2015 – the same month in which Zwane helped the family acquire the Optimum coal mine – Absa closed the Guptas' bank accounts. FNB, Standard Bank and Nedbank followed suit in April, all citing questionable transactions, transfers and payments amounting to billions of rands. Not wanting to fall foul of local and American laws about money laundering and illegal capital flows, the banks decided to end their relationship with the family and its businesses. But the Guptas knew where to go knocking, and found sympathetic ears in Zwane, Mantashe, Duarte and Enoch Godongwana (a member of the NEC), who tried to bully and coerce the banks into reinstating services to the family business, Oakbay.[15]

Zwane – an obscure figure now energised by his patrons' eager support – took it upon himself to announce that an inter-ministerial committee had recommended to Cabinet that a judicial commission of inquiry be established to look at the Financial Intelligence Centre and the banking sector. It was an extraordinary announcement, which not only circumvented accepted Cabinet practice, but was also a pure fabrication and confirmed that Zwane was nothing more than the Minister of Gupta Affairs. The 'inter-ministerial committee' in actual fact was nothing more than a couple of ministers tasked by the president to look into the banks' decision, something Gordhan as finance minister wanted no part of. Zwane's statement about the committee was removed from the Department of Minerals and Energy's website on the same day and his spokesperson couldn't give any answers when questioned about it. Zwane's announcement was later denounced by the Cabinet.

On 22 August 2016, a letter was delivered to the offices of Gordhan's lawyer, Tebogo Malatji, of Gildenhuys Malatji Attorneys. Signed by Major General Sylvia Ledwaba, head of organised crime at the Hawks, it demanded that the Minister of Finance report to room 240 on the second floor of the Hawks HQ, the General Piet Joubert Building in Pretoria, to give a statement. This was in connection with a completed investigation into Gordhan's alleged contravention of the Public Finance Management Act, the Prevention of Corrupt Activities Act and the National Strategic Intelligence Act, and related to Pillay's early retirement and the so-called rogue unit.

There was no way Gordhan was going to play their game. He refused to present himself to the Hawks, insisting that there was no basis in law or in the facts that dictated that he had to comply with Ledwaba's letter: 'I have a job to do in a difficult economic environment and serve South Africa as best I can. Let me do my job.'[16] De Vos said that the letter displayed 'at best, astonishing incompetence, at worst, deeply dishonest abuse of process'.[17] The rand immediately lost 4% against the dollar and 5% against the pound. Trevor Manuel said Gordhan's dismissal would 'destroy' the economy, while analysts added that market reaction would be 'profound' should Zuma fire Gordhan. It was speculated that the move against the minister was about stopping Treasury investigations into SAA, Prasa and certain Eskom contracts, as well as to remove blockages related to the planned nuclear programme.[18] Gordhan's co-accused, including Pillay and Van Loggerenberg, were greeted by a number of supporters at the Piet Joubert Building on 25 August 2016, including former Constitutional Court judge, Johann Kriegler, advocate George Bizos and representatives of civil-society groups, including Corruption Watch and Section 27. Bizos said they were 'concerned about the future of justice and law'.[19] Zuma, after keeping his own counsel (and possibly

the Guptas') for 48 hours, broke his silence on the same day and said he
had 'full confidence' in his finance minister, but that there was nothing
he could do about the situation. This was 'a battle between "Mandela
values" and those who steal,' Gordhan told staff at the Treasury.[20]

Questions around 'those who steal' became apparent a day later, when
the Treasury was forced to call out Eskom in public, saying its investigations into the deal between the electricity parastatal and the Guptas'
Tegeta Resources had been blocked by Eskom CEO Brian Molefe and
board chairperson Ben Ngubane. 'Members of the public also deserve to
know how public finances are spent. It should therefore concern all South
Africans that there are efforts to block and undermine the reviews,' the
Treasury said in a statement.[21] Gordhan was clearly not backing off, and
followed it up with a stern meeting with Myeni's SAA board two weeks
later, declaring that it would not be 'business as usual' for the airline and
setting out an 11-point frame of reference within which Myeni was to
manage the airline's affairs.[22]

Two weeks before he was to deliver the mini-budget to Parliament,
Gordhan was served with a summons by the NPA on charges relating to Pillay's pension agreement. It was all the prosecutors had left,
having decided that charges relating to the SARS unit were too flimsy.
Abrahams announced his decision to nail the finance minister at the
NPA headquarters in Pretoria, confidently grandstanding and barking
his way through a press conference in front of a stunned media corps.
'The days of disrespecting the NPA are over. The days of not holding
senior government officials accountable are over,' he harrumphed victo-
riously, shortly after he had appealed a decision by the High Court that
corruption charges against Zuma should be reinstated.[23] Abrahams said
he had every confidence in the planned prosecution of Gordhan, Pillay
and Oupa Magashula, but would not resign if it failed. Gordhan, who
had just returned from the second investors' roadshow of the year said:
'South Africans need to ask whose interests these people in the Hawks,
the NPA and the NDPP are advancing. Where do they get their political
instructions from and for what purpose?'[24]

Just over two weeks later, on the same stage at the NPA's head office where he had announced the charges against Gordhan, a squirming, nervous and ill-at-ease Abrahams dropped the charges against the three. Abrahams, sweating and twitching, launched into a long and tedious explanation as to why the initial decision to prosecute had been taken, adding it had been made 'lower down' in the NPA chain of command. 'I will not resign … Am I incompetent? That's an unfair question … Does the economy depend on one man?' Abrahams stammered, a far cry from his self-satisfied, bellowing delivery two weeks before.

But Gordhan had already moved on and gone on the offensive. In mid-October he challenged the Guptas directly, launching a High Court bid to force the family to back off from the Treasury. In an affidavit Gordhan gave explosive details about how the family tried to use their political connections to force the Treasury to intervene with the banks on their behalf – he also blew the lid off almost R7 billion worth of 'suspicious transactions' identified by the Financial Intelligence Centre.

By exposing every skirmish to the harsh glare of public opinion, Gordhan had survived sustained, carefully planned attacks on him and the Treasury. He had firmly dealt with Ntlemeza and the Hawks, as well as Abrahams and the NPA. And he had targeted the Gupta family. In late November, agencies Fitch and Moody's retained South Africa's credit rating at investment grade, and Gordhan was named business leader of the year at the *Sunday Times* Top 100 Companies awards. Accepting the award from Bongani Siqoko, who succeeded Phylicia Oppelt as editor, Gordhan called for justice for members of the SARS 'rogue unit' and said that greed was behind corruption and rent-seeking. 'I think it is important that we do everything possible to make sure that at the end of the day justice is in fact done,' he told the audience, before refusing to accept a bottle of Johnnie Walker whisky as a gift.[25]

The firing of Nene was supposed to be easy and the scaling of Treasury's ramparts a foregone conclusion. But Zuma and the Guptas' plans of a hostile takeover at 40 Church Square had been thwarted through a combination of Gordhan and his cavalrymen's bloody-mindedness and civil society's activism. The Hawks and the NPA had failed. It was back to the drawing board.

PART 5

We the people

CHAPTER 16

The rise of civil society

—

'The forces that are opposed to us are hard at work. Our non-governmental organisations play an important part in South Africa, but there are those who work to destabilise the state. They are just security agents that are being used for covert operations. We know who they are. Government will not be shy in dealing with them.'
– David Mahlobo, Minister of State Security and a confidant of Zuma, 26 April 2016

On 18 July 2017, the 99th commemoration of the birth of Nelson Mandela – Pravin Gordhan stood quietly at the back of the massive Rhema Bible Church in Randburg listening to representatives of more than 100 civil-society organisations. They were giving feedback after meetings to discuss a national plan of action to combat corruption and an errant governing party.

The conference, attended by a number of ANC elders as well as former senior civil servants hounded out of government, was organised by the Save South Africa campaign and the Ahmed Kathrada Foundation, which emerged as one of the prime movers behind uniting disparate and often disorganised civil-society groups. Non-governmental actors in South Africa have always been part of the political landscape. The ANC government got a largely free ride in the post-apartheid glow, until the Treatment Action Campaign became the first major civil-society organisation to take on the government, forcing the Mbeki administration to backtrack on its refusal to provide antiretroviral medicine.

Zuma's vice-like grip on state power and the belief in many quarters that traditional political actors cannot be relied on to keep the executive accountable led to a proliferation of organisations in the latter half of Zuma's presidency. All of these entities have as their main focus the rooting out of corruption and keeping a check on the abuse of state power – very often forcing government to implement its own laws. These groups have become very adept at using the courts to coerce government into obeying the law and have earned the ire of government and the ANC, who time and again after defeats in the courts accused them of fomenting regime change or being in cahoots with 'foreign powers'.

Gordhan, chatting and laughing with his comrade Derek Hanekom, however, knew better. Ever since he and Hanekom were dismissed as ministers in March 2017, Gordhan had been active in trying to mobilise ground-roots activism, spurred on by the growing anger at state capture. 'This is not new to me,' he grinned. 'Some of us have seen this [mass mobilisation] before,' he said, referring to the formation of the United Democratic Front in the 1980s.

The offices of the Helen Suzman Foundation, named after the lone liberal voice in the apartheid Parliament in the 1970s and early 1980s, are in a grand old whitewashed building in Parktown, Johannesburg. The foundation is led by the eccentric (and flamboyant) Francis Antonie. It was initially established as a think tank, researching democracy and advancing the liberal and progressive ideas Suzman stood for. In recent times, however, it has emerged as one of the prime civil-society organisations that have used the courts to claim civil liberties, joining forces with Freedom Under Law, the organisation chaired by former justice of the Constitutional Court, Judge Johann Kriegler, by challenging government decisions. On the afternoon of Monday 21 March 2016, the normally boisterous Antonie was subdued. Late on Saturday night, thieves had broken into the foundation's offices, tied up a security guard and fled with a number of computers. 'This was no ordinary robbery […] The thieves knew exactly what they were after. We obviously do not know who they were, but we have our deep suspicions,' Antonie said.[1]

The Helen Suzman Foundation and Freedom Under Law had been involved in litigating Zuma's appointment of the perjurious Ntlemeza, one of the president's henchmen, as commander of the Hawks. Both organisations were objecting to Ntlemeza's appointment after its previous head, Anwa Dramat, was seemingly forced out by his enemies because of certain 'high-level investigations' he was conducting. Ntlemeza, after having been appointed permanently, proceeded to restructure the unit and cleaned out Dramat's management team. Both the Helen Suzman Foundation and Freedom Under Law argued that the Hawks are an 'indispensable investigative organ, whose reach extends into the highest office in South Africa'[2] – and hence Ntlemeza was wholly unfit for the job.

Ntlemeza – such an important cog in Zuma's protection racket – was eventually removed by the High Court in Pretoria, citing an earlier decision by Judge Elias Matojane in the same court: 'In my view, the conduct of the third respondent (Ntlemeza) shows that he is biased and dishonest. To further show that the third respondent is dishonest and lacks integrity and honour, he made false statements under oath.'[3]

The same organisations also exposed NDPP Shaun Abrahams's half-baked decision in October 2016 to charge Gordhan and former SARS colleagues with fraud. Abrahams embarrassingly backtracked on his decision before the North Gauteng High Court could hear the organisations' application to declare the intended prosecution 'irrational, illegal and unconstitutional'. The decision to charge Gordhan, they argued, displayed a 'dizzying incompetence at the NPA and the Hawks'.

But the increased public activity of civil-society organisations wasn't merely focused on litigation and urgent High Court applications. South Africans, mobilised by the power of social media and increasingly slick awareness campaigns, started to take to the streets to voice their displeasure with the state of affairs in the country. Zuma's decision to fire Gordhan as finance minister in March 2017 led to nationwide protests and two marches on the Union Buildings. The day after Zuma installed

Gigaba in the National Treasury as the lackey he wanted but could never get, Save South Africa, an organisation established by business-man Sipho Pityana, amassed thousands of people on Church Square before leading protestors to the seat of government days later. Similar scenes played out in Cape Town, as a sea of unhappy citizens descended on the legislature to protest against the president.

Even though the governing party has a history as an organisation of mass mobilisation, it saw the seeds of so-called 'regime change' in the #ZumaMustFall movement, which sprang up after Zuma fired Nene in 2015. Ever since then, marches have been regularly held nationwide – during the opening of Parliament, on Freedom Day and other public holidays, like Youth Day. But Mantashe and Mahlobo repeatedly ques-tioned these gatherings, both saying the influence of foreign agitators could not be discounted. At the party's national policy conference in June 2017 both explained that the governing party was investigating how the characteristics of 'colour revolutions' – which saw governments in countries like Libya and the Ukraine being toppled by mass social movements – manifest in South Africa.[4] This, they said, entailed the establisment of non-governmental organisations as fronts for foreign powers' efforts to infiltrate society, the use of slogans and terminology to popularise revolt, the creation of 'celebrity leaders' and propaganda about government failures. It echoed Mahlobo's budget speech the pre-vious year, in which he told MPs that even though NGOs played an important part in the struggle against apartheid, some were working hand in glove with foreign governments – and that the state wouldn't hesitate to act against them.

But civil society wasn't standing for it, and Right2Know, an organisa-tion working to ensure transparency and freedom of speech, slammed Mahlobo, demanding he identify those organisations committing 'trea-son' – or shut up. 'Mahlobo must give evidence or stop making bogus claims of a "regime change" plot,' R2K's Murray Hunter retorted:

> This is now a regular claim of the minister. To this day, no evidence
> for the claims has been presented. No persons have been arrested.

Therefore, we believe these claims seek to cast suspicion on people across the country who are mobilising against corrupt government leaders and a failure to deliver on people's basic needs. Instead of addressing the needs of the people, there is an increasing tendency to frame such people as a 'threat'. Too many times have legitimate movements, organisations and causes been labelled as 'threats', and activities of some 'third force'. It is an old formula for suppression.

State capture proved to be a catalyst for civil society to try to unearth the extent of corruption in the state, and in May 2017 a landmark academic paper recommended that an official probe be launched to determine exactly how much the Guptas had fleeced the state.

The investigation – conducted by nine academics from four universities and dubbed the State Capacity Research Project – estimated that the Gupta family was involved in transactions of almost R7 billion in 2016 although their declared income was in the region of R2,6 billion. The 63-page report details the emergence of a 'shadow state', a parallel state structure, where institutions are hollowed out to protect factional interests while SOEs are retooled to serve as enrichment vehicles. And Zuma and the Guptas were at the centre of this system of patronage. The report reads:

> At the nexus of this symbiosis between the constitutional and shadow states are 12 companies and 15 individuals connected in one way or another to the Gupta-Zuma family network. The way this is strategically coordinated constitutes the shadow state. Decisions made within this nexus about what happens within the constitutional state are executed by well-placed individuals located in the most significant centres of state power (in Government, at SOEs and the bureaucracy).[5]

The investigation drew on information available in the public domain and, along with further original research, found that state capture started as relatively low-level corruption but 'eventually evolved into state capture and the repurposing of state institutions'. The researchers, attempting to draw together all available strands and pieces of evidence, concluded that a 'silent coup' had taken place in South Africa, and said the removal of Gordhan from the National Treasury was evidence of this.

At the same time, the South African Council of Churches announced that it had also been conducting an investigation into state capture. The council established an 'unburdening panel', a confessional of sorts for civil servants and private citizens involved in corruption but who want to come clean. The release of the clergy's report was attended by Gordhan, Dramat, former government spokesperson Themba Maseko, who was strong-armed by Ajay Gupta, and Pillay. The details contained in the confessions are confidential, but inform the manner in which churches across the country approach the state.

The barrage of reports by civil society into state capture increased in June 2017, when Wayne Duvenage, the crusader against e-tolls in Gauteng, released charge sheets compiled by OUTA. It was based on advice by legal counsel on what charges Zuma could face relating to various crimes, including corruption. 'It is not a hearsay document. It is not a thumb suck. The proof is there,' Duvenage said.[6]

Every major former South African statesman in the country has a foundation. Nelson Mandela's is focused on managing his legacy and memories of the struggle against apartheid, Thabo Mbeki's on academic development, FW de Klerk's on constitutional issues, while the Sisulu and Tambo foundations look to preserve the legacies of their patrons. But no other foundation has been as involved or as vocal in uniting civil society as the Ahmed Kathrada Foundation. The organisation and its director, Neeshan Balton, had been heavily involved in facilitating anti-racist dialogue at community level, but the assault on the Treasury by Zuma and the Guptas in the week of Kathrada's death led to the foundation taking a leading national role among civil-society organisations.

After the controversial Cabinet reshuffle of 30 March 2017, the foundation hosted a joint press conference with the Mandela Foundation where Kathrada's widow, Barbara Hogan, whom Zuma earlier fired as Minister of Public Enterprises, angrily dismissed Zuma as a 'rogue' president. The Ahmed Kathrada Foundation subsequently provided a platform for Gordhan to speak about state capture at events around the country. Balton also took the lead with the launch of Future SA, an umbrella body that sought to bring order to the plethora of civil and public-awareness campaigns that sprouted in the wake of the Cabinet reshuffle. This was part of an effort to establish a 'broad front' and to 'recapture the state' Balton said.[7]

The Cabinet reshuffle and the resultant political crisis also led to the launch of a National Foundations Dialogue initiative, supported by the Mbeki, De Klerk, Tutu and Luthuli foundations. At its inaugural meeting, former presidents Mbeki, De Klerk and Kgalema Motlanthe agreed that South Africans need to unite to defend the Constitution. Mbeki said it was impossible to argue against the notion that there was a 'national sickness' in politics. 'After serious reflection, proceeding from their different positions, our National Foundations have concluded that our country is immersed in a general and worsening crisis which impacts and will continue to impact negatively on our country and the rest of our continent,' Mbeki said.[8]

The free press – a vital part of civil society – has exerted enormous influence on the political climate in the country, routinely revealing evidence of malfeasance and misdeeds related to state capture and grand corruption. Without doubt, the publishing of the so-called #GuptaLeaks, a trove of emails and documents from the heart of one of the Gupta companies, has piled the pressure on the ANC, the president and the Guptas, who towards the end of 2017 were facing an increasingly hostile South African public.

The rolling coverage of the leaked emails, initially published by *City Press* and the *Sunday Times*, and later by amaBhungane, the *Daily Maverick* and News24, may have been overwhelming but helped expose the anatomy of state capture. The emails confirmed many earlier revelations and reports, backed up by documentary evidence, such as the fact that Duduzane Zuma was helped to buy a multimillion-rand apartment in Dubai, where the Saxonwold family have their foreign lair. The emails completed the picture of a captured state, revealing how ministers, senior government officials and executives beat a path to Dubai, feasting on the Guptas' largesse in exchange for access to state resources.

But, despite the deep reporting and detailed accounts of irregularities, authorities had for months refused to act. *City Press* reported that the Hawks don't believe there is enough evidence against the president or his close friends, the Guptas, to ensure success in a prosecution.[9]

CHAPTER 17

Ten trials that changed our history

'*The Constitution itself cannot save South Africa from crime, corruption, misgovernance, governmental inefficiency and police brutality. What can save us is the Constitution in a combination with a proud, deeply sceptical population, together with principled lawyering.*'

– Constitutional Court Judge Edwin Cameron, address to the Johannesburg Bar,

1 November 2014

On the occasion of his 60th birthday, in January 2008, then Deputy Chief Justice Dikgang Moseneke hosted a private celebration for family and friends. As one would expect at such an occasion, Moseneke delivered a short speech, referencing his time on the bench and what he had planned for his last years as a judge.

'I chose this job very carefully. I have another 10 to 12 years on the bench and I want to use my energy to help create an equal society. It's not what the ANC wants or what the delegates want; it is about what is good for our people,' Moseneke was reported as saying, possibly referring to the outcome of the ANC's 2007 elective conference in Polokwane a month or so earlier where Jacob Zuma roundly defeated Thabo Mbeki as party president.[1]

Moseneke probably didn't expect one of his guests to leak the notes of his birthday speech to the *Sunday Times*. Nor did he expect these notes to become a political bombshell in the ANC. The ANCYL called on him to apologise and said his quoted words proved that Zuma would 'never get a fair trial'.[2] Probably never in the history of South African jurisprudence had a birthday-party speech caused such a tumult. The ANCYL claimed that the former NPA head, Bulelani Ngcuka, who had 'led a crusade of suicide bombers against comrade Jacob Zuma', was in attendance.[3]

After meeting the then ANC deputy president, Motlanthe, Moseneke issued a statement clarifying what he had meant: 'Talking in the context of social justice and equality required by our constitutional democracy, I emphasised that we must all strive to achieve what is good for all our people. There is nothing in what I said which is inconsistent with my responsibility as a judge and as a citizen.'[4]

The ANC also clarified the matter: 'Having listened to Justice Moseneke's account of his speech and the context of his remarks, the ANC accepts that no ill was intended. The ANC confirms its confidence in the integrity of the Deputy Chief Justice, and reaffirms its confidence in the courts to uphold the law and safeguard the rights of all citizens.'[5]

This episode, however, illustrated the tension that existed between Zuma's ANC and the judiciary almost immediately after the Polokwane victory. In one of his first interviews with the media after Polokwane, newly elected ANC secretary general Mantashe called some Constitutional Court judges 'counter-revolutionary forces' who conspired to undermine the ANC.[6] Referring to the handling of the complaint against Western Cape judge president John Hlophe, who allegedly had tried to interfere in the adjudication of a case involving Zuma by the court, Mantashe lashed out at the judiciary for creating a 'hullabaloo' about Zuma and dragging the case into the open.[7]

Three years later, Mantashe's criticism of the Constitutional Court had intensified. He just couldn't stomach the idea of an opposition party or civil-society group heading off to court when they were not happy with a decision by the legislature or the executive. 'You can't have a judiciary that seeks to arrest the functioning of government. For every small disagreement in Parliament, the opposition threatens to take matters to the court,' Mantashe said in an interview. 'Once you have that, then you will have a perception that says the judiciary is actually consolidating opposition to government.'[8]

Despite Mantashe's disapproval, opposition parties and civil society intensified their efforts to challenge problematic appointments and decisions by the executive in the courts. The Zuma era saw an explosion of legal activism through numerous court challenges, which often ended up in the Constitutional Court in Braamfontein. Organisations like Freedom Under Law and the Helen Suzman Foundation focused on specific cases in their litigation. Others, like the DA, brought various applications to set aside appointments and decisions.

Critics of the DA in particular and other opposition parties' legal battles against the government have referred to this strategy as 'lawfare', whereby a party or organisation without sufficient popular support ties up its opponents in never-ending litigation to ultimately weaken them politically. One can imagine that Mantashe would be attracted to this school of thought. There is, however, another side of the debate, which is that the Constitution affords South Africans protection from state abuse, for which you don't need popular support. And this is the beauty of our Constitution: that any child, woman, man or non-governmental organisation can take on the president, a minister or state department in court if you believe they have transgressed their constitutional duties (and you can find a lawyer, of course). Such cases have been central to the fightback against Zuma's misrule.

The president grew increasingly annoyed with the strategy by the DA and others to drag him to court. Zuma is paranoid of having to appear in court and through his lawyers exercised every technical trick in the book to avoid standing trial on corruption charges. During his opening address at the ANC's mid-year policy conference in 2017, Zuma lashed out at opposition parties. He said the practice of lawfare was contradictory to his definition of democracy and was hindering the state from implementing its policies.[9] 'I have never seen such democracy. ... People will vote for you in majority because of programmes you present, but once your programmes are there, you try to implement them, some people take you to court,' Zuma complained.[10]

Meokgo Matuba, the ANC Women's League secretary general, said it felt as if the ANC was 'co-governing with the courts'.[11] ANC chairperson and speaker Baleka Mbete joined the judges-bashing, saying the party knew they would lose their cases if they landed up with certain judges. 'It has nothing to do with merit, with correctness or wrongness,' Mbete said. 'Some names pop up in the head already.'[12]

The judiciary stood firm, though, and would not be intimidated by Zuma and his colleagues. When Zuma appointed the relatively unknown Judge Mogoeng Mogoeng as Chief Justice over Moseneke, who many had thought was a dead certainty for the job, there were fears that Mogoeng (who was judge president of the North West at the time) would be softer on the executive – even pliable. These fears were later proven to have been wholly unfounded when Mogoeng himself penned some of the harshest judgments that have gone against Zuma. Like Madonsela, Mogoeng turned out to be fiercely independent and did not bow to pressure from Zuma or his defenders in the ANC.

Although many more public-interest cases went to court during Zuma's term in office, the following ten trials stand out as having a fundamental impact on the body politic of South Africa. They shone a spotlight on decisions that Zuma and his lieutenants would have preferred to keep behind closed doors.

1. *Democratic Alliance* v *President of South Africa and Others* (the Menzi Simelane case)

Judgment: 5 October 2012, Constitutional Court
Judge: Zak Yacoob (on behalf of a unanimous bench)

Shortly after Advocate Menzi Simelane's appointment as NDPP, the DA challenged his candidacy and ultimately succeeded in having him removed from the NPA.

Before being appointed by Zuma to the NPA, Simelane was the director general of the justice department. It was in this role that he got involved in the corruption investigation against the late police chief Jackie Selebi. The Scorpions were still in existence and had successfully prosecuted Selebi for accepting bribes from drug dealer Glenn Agliotti in exchange for providing him with police protection and intelligence.

But before the case could get to court, there was serious pressure on Advocate Vusi Pikoli, the then NDPP, to drop the case in the national interest. Pikoli refused and fully backed the Scorpions, which fell under the NPA. In the end, Pikoli was suspended by Mbeki and dragged in front of a commission of inquiry, chaired by former speaker Frene Ginwala, where Simelane had to present the state's case. Ginwala cleared Pikoli, but made character findings against Simelane, including that he was dishonest in his response to important questions at the inquiry.

Yacoob and his colleagues found that Zuma and Radebe (then justice minister) acted irrationally when they appointed Simelane to the position of NDPP, without taking into consideration Ginwala's findings of dishonesty against him. 'It is obvious that dishonesty is inconsistent with the hallmarks of conscientiousness and integrity that are essential prerequisites to the proper execution of the responsibilities of a National Director,' they found.

Simelane was subsequently removed from his position.

2. *Freedom Under Law* v *National Director of Public Prosecutions and Others* (the Richard Mdluli case)
Judgment: 23 September 2013, North Gauteng High Court
Judge: John Murphy

The withdrawal of criminal charges against crime-intelligence head Lieutenant General Richard Mdluli exposed the deep flaws at the NPA and eventually led to two senior prosecuting bosses, Nomgcobo Jiba and Lawrence Mrwebi, being struck off the role of advocates (for details, see Chapter 7).

Freedom Under Law, headed by former Constitutional Court Judge Johann Kriegler, challenged the dropping of murder and fraud charges against Mdluli, who had considerable influence at the NPA through Jiba and Mrwebi, and was closely linked to Zuma's rise to power.

Murphy ruled that the dropping of charges against Mdluli was unlawful and that they should be reinstated by the NPA, which then NPA boss Mxolisi Nxasana decided to do. In reaction to arguments in court that the prosecution may be difficult, Murphy remarked: 'Where there is a will there is a way.' He added that, in the hands of skilled prosecutors, defence counsel and an experienced judge, he was confident that justice would be done on the evidence available, 'leading as the case may be to convictions or acquittals on the various charges in accordance with the law and justice. But more than ever, justice must be seen to be done in this case.'

Disciplinary charges against Mdluli were also reinstated after this ruling and he has been on suspension while the criminal trials against him proceed.

3. *Southern Africa Litigation Centre* v *Minister of Justice and Constitutional Development and Others* (the Omar al-Bashir case)
Judgment: 24 June 2015, North Gauteng High Court
Judges: Dunstan Mlambo, Aubrey Ledwaba and Hans Fabricius

In June 2015 the Sudanese president, Omar al-Bashir, visited South Africa to attend an African Union summit in Sandton. Al-Bashir is a wanted war criminal and an arrest warrant has been issued by the International Criminal Court for alleged war crimes and genocide in Sudan's Darfur region.

As a signatory to the Rome Statute of the ICC, South Africa was supposed to act in accordance with the statute's legal requirements.

After Al-Bashir's presence in South Africa was publicly confirmed, and the government refused to arrest him, the Southern Africa Litigation Centre, an organisation that promotes human rights and the rule of law, approached the court with an urgent application to prevent Al-Bashir from leaving South Africa. The interim application was granted and the parties had to come back the next day for a final order to be decided upon.

During argument, Advocate William Mokhari for the government repeatedly assured the court that Al-Bashir was still in the country. Shortly after a final order for Al-Bashir's arrest was handed down,

Mokhari told the court that the Sudanese leader had in fact left the country. The judges ruled that this was a clear violation of the court order and asked for an explanation from the government as to how it had occurred. The SCA, in hearing the matter, called it 'disgraceful conduct'. There were only two options: either Mokhari had lied to the court, or his clients had misled him.

4. *Economic Freedom Fighters* v *Speaker of the National Assembly and Others* (the Nkandla case)
Judgment: 31 March 2016, Constitutional Court
Judge: Mogoeng Mogoeng (on behalf of a majority bench)

Chief Justice Mogoeng delivered what was probably the most closely watched Constitutional Court judgment ever in the history of South African jurisprudence. It was also the most damaging court ruling for Zuma to date. The court found the president had neglected his constitutional duties by not giving effect to Madonsela's findings in her report on the state's R246 million splurge on Zuma's private homestead at Nkandla, thereby violating his presidential oath of office.

The case was brought to court by the EFF, who took a clever chance by seeking direct access to the Constitutional Court. The DA and Corruption Watch subsequently joined the matter.

Mogoeng started off his judgment by explaining the importance of checks and balances to prevent the abuse of state power and resources, as happened under apartheid. Public office bearers ignore their constitutional obligations 'at their peril', he ruled, adding that constitutionalism, accountability and the rule of law were the 'sharp and mighty sword that stands ready to chop the ugly head of impunity off its stiffened neck'.

Mogoeng's dramatic ruling resonated with South Africans, who for months had been subjected to a massive cover-up over Nkandla, which boomeranged when Zuma accepted he had to pay a portion of the costs. Zuma eventually paid back R7,8 million and apologised to South Africa for the 'frustration and confusion' he had caused.

5. *Democratic Alliance* v *Acting National Director of Public Prosecutions and Others* (the 'spy tapes' case)
Judgment: 29 April 2016, North Gauteng High Court
Judges: Aubrey Ledwaba, Cynthia Pretorius and Billy Mothle

The so-called 'Zuma spy tapes' case has occupied our courts since April 2009 when Advocate Mokotedi Mpshe, then acting NDPP, decided to drop corruption charges against Zuma relating to the arms deal and his financial relationship with Schabir Shaik based on a set of transcripts of leaked intercepted recordings. Mpshe acted against the advice of Advocate Billy Downer, the prosecutor in the trial, when he decided 'it would not be in the interest of justice' to proceed with the matter. At that point, Zuma was facing 18 charges of racketeering, corruption and fraud, relating to 783 payments he had received from Shaik.

Mpshe's decision opened up the way for Zuma to become president in May 2009. The DA, under then leader Helen Zille, decided to take Mpshe's decision on review on the basis that he had acted irrationally when he dropped the charges. Zuma and the NPA fought the review application tooth and nail, first arguing that the DA did not have legal standing to bring the case to court, and then they refused to hand over the transcripts of the so-called spy tapes, which were recorded telephone calls between Advocate Bulelani Ngcuka and Advocate Leonard McCarthy, the former Scorpions head, during which they discussed the timing of the Zuma charges.

Finally, seven years later, the North Gauteng High Court in Pretoria ruled in the DA's favour and set aside Mpshe's decision. Judges Ledwaba, Pretorius and Mothle found that Mpshe had been 'under pressure' and made an 'irrational decision' to terminate Zuma's prosecution. Mpshe, the judges said, had 'ignored the importance of the oath of office, which demanded of him to act independently and without fear or favour'. The judges ruled that the phone calls did not taint the case against Zuma and that he should have faced the charges.

Zuma and the NPA petitioned the SCA to appeal the judgment, which was heard in the latter part of 2017.

6. *Democratic Alliance* v *SABC and Others* (the Hlaudi Motsoeneng case)
Judgment: 12 December 2016, Western Cape High Court
Judges: Owen Rogers and Andre le Grange

This decision ended the catastrophic misrule of Motsoeneng as an executive at the public broadcaster, the SABC. The DA had been doggedly pursuing a case against Motsoeneng since his appointment as acting chief operating officer, for which job requirements were changed to accommodate him.

The DA argued that Madonsela's findings against Motsoeneng were binding and should have been implemented before he could have been considered for permanent employment. Among her findings, Madonsela found that Motsoeneng had misled the SABC by falsifying his qualifications and pretending he had matric.

Rogers and Le Grange ruled that Motsoeneng's appointment was unlawful and irrational, and ordered the SABC to institute fresh disciplinary proceedings against Motsoeneng, because an earlier process was flawed.

Motsoeneng had to vacate his office and was subsequently fired after a new disciplinary hearing.

7. *Black Sash Trust* v *Minister of Social Development and Others* (the social-grants case)
Judgment: 17 March 2017, Constitutional Court
Judge: Johan Froneman (on behalf of a majority bench)

Over 17 million South Africans – pensioners, caregivers to children and the disabled – receive a social grant from the government every month. Most of the recipients are dependent on this grant, totalling R150 billion a year, for their livelihood.

In 2012 the Constitutional Court declared the awarding of a tender for administering the monthly payment of the grants to Cash Paymaster Services invalid. The court realised, however, that the payment of the grants could not be halted and suspended the implementation of the ruling after an assurance by the South African Social Security Agency (Sassa) that the state would develop its own technologies and systems to administer the payments.

Sassa is the entity responsible for grant payments, and falls under the Department of Social Development.

The department and the agency miserably failed to deliver on their promise, and a month before the Cash Paymaster Services contract was due to expire, the state had not put in place mechanisms to take over the payment of the grants. With a national catastrophe looming, Black Sash, a women's resistance movement during apartheid, took up the matter and asked the court to intervene in the crisis.

Froneman held that Bathabile Dlamini, the Minister of Social Development and a close Zuma ally, was responsible for the mess and found that her conduct, as well as that of Sassa, placed the social-grants system in jeopardy. The court allowed Cash Paymaster Services to continue with payments for one year, but at a capped fee determined by the Treasury.

The court further ordered Dlamini and Sassa to report to it on a quarterly basis on progress with taking over the payment of grants. This was an extreme example of a broken state that eventually led the judiciary to intervene in a matter from which it would have ordinarily stayed clear.

8. *Helen Suzman Foundation and Freedom Under Law* v *Minister of Police and Others* (the Berning Ntlemeza case)
Judgment: 17 March 2017, North Gauteng High Court
Judges: Peter Mabuse, Jody Kollapen and Selby Baqwa

Ntlemeza's disastrous tenure as head of the Hawks came to an abrupt end after a successful court application by two of the most vocal civil-society organisations against the capture of the criminal-justice system.

The Helen Suzman Foundation and Freedom Under Law challenged Ntlemeza's appointment by then police minister Nathi Nhleko on the grounds of irrationality after a court found that he was dishonest and acted in bad faith in his handling of the suspension of former Hawks Gauteng boss Shadrack Sibiya.

The North Gauteng High Court overturned Sibiya's suspension based on Ntlemeza's actions. The court found that the Sibiya court judgments were 'replete with findings of dishonesty and mala fides' against Ntlemeza and that they constituted direct evidence that Ntlemeza lacked the 'requisite honesty, integrity and conscientiousness to occupy the position of any public office, not to mention an office as important as that of the National Head of the [Hawks].'

Ntlemeza appealed the matter, but was subsequently ordered by Minister of Police Fikile Mbalula to vacate his office pending the appeal.

9. *Earthlife Africa Johannesburg and Southern African Faith Communities' Environment Institute* v *Minister of Energy and Others* (the nuclear case)
Judgment: 26 April 2017, Western Cape High Court
Judges: Lee Bozalek and Elizabeth Baartman

The South African Government's controversial plan to build nuclear power stations at a cost of R1 trillion was stopped in its tracks by two small non-governmental organisations that challenged Goliath in court. And won.

Earthlife Africa and the Southern African Faith Communities' Environment Institute successfully opposed the controversial transaction by challenging the unlawful process that was followed in the request-for-proposal phase. The country had signed cooperation agreements with Russia, the US and South Korea, which were set aside in a landmark ruling by Judge Bozalek.

The court found that the former energy minister, Tina Joemat-Pettersson, had not followed due processes when she handed over the nuclear procurement to power utility Eskom in late 2016 and declared the government's intention to buy 9,6 GW of nuclear energy unlawful.

Although this didn't mean the end of the road for nuclear, it was a significant setback for Zuma's administration, who had rushed to push through the deal before the end of their term. Numerous economists have warned that the transaction would effectively bankrupt South Africa.

After a foreign trip by Joemat-Pettersson in 2014, the Russian nuclear corporation Rosatom announced that it had secured a deal with South Africa. The company had to paddle back when a storm erupted in South Africa over the complete lack of transparency in the process. The government then initiated a process whereby agreements were signed with a number of interested countries, although those in the know still believed Zuma had already promised Putin the deal during his bizarre 'medical visit' in August 2014.

Zuma's son Duduzane and the Guptas would be in prime position to score from a nuclear transaction by supplying uranium from their Shiva mine.

10. *United Democratic Movement v Speaker of the National Assembly and Others* (the secret-ballot case)
Judgment: 22 June 2017, Constitutional Court
Judge: Mogoeng Mogoeng (on behalf of a unanimous bench)

After increasing revelations about the extent of state capture, Zuma's proximity to the Gupta family and numerous protests asking for Zuma to go, the country's opposition parties united in bringing another motion of no confidence in the president in Parliament. It was the eighth vote of its kind, but, this time, the opposition realised it had a better chance of success if ANC MPs had the opportunity to vote in secret.

It's an open secret that the majority of ANC leaders fear Zuma – either because they are beholden to him for their jobs, or because he's got dirt on them. The opposition realised that it would be easier to remove Zuma through a secret ballot and took Speaker Baleka Mbete, who argued she did not have the powers to call for a secret ballot, to court.

In a unanimous decision by Mogoeng, the Constitutional Court ruled that Mbete in fact had the power to call for a secret vote. 'South Africa is a constitutional democracy – a government of the people, by the people and for the people through the instrumentality of the Constitution. It is a system of governance that "we the people" consciously and purpose-fully opted for to create a truly free, just and united nation,' Mogoeng said at the beginning of the judgment. The court found that it was for Mbete to decide whether a secret vote would ensure that MPs exercise their oversight power 'most effectively'.

This ruling opened the way for Mbete to rule in favour of a secret vote, which took place on 8 August 2017. Zuma narrowly escaped being removed by attracting 198 votes against the motion versus 177 votes in favour of it. There were nine abstentions.

CHAPTER 18

Losing the vote

'The people have been liberated now ... hence the ANC will rule
until Jesus comes back to save us.'

– President Jacob Zuma, Soweto, 7 January 2017

The municipal elections of 2016 were nothing short of a disaster for
the ANC. The governing party, used to overwhelming majorities in
every election since the advent of democracy in 1994, spent more than
R1 billion on its campaign but lost three major metropolitan municipalities to the opposition, including South Africa's administrative capital of
Tshwane and the economic hub of Johannesburg. Its popular support
collapsed to 53,9% from 61,9% in the previous municipal election in
2011 (and was down from 62,15% in the general election in 2014).

It was a major shock for a party whose leader had for years been telling its supporters that the ANC would rule 'until Jesus comes'.[1]

In the aftermath of the elections – and under the glare of the spot-
lights at the Independent Electoral Commission's national results centre
in Pretoria – the ANC promised to do introspection and said that voters
had given the party a message it wouldn't ignore.

In reality, however, the party had been ignoring popular sentiment for
a good while by the time the election day arrived on 3 August. A series
of polls in the run-up to the election revealed that the party was set to be
rocked back in Gauteng, while control of the metropolitan municipality

of Nelson Mandela Bay, which includes Port Elizabeth and the historical ANC strongholds New Brighton, Motherwell and Zwide, was also set to change hands. This wasn't a bolt out of the blue either: electoral trends had been indicating in which direction the ANC was headed for a while. Analysts had warned that Zuma's poor leadership and party factionalism were going to hurt. But nobody was prepared for how much support the party was going to shed.

The portents had been there as early as April, when less than half of the expected 100 000 supporters pitched up for the launch of the ANC's election manifesto at Nelson Mandela Bay Stadium. The ANC's campaign management team, led by Nomvula Mokonyane, the Minister of Water and Sanitation, and a staunch Zumaite, had descended on the city to try to stave off the DA's campaign to claim the council. The event, normally a loud and busy celebration of the party, was devoid of energy and enthusiasm. Zuma's speech started way behind schedule as organisers were scrambling to get supporters into the stadium. His speech rang hollow: he spoke of a vote for the ANC being a vote for the Constitution and how government planned to hold corrupt and errant civil servants to account – this just two weeks after the Constitutional Court's scathing judgment that he, the president, had failed to uphold, defend and respect the Constitution.

By the time the ANC caravan rocked up in Port Elizabeth, the Nelson Mandela Bay Metropolitan Municipality was in chaos. Corruption had become endemic, with syndicates running various service-delivery programmes and raiding the city's coffers.[2] The ANC had parachuted in Danny Jordaan, the country's soccer boss and organiser of the 2010 FIFA World Cup, as mayor to try to save what was left. Jordaan, a native of the Windy City, had no political experience to speak of and was himself embroiled in the FIFA corruption scandal. Jordaan has consistently denied any wrongdoing.

North of the city, in Uitenhage and KwaNobuhle, the United Front (the National Union of Mineworkers' political vehicle) was making inroads, and anger over ANC corruption and service-delivery failures was reaching fever pitch. The DA had targeted the city as its second metropolitan conquest outside Cape Town and had actively campaigned there for more than a year. It came as no surprise when Bathabile Dlamini, the president of the ANC Women's League, who sometimes moonlights as Minister of Social Development, was sent packing when she went on the campaign trail in New Brighton the day before the manifesto launch. Heckled and shouted down, Dlamini retreated in tears after residents chased her away and accused her of being drunk on 'expensive whisky'. The signs were there for all to see.

The ANC's election machine is formidable. Putting aside historical sentiment and emotional attachment, the party has over the years been able to rally a network of organisers and activists ahead of every election to spur involvement and mobilise support. This has led to total electoral dominance for more than two decades, with voters heading to the polls in their droves, election after election. The ANC knows how to get voters and has a political brand without equal on the continent. Its role as one of the prime movers behind the coming of democracy in South Africa, coupled with incomparable leaders like Nelson Mandela, Walter Sisulu and Oliver Tambo, meant it went unchallenged when it called on history. Even disgruntled ANC supporters are routinely overwhelmed by the party's struggle credentials when they enter the voting booths, finding it almost impossible under even the most testing of circumstances to break with the party that helped bring freedom to black South Africans.

ANC rallies in the country's various stadiums are also a sight to behold – carnivals of colour, sound, singing and dancing, and political oratory and pageantry. The governing party has perfected the art of stadium rallies. From the logistics of bussing in thousands of supporters from all over the country to the ear-popping roar of nouveau riche ANC supporters revving their Harley Davidson motorbikes before the arrival of dignitaries, these events are meant to instil shock and awe. Massive stages accommodating the whole of the NEC, messages of support from within and outside of the country's borders and a cast of artists and political celebrities, all dancing to the tune of struggle and ANC election songs, create an atmosphere in which supporters and leaders alike bask in ANC invincibility.

The ANC reached its zenith during the general election of 2004, when under Mbeki it secured 69,69% of the almost 16 million votes cast. It was the tenth anniversary of democracy, GDP growth was accelerating and the country was starting to develop a consensus around national identity. The ANC was also more than three percentage points clear of the required two-thirds majority needed to change the Constitution, but opted not to tamper with the country's founding document.

But by 2009 the picture of total ANC dominance had started to change. In May that year, Zuma, who had won the bloody battle of Polokwane and had corruption charges against him dropped, took over a government with rising debt and less fiscal space. The ANC found it harder to consolidate its support and came in under the two-thirds mark with 65,9%. The ANC offshoot Congress of the People, led by Lekota and Shilowa, polled 7,42% in its first outing. The DA, under Zille for the first time, increased its support from 12,37% in 2004 to 16,66%.

Municipal elections are a different beast from general elections, however. Voter turnout tends to be much lower, which favours opposition parties, and voting patterns differ too – traditional ANC voters often tend to vote differently in order to keep the governing party in check. Opposition parties have therefore performed better in local government than national government elections. The DA, for example, gained 7,3 percentage points more in the 2011 municipal election than it did in the general election two years before. Municipal and general elections therefore cannot be directly compared, even though there are identifiable trends between the two. On the whole, the ANC had been on a sharper decline in municipal elections than in general elections, steadily shedding support between the general election in 2009 and the municipal election in 2011.

The general election in 2014 was when the ANC's decline really should have hit home. Even with a higher voter turnout and more registered voters, it received fewer votes (11,4 million) than in 2009 (11,6 million), for a tally of 62,15%. Newcomers the EFF made an immediate impact, garnering 1,16 million votes (6,35%), while the DA continued on their steady march, breaching 4 million votes for a share of 22,23%, a significant figure. The looming electoral disaster in 2016 was foretold by the Gauteng results, where the ANC's support in the country's economic and industrial heartland shrank from 64% in 2009 to 53,6% in 2014 – a quarter of a million votes down.

The cumulative effect of the Nkandla and Guptagate scandals, as well as the Marikana killings and the expulsion of the metalworkers' union NUMSA, was slowly starting to bite. In 2004 the party had 279 seats in the 400-seat National Assembly; in 2014 that was down to 249. At the provincial level, which closely mimics votes at the municipal level, the ANC was down in Johannesburg (from 62% to 52%), Tshwane (59% to 49%) and Nelson Mandela Bay (49% to 48%). And even though both Zuma and Mantashe admitted afterwards that the ANC was struggling, nothing was done to implement a turnaround strategy. The reality of a party in decline was there for everybody to see and Zuma said as much when he admitted the party had been 'shaken'. 'I can guarantee you that if everything goes wrong with the ANC, everything will go wrong in this country,' he said.[3] Mantashe identified the party's Achilles heel: the middle class and unemployment. 'The concerns of youth regarding employment are used as a mobilising tool … The urban constituency, as seen with our middle class in recent elections, is another soft spot.[4]

The run-up to the August 2016 municipal elections could not have been more calamitous for the ANC. The Nenegate debacle in December 2015, when Zuma dismissed the respected finance minister in favour of a Gupta appointment, was an epic disaster that cost the economy billions of rands, thrust state capture into the spotlight and exposed deep divisions among the ANC's leaders. Things got worse a couple of months later when the Constitutional Court delivered the most devastating and strongest rebuke of the executive since 1994, saying that Zuma and Parliament had neglected their constitutional duty to ensure the implementation of the Public Protector's findings on Nkandla. It was a devastating ruling, which in any other country would have resulted in the abdication of the president and the resignation of the speaker. Their absolute refusal to adhere to the findings of a constitutional body, which had followed due care and exercised its authority, was unacceptable to the country's apex court, which ordered the head of state to reimburse the state in a process to be overseen by the National Treasury. Amid this constitutional crisis, Jonas, the Deputy Minister of Finance, and Vytjie Mentor, a respected former ANC MP, revealed how they had both been offered jobs as ministers by the Guptas. Mentor claimed Zuma was in the same house while the offer was being put to her, saying he emerged from another room after she had rebuffed the Guptas' advances.

The ANC was at a loss as to what to do. Its president, described as a 'one-man wrecking ball',[5] was muscling in on crucial state institutions to protect himself while inflicting damage on the government, party and country as a whole. In April 2016, four months before the local elections, a survey by market-research company TNS found Zuma's approval rating had declined from 43% in March 2015 to 27% in February 2016.[6] A month later a poll by Afrobarometer found trust in Zuma had dropped to 34% from the 62% recorded in 2011.[7] The ANC found it difficult to shrug off Zuma's scandals and controversies as election day approached, and the party in Gauteng put up election posters without Zuma's image on them. Polling by research firm Ipsos revealed that the ANC might very well lose Pretoria, Johannesburg and Port Elizabeth, but these predictions were dismissed as fanciful by the ANC and many analysts. There was broad agreement that the corruption-ridden Nelson Mandela Bay might be up for grabs, but Tshwane and Johannesburg were considered by many a bridge too far. But Ipsos's final predictions – released two days before voting day – were to prove spot on.

Parks Tau, Mayor of the City of Johannesburg, had been fighting an uphill battle in the country's largest city. He had started to tackle the dysfunction of municipal contractors, like Pikitup and City Power, left in tatters by his predecessor, Amos Masondo, whom the ANC 'redeployed' to Parliament (party lingo for fired and given a soft landing). With a budget of R55 billion – the metropolitan municipalities have a total budget of R228 billion[8] – Tau and the ANC had been in control of a rather hefty purse with which to manage service delivery and change. Zuma, however, had been steadily eroding the ANC's support in the urban areas in and around Johannesburg and Pretoria. Try as they might, the ANC in Gauteng just couldn't put clear blue water between itself and the party's leader, and voters made their feelings clear wherever Tau and his colleagues went to campaign. It was starting to shape up as a local election decided on national issues.

North of the Hennops River, in Tshwane, the ANC was in disarray. Competing factions were vying for the party's regional leadership in a city beset by corruption and major billing problems. The mayor, Kgosientso 'Sputla' Ramokgopa, had also embarked on a multimillion-rand vanity project, building a swanky new civic centre while kitting out City Hall as the mayor's parlour. The internal warring in the municipality led to the ANC imposing a mayoral candidate, Thoko Didiza, a former minister in the Mbeki government. Violence erupted in protest at the choice, with ANC members questioning Didiza's nomination because she was not from the city. 'They've embraced me as their child,' Didiza said amid widespread violence in Atteridgeville, Mamelodi and Mabopane.[9]

The ANC's losses on 3 August 2016 were severe. It ceded its status as the biggest party in Nelson Mandela Bay and Tshwane, and racked up double-digit losses in those councils as well as in Johannesburg.

- ❏ In Johannesburg the ANC lost 14 percentage points from 2011 and secured 44,5% of the vote. The DA increased its share by 3,8 percentage points to 38,4%, while the EFF made a rousing entry into local-government elections by convincing 11,09% of the city's electorate to vote for it.
- ❏ In Tshwane the ANC gave up 14 percentage points for a tally of 41,2%. The DA, however, eclipsed that by adding 4,45 percentage points to muster 43,1% of the vote, while the EFF replicated their Johannesburg success with 11,6% of the vote.
- ❏ In Nelson Mandela Bay, Jordaan's ANC failed to convince voters and gave up 11 percentage points to poll 40,9%. Athol Trollip from

the DA led the party to 46,71%, an increase of 6 percentage points. The EFF put the opposition over the top with 5,1% on its debut.

❏ The DA increased its majority in Cape Town to 66,62%, while the ANC kept control of Buffalo City (East London), eThekwini (Durban), Mangaung (Bloemfontein) and Ekurhuleni (the East Rand).

The ANC's defeats in Johannesburg, Tshwane and Nelson Mandela Bay were larger than the downward trend in national support between the 2011 and 2016 municipal elections (-8 percentage points) or the 2014 general and 2016 municipal elections (-8,25%), which signalled that urban voters were starting to warm up to the idea of opposition-run councils. The results also signalled a new era in South African politics with horse trading, cajoling and threats becoming the order of the day as new coalition city governments started to take shape. During the weeks that followed the hotly contested polls, the EFF, who emerged as kingmakers in a number of councils, played both sides of the fence and indicated to the ANC that it would be willing to work alongside it as long as Zuma was dumped as president. When Mantashe, very respectful of Malema and his party, declined the proposition, the EFF promptly reached an agreement with the DA in all three metros, handing the mayoralties by prior agreement to the DA. Herman Mashaba, a millionaire businessman from Soweto, took over in Johannesburg; Solly Msimanga, a young, bright party activist, took over in Tshwane; and Trollip, the white, Xhosa-speaking former parliamentary leader, ousted Jordaan in Port Elizabeth. Malema explained his decision at a carefully choreographed media conference in Johannesburg, with the grim vista of Alexandra as backdrop. He explained the EFF was in a difficult position, but wanted to ensure continued delivery of services: 'The DA is the better devil. We couldn't be neutral, we had to take sides. This is history. We were caught between two devils.'

Maimane hailed the election as a 'historic moment' and a tipping point, with voters punishing the ANC who had up until then governed 'with absolute impunity'.[10]

The ANC's final humiliation came at the electoral commission's massive results operations centre on 6 August 2016, when Zuma delivered a speech after the final results had been declared. Four young women stood up in front of the stage, facing the audience and holding up posters saying 'remember Khwezi'. (Fezekile Kuzwayo, nicknamed Khwezi, was the young woman who accused Zuma of rape, of which he was later acquitted.) She died on 9 October 2016. Unfazed, Zuma carried on with his speech as dignitaries scurried around in the background, unsure what to do with television cameras trained on them and the whole country watching. It was an audacious protest, embarrassing Zuma further and enraging his supporters in the Women's League.

There was no doubt that the political tectonic plates had shifted. The rate at which the electorate was rejecting the party of liberation was accelerating at an alarming pace. The DA now held the mayoralties of Tshwane, where the ANC government has its seat, Port Elizabeth, the home of so many struggle heroes, and Cape Town, where the ANC-dominated Parliament meets.

But it was the loss of Johannesburg that hurt the most: Egoli, the city of gold, or Maboneng, the city of light, was the political heart of South Africa during the struggle. It was the city of promise that lured the young Mandela to it and where he and Oliver Tambo established their law firm. It was in Soweto, on the outskirts of Johannesburg, where the struggle violently and murderously exploded on 16 June 1976. It was in Rivonia, to the north of the city, where Mandela and others were arrested and it was to Johannesburg that the ANC returned after it was unbanned. And it was the city on the high veld that hosted the multi-party negotiations that prevented a bloodbath in the early 1990s in the run-up to democracy.

Johannesburg had long represented the beating heart of the ANC, and now its residents had rejected the party.

PART 6

Zupta fights back

CHAPTER 19

Stalingrad and state capture

—

'Please … can you stop talking for the president? Mr Hulley,
I am forbidding you from speaking. I'm not giving you an
opportunity. I'm asking Mr President to address me …
you are here to support the president, but President Zuma is the
one employed by the state. You are employed as his advisor,
but not as his mouth.'

– Thuli Madonsela to Zuma's legal advisor, Michael Hulley, 6 October 2016

Advocate Thuli Madonsela, the country's third Public Protector, was struggling to hold it together and keep calm. It had been almost seven months since her office had sent a letter to Zuma informing him of three complaints to her office about the head of state's alleged breaches of the Executive Members' Ethics Act. She had received no reply. She followed it up with another letter, on 22 April 2016, to which she had also received no reply. On 13 September 2016 she forwarded another letter to the Presidency, requesting a meeting with the president about her investigations into state capture, the Guptas and Zuma's son Duduzane. The Presidency finally agreed and a date was set for 6 October 2016, nine days before the end of Madonsela's seven-year term.

During the meeting, Madonsela tried her best to remain polite and measured while Michael Hulley, the lawyer who had been the architect of Zuma's legal defences over the years, raised objection after objection.

She had explained the legal basis of her investigation, the history of her efforts to engage the president and the general thrust of the questions to Zuma. But the president remained quiet, letting the trusted Hulley put up legal roadblocks and barriers. As with the 'spy tapes' issue, Nkandla and every other legal wrangle he has been involved in, Zuma was fighting the battle street by street. Madonsela was slowly reaching the end of her tether, but remained committed to having a meaningful engagement with Zuma, even if it meant indulging Hulley for the time being.

During the months that had elapsed between her first letter and meeting the president, there had been no willingness from the head of state to acknowledge the gravity of the allegations or to offer assistance to Madonsela's office. And the allegations were serious. In March, reports surfaced that the Gupta family had offered Mcebisi Jonas the position of Minister of Finance. Weeks later, Nene was replaced by an unknown backbencher, who promptly arrived at the National Treasury with two Gupta-linked advisors in tow. And shortly after this the Guptas bought a coal mine with ample financial assistance from Eskom. It was all very, very dodgy. State capture was in the air.

'It is not just President Zuma's reputation that is on the line,' Madonsela said to Hulley, with Zuma listening on. 'The reputation of young Mr Zuma is on the line, the reputation of Mr Gupta, Ajay Gupta, who was very much sad about what has happened and incredibly emotional about this matter, is also on the line and so are the reputations of the accusers.'[1]

Zuma had, on that very day, confirmed the appointment of Busisiwe Mkhwebane as Madonsela's successor. Rumours had it she was handpicked by Mahlobo, Zuma's faithful Minister of State Security, for whom she had earlier worked, and Hulley argued that the new Public Protector would be perfectly capable of finalising the investigation after Madonsela had vacated her office.

'Well, maybe we should just cut to the chase and find out why there is a rush?' Hulley asked an increasingly irritated Madonsela.

Ever since she had been appointed Public Protector, Madonsela, who was involved during the multi-party negotiations at Kempton Park as a legal advisor and later worked for the South African Law Reform Commission, had been lauded for her commitment to justice. She was targeted by the ANC during the Nkandla investigation, repeatedly denigrated and her office insulted. Now it became abundantly clear that Zuma wanted to kick the investigation down the road. He was not going to subject himself to an investigation that might produce another adverse finding, like Nkandla. And what better way than to stall and stall until Mkhwebane took over the reins?

'I'm rushing it because I'm the Public Protector until the 14th of October. I'm rushing it because I am supposed to have finished this matter within 30 days. I'm rushing it because I have institutional memory relating [to] this case ... why are you so persistent on having the new Public Protector complete the case? But I don't even want you to answer it ... There were 7 months for us to receive a version from the President,' Madonsela said.

Through all of this Zuma remained quiet.

On 8 March 2016, Andrew England of the *Financial Times* published a story in the venerable London broadsheet about the friendship between the Gupta family and Zuma, alleging that the family had offered the job of finance minister to Jonas.[2] Then, on 13 March 2016, the *Sunday Times* published a bombshell: 'How Guptas shopped for new minister', read the headline. The report gave details confirming the earlier *Financial Times* version, adding how Jonas had turned the Guptas down. 'This was not before telling them that they do not run the country.'[3]

The ANC led the outcry – not by condemning the family's overt and growing influence in the country's executive, but rather by attacking the newspaper for 'portray[ing] the leadership of the ANC ... as collaborators to fit the fictitious narrative of a Gupta-controlled country'.[4] Two days after the *Sunday Times* report, Vytjie Mentor, the straight-talking and brash former ANC MP, added that she, too, had been offered a job by the Guptas, as Minister of Public Enterprises.[5] What's more, Jonas confirmed the newspapers' versions the following day in a written and video statement released by the National Treasury. 'The narrative that has grown around the issue of "state capture" should be of concern to all responsible and caring South Africans, particularly those of us who have accepted the task to lead our people,' Jonas said.[6]

Three complaints were forwarded to Madonsela's office: one by the DA's Maimane, another by a certain Father Mayebe of the Catholic Dominican Order and the last by a member of the public. They asked the Public Protector to investigate the details around the offer to Jonas, whether or not the Guptas benefited improperly from government contracts and what the president's role in the affair was.

Madonsela and her team had been in the spotlight for the better part of four years, ever since she had launched her investigation into the lavish alterations to the president's homestead. That investigation and its findings were a watershed. Not only did the previously impotent and anonymous Office of the Public Protector start to live up to its constitutional prescripts, but Madonsela also became somewhat of a folk hero, and the Public Protector feted as one of the last effective state institutions (alongside the Treasury) to keep executive power in check. In the public eye, Madonsela became the embodiment of constitutionalism and the rule of law, resisting the ANC, Parliament and Zuma when they started attacking her integrity and calling her a CIA agent, accusing her of wasting money and undermining Parliament. Her powers – up until then disputed by a hostile ANC and obstructionist government – were confirmed by the Constitutional Court on 31 March 2016, mere weeks after Jonas had confirmed the sensational claims of the Guptas' offer to him, when it ruled that the Public Protector's findings are binding and reviewable only by the courts.

Madonsela acted immediately after she received the complaints and notified the president of her intentions to investigate the allegations. She tasked the Good Governance and Integrity branch of her office to do the legwork and asked for more funds from the Department of Justice to rope in extra resources. The allegations were far-reaching and those implicated were senior government officials, including three ministers, Lynne Brown (public enterprises), Mosebenzi Zwane (mineral resources) and Des van Rooyen (cooperative governance and traditional affairs) – all with demonstrable ties to the Guptas. Besides the ministers, the president's most enterprising son, Duduzane, as well as the Gupta brothers were all in Madonsela's cross hairs. As were Eskom, Transnet, Denel, SAA, the SABC – state entities suspected of being repurposed in service of the Guptas.

The investigating team interviewed everyone involved or implicated in the claims made by Jonas, Mentor and Themba Maseko, a respected former Cabinet spokesperson, who also came forward with revelations about Zuma and the Guptas' improper relationship. Everyone spoke to Madonsela, except the president and his son, that is.

As discussed in an earlier chapter, Mentor told Madonsela how she had flown to Johannesburg for a meeting with Zuma but instead was taken to the Guptas' garish Saxonwold mansion where she turned down their offer of a ministry.

During his interview, Jonas confirmed that Duduzane acted as the fixer between him and the Guptas and had arranged for a meeting at a swanky hotel in Rosebank, before going with him to Saxonwold, where Ajay Gupta held court. Gupta told Duduzane and Fana Hlongwane, who was a middleman in the equally calamitous arms deal and ostensibly a friend of Zuma Jr, to sit down during his conversation with Jonas. They never uttered a word while Gupta boasted about how much money they had made from the state or when he threatened Jonas, telling him he was 'well aware of his activities' as part of a faction undermining the president.[7] When Jonas was leaving, Gupta asked him for a bag in which he could place R600 000 in cash as a show of faith to the deputy minister. Gupta denied this account later.[8]

Zuma was again implicated by Maseko, who told Madonsela how he had received a call from the president asking him for his help on behalf of the Gupta brothers. As head of the government's communications arm, he controlled a budget of several millions of rands, which the Guptas wanted channelled to their newspaper, *The New Age*. When he resisted, Ajay Gupta had threatened to speak to Maseko's seniors in government (see Chapter 5).

The president was never going to subject himself to questioning by his arch enemy, Madonsela. He had waited until the absolute last minute, when her term was about to expire, before granting her a slot in his schedule and even then, during their October meeting,[9] which lasted more than four hours, he never spoke about the merits of the allegations. Hulley expertly obfuscated and obstructed, badgered and retreated and managed to keep his man out of harm's way.

The lawyer, who perfected Zuma's proven Stalingrad strategy of contesting every little detail and seeking recourse in every available legal avenue, very politely argued that the president had had insufficient time to study a number of questions forwarded to him ahead of the meeting. He added that Zuma would like access to all documentation available to Madonsela and that he would also like to question witnesses already interviewed by the Public Protector before he would be able to assist fully in the investigation. Madonsela, equally politely, rejected Hulley's arguments and made the point that everything she was to question the president about had been in the public domain since March. All the while during Madonsela and Hulley's sparring, Zuma sat in silence, not uttering a word. When Hulley asked for a break so that he could consult with the president, Madonsela addressed Zuma directly: 'I am concerned though that ... you are the president of the Republic of South Africa and you are employee number one. Normally when we are dealing with people who are responsible for the state, we deal with them, and their lawyers come in where necessary, because it is you who is accountable.'

Madonsela demonstrated remarkable calmness and exceptional emotional intelligence after Zuma finally spoke to her, explaining why he needed time to consider his answers before submitting them to the Public Protector. 'Thank you, Mister President,' she replied. 'I note with gratitude your response, your willingness to respond at a future date, which basically was what Mr Hulley was asking, that we postpone today's proceedings and rather go at a future date.'

She was determined not to be denied, reiterated the importance of the engagement and elbowed Hulley out of the way, asking the president:

❏ Can you explain your relationship with the Gupta family? How did it start?

❏ Describe your relationship? How long have you been friends?

❏ How often do you visit them? Have you been to Saxonwold?

❏ Do you know about Duduzane's appointment as a director in some of the Guptas' companies?

❏ Do you know that Duduzane lives in the Guptas' Saxonwold home?

❏ Are you aware of the allegations against the Guptas?

❏ Were you in their Saxonwold home when the offer of a ministry was made to Mentor?

❏ What is your reaction to the statements by Jonas and Maseko?

❏ Why did you remove Nene and appoint Des van Rooyen?

❏ Have you ever considered your or Duduzane's relationship with the Guptas as a conflict of interest?

❏ Please provide details of your property ownership.

But Hulley was relentless, insisting that Zuma needed time to consider his replies even though Madonsela contended the questions were purely factual and not legal in their basis. 'With respect, Madam, the fact of the matter is that those ... or the answer to those have legal import. There are provisions in Parliament ...' he protested, but Madonsela was fed up.

'All I'm asking for is honest answers. These answers can't change with legal advice ... they can't. The president will give me the honest facts of why he removed Nene and why he appointed Van Rooyen,' she told her adversary before again turning to Zuma. 'Sir, why do you need a lawyer to advise you [now], because lawyers advised you before you did that?' Zuma said nothing. Madonsela repeated her question, ignoring Hulley's protestations: 'Now, why do you need a lawyer to be able to tell me why you removed any of those ministers?'

Hulley refused to budge. Exchanges became so heated that Madonsela at one point said she refused 'to be bullied' by him and rejected his subsequent apology, saying Hulley was 'not even allowing the president of the Republic of South Africa to speak for himself'. She then made a last-ditch attempt to compel Zuma to comply with the law by answering her questions and implored him to answer her honestly and truthfully. Zuma, the product of hours of coaching by Hulley, refused. His contention was telling and gives fascinating insight into the head of state's flexible relationship with the truth:

> **Madonsela:** 'Okay, perhaps I should ask one question, Sir. Would the answers that you give me, after I have given you an opportunity to reflect, differ from the answers that you have given to the media or any other person who has ever asked you about the issues of Jonas, Mentor, Maseko and [the] Guptas?
> **Zuma:** No, they would not differ …
> **Madonsela:** Would you offer a different answer?
> **Zuma:** No, I would not offer a different one …
> **Madonsela:** So why do you want to defer it then if you are going to give me the exact answer you have given to the media?
> **Zuma:** No, as I say, giving an answer to a journalist or to somebody is different than giving an answer to a Public Protector …
> **Madonsela:** That is why I was asking Sir, if it would differ from the one you have given to the media? If it won't differ, what then would change from today to the time we have that interview, if you are going to give me exactly the same answer you have given to the media or any other person who has ever asked you about these matters?
> **Zuma:** Well, I don't know how to answer it again, because I say …
> **Madonsela:** I'm trying to understand you, Sir …
> **Zuma:** No, no …
> **Madonsela:** If you are saying you have answered these questions before and I'm going to ask you the same questions, I'm struggling to understand it and you are saying the answer won't be different from the one you have given to the media, I'm struggling to understand then what do you need to rethink?
> **Zuma:** No, if I give an answer to a friend or to a journalist I can phrase it anyway, saying exactly the same thing, but the words I use there … the Public Protector might say, 'But what did you mean by

this word?' as you phrase your question. The Public Protector has got to consider this at the end and take a decision.

Zuma wanted to reconsider and rephrase answers to questions of fact. And he and Hulley were immovable in their contention that they did not have time to consider Madonsela's questions.

'I just think we keep going around in circles about what exactly did the President know about what he was being asked to answer for,' Madonsela said.

She again addressed Zuma: 'It was always about your ethical conduct, Sir.'

Zuma cancelled a follow-up meeting with Madonsela on 10 October 2016, on the morning it was scheduled to take place. In his letter, Zuma repeated all the objections from four days earlier and requested an undertaking by Madonsela that she would not finalise her report before getting his side of the story first. She fired a letter back, saying her office had gone to great lengths to obtain the president's version of events and noting that he had twice agreed, but failed, to assist the investigation. Two weeks after Madonsela vacated the Public Protector's office – on 2 November 2016 – the High Court in Pretoria ordered the release of the report after Zuma, Zwane and Van Rooyen had attempted to prevent its release.

The 355-page report, titled 'State of Capture', which includes the full transcript of the 6 October interview, found that neither Zuma nor government made any attempt to investigate the very serious allegations by Jonas, Mentor and Maseko about the manipulation of the state. It also found that the Guptas benefited from Eskom's assistance in the purchase of a coal mine and that its board 'acted solely for the benefit of one company'.

The report advised the president to establish a judicial commission of inquiry into state capture, to be appointed by the chief justice. Zuma balked at the findings, preferring to appeal Madonsela's remedial action.

Neither the president nor the ANC publicly dismissed either Jonas, Mentor or Maseko's accounts of their meetings with the Guptas, or their influence on the state, or Zuma's actions. The report was forwarded for further action and investigation to Shaun Abrahams, the NDPP, and Berning Ntlemeza, head of the Hawks. They never lifted a finger.

At paragraph 5.28 in the report, Madonsela states: 'I met with the President on 6 October 2016 to solicit his response to the above allegations. He did not respond to any of my questions.'[10]

State capture was real.

CHAPTER 20

Fake news and dirty tricks

*'Bell Pottinger is keen to build a long-term partnership
with you and the South African team. We want to stand shoulder-
to-shoulder in communicating such a vital message for
South Africa. The future of the country, in terms of fair economic
growth, an inclusive society and political stability, depends on it.'*
– Victoria Geoghegan, former partner of British PR firm Bell Pottinger, in an email to
Duduzane Zuma, 19 January 2016

Ｄecember 2015 was not a good month for the Zuptas. The 'silent coup' to capture the National Treasury using Van Rooyen and his Gupta-linked advisors had boomeranged and the campaign to install a Zuma-friendly fiscus was back to square one. The notion that the state was being captured was strengthening in people's minds as more evidence emerged of how Zuma and the Guptas planned to take control of public spending. Playing the victim role he so loves, Zuma would later tell his supporters how 'monopoly capital and their stooges' had attacked him, and how they had fired Van Rooyen and reappointed Gordhan as finance minister.[1] Months after he removed Van Rooyen after his three-day spell as finance minister, Zuma continued to defend him.

The Zuptas needed a fightback plan – and they needed it fast. It was well known at the time that Nene had refused to sign a guarantee for procuring nuclear power – most likely from Russia's Rosatom – at a cost of R1 trillion, which would have bankrupted South Africa. The Guptas and Duduzane Zuma, through their shareholding in Shiva Uranium, stood to benefit handsomely from supplying uranium to the new nuclear plants. With Gordhan, the disciplinarian, back at the Treasury, there was absolutely no chance Zuma, his son or their friends would ride roughshod through finance-management legislation, budgets and common sense. They needed Gordhan out and a new narrative that would counter the rapidly unfolding revelation of state capture at the highest level.

Enter Bell Pottinger. Co-founded by former British prime minister Margaret Thatcher's public-relations advisor, Lord Timothy Bell, the PR firm had gained a notorious reputation for its 'dark arts' campaigns for dubious clients. Some of the people whose images were polished by Bell Pottinger over the years include Belarusian president Aleksandr Lukashenko, known as Europe's last dictator; Chilean dictator Augusto Pinochet and the ruling Assad family of Syria.[2] And, in October 2016, the UK's Bureau of Investigative Journalism revealed how Bell Pottinger had set up a top-secret propaganda programme in Iraq for the US military and the CIA, which included producing false-news videos.[3]

Closer to home, Bell Pottinger advised FW de Klerk during the 1994 election and had contacts with political parties in Zambia, Malawi, Kenya and Nigeria.

Details about how the PR firm was introduced to the Zuptas are sketchy, but a former employee told the *Sunday Times* that contacts had been made 'by a gentleman called Fana'.[4] The 'Fana' he referred to is Fana Hlongwane, the so-called 'arms deal playboy' who was at the heart of South Africa's controversial armaments transaction with a number of European companies, including British Aerospace (now called BAE Systems). During the arms deal, Hlongwane, who has a penchant for pretty women and fast cars, was a special advisor to Joe Modise, the then defence minister. At the same time, he received commissions from BAE front companies, totalling tens of millions of rands. BAE Systems was awarded the contract to supply 24 Hawk jet trainers to the South African Air Force.

Although Hlongwane, who is close to the ANC, has been named in numerous investigations into the arms deal, he has never been charged. He denied any wrongdoing in his evidence before the Seriti Commission in 2015. He keeps a very low profile and is seldom seen in public, outside of luncheon appearances at luxury Sandton establishments. Those in the know say Hlongwane had 'repositioned' himself after the arms deal fall-out and made inroads into the Zupta network, with a particular focus on befriending Duduzane Zuma.

While Hlongwane was a BAE agent during the arms-deal years, his paths would have crossed those of Christopher Vincent Geoghegan, a BAE veteran and board member until his resignation in 2007. And so the story goes: Chris Geoghegan introduced Hlongwane to his daughter, Victoria, who was a partner at Bell Pottinger. Hlongwane introduced Victoria Geoghegan to the Guptas and she became the lead partner on the Oakbay/Gupta account – at a fee of £100 000 (about R2,3 million at the time) a month for the account. The well-educated Victoria oversaw arguably the most destructive campaign in the PR firm's scandal-ridden history – one that would eventually claim her career and reputation.

Interestingly, the Gupta leaks show that Hlongwane was in Dubai in December 2015, at the same time that a flurry of South African ministers and civil servants descended on the desert city to meet the Guptas. Was this a gathering of the wounded, after Van Rooyen's short-lived tenure at the Treasury? Hlongwane checked into Dubai's Oberoi Hotel on 16 December 2015 and paid the hotel bill of Ayanda Dlodlo, the communications minister, who was staying at the hotel at the same time.

A month later, Victoria Geoghegan, Lord Bell and other Bell Pottinger staff jetted into Johannesburg to meet Duduzane Zuma and the Guptas. A secret intelligence report, released by the SACP (who had since asked Zuma to step down) in April 2017, claimed that President Zuma attended a meeting with Bell Pottinger, so that he could explain to the PR team 'the priorities of the project as he saw them, as well as to outline any other communication request that he might like them to focus on'. The author of the report is unknown, but it quotes a former Bell Pottinger partner as its source. Zuma has not confirmed attending such a meeting and it could not be independently verified that he did. According to this 'former partner', Zuma asked Bell Pottinger to help Duduzane clean up his reputation and for communication assistance 'to create an environment which would be advantageous to enabling his ex-wife, Nkosazana Dlamini-Zuma, to replace him as leader of the ANC when the time was right'.

The Gupta leaks show that on 19 January 2016, Geoghegan sent the young Zuma a gushing email, thanking him for 'sparing us so much time'. This correspondence reveals the original, formal aim and purpose of the fightback campaign. 'Bell Pottinger is keen to build a long-term partnership with you and the South African team. We want to stand shoulder-to-shoulder in communicating such a vital message for South Africa. The future of the country in terms of fair economic growth, an inclusive society and political stability, depends on it,' Geoghegan wrote to Zuma, attaching a document to her email in which she detailed the focus of that long-term partnership.

'1994 was a seminal year in South Africa's history,' she wrote at the beginning of the document. 'The peaceful handover of power raised the hopes of many, and the expectation of imminent political AND economic enfranchisement was justified. The reality is that whilst political freedom has been attained there is a feeling that expectations of economic empowerment have not been met, with the wealth of South Africa sitting within a small grouping.' Up to this point, few South Africans would argue with her: her words could have been lifted from a DA pamphlet.

Geoghegan went on to explain that economic empowerment was the 'next big key issue' facing South Africa, 'expressed to us in emotive language using phrases such as "economic apartheid" and "economic emancipation"'. And then the sting: Zuma is blamed for 'almost all of South Africa's ills'; there was a need for a new campaign that focused on 'economic emancipation'. Effectively, they had to create a scapegoat for South Africa's woes that wasn't Zuma or the ANC. Although the phrase isn't mentioned in these early documents, the result of this was the birth of the WMC – white monopoly capital – campaign. Geoghegan warned, however, that this shouldn't look like a 'Mugabe-style programme of asset seizure' because 'then it is all South Africans who will suffer'.

The WMC campaign, Geoghegan cautioned, cannot be sold 'overnight' and she suggested that 'discipline, continuity and consistency' were needed to gain credibility. 'The key to any political messaging is repetition and we will need to use every media channel that we can, to let our message take seed and to grow,' she wrote.

Geoghegan, one editor quipped, almost started to style herself as 'South Africa's new Mandela'. It seems that the irony was completely lost on her that she was not sitting with the leader of a small, oppressed opposition party but with the son of South Africa's president, who had been in power for seven years at the time of their meeting. For at least 20 years, Jacob Zuma had been in powerful positions in the ANC and government, during which time he could have had a meaningful impact on economic development and policy. Instead, he chose to enrich himself and his family by using his power and influence in exchange for financial benefits from opportunistic benefactors. In the case of Nkandla, money was literally diverted from building houses for South Africans to building a palace for the president and his family.

Geoghegan listed some recommendations, which would be developed into a full and comprehensive strategy:

❏ To create a 'non-party political narrative around the existence of economic apartheid and the vital need for more economic emancipation'. This narrative should appeal to business, academia and 'grass-roots population'.
❏ To establish a political party agnostic 'vehicle' that would become the 'public face of the narrative'.
❏ That Bell Pottinger would 'package the narrative' into speeches, slogans, press releases and other content.
❏ To use data and case studies that show that 'apartheid still exits'.
❏ To speak to local and international media.
❏ To use radio, social media and slogans to 'unite' the 'grass roots population' around the narrative.

In this document, Geoghegan stated that the Oakbay support team would include her, Jonathan Lehrle (who later left Bell Pottinger with Lord Bell), Nick Lambert and Darren Murphy, a special advisor to former prime minister Tony Blair. Lord Bell would be available 'for strategic counsel as and when required,' she said.

Duduzane Zuma responded enthusiastically to Geoghegan's email. 'The pleasure of meeting you and your team is mine. Once again, I'd like to thank you for making the trip [to] South [Africa] on such short notice ... You come highly recommended and you represent a powerful brand, I do not take that for granted,' he wrote. That high recommendation, in all probability, came from Hlongwane.

The young Zuma wrote that he was 'enthused' by Geoghegan's understanding of the brief. 'I have to reiterate that, which you correctly put it, this "journey" is not primarily one to affect the outcome of the elections but to turn the tide of our country's trajectory in the long term.' It is unclear to which election Zuma referred: the 2016 local-government election, the 2017 ANC leadership election or the 2019 national election.

Duduzane proceeded to ask Geoghegan for help with a 'campaign' he was working on 'in line with the broader plan'. It would have a 'hard hitting message along the lines of the #EconomicEmancipation' and it would need printed T-shirts and banners.

It is not clear what happened to Duduzane's 'campaign', but early in 2016 two organisations, which many believe were the 'vehicles' Geoghegan referred to, gained prominence in South Africa on social media and in the press: Mzwanele 'Jimmy' Manyi's Decolonisation Foundation and Andile Mngxitama's Black First Land First. Both rejected the notion that they were funded by the Guptas, but the Gupta leaks show that both were in contact with the Guptas. Mngxitama attended meetings with Gupta lieutenants and was briefed on an article, while Manyi sent his CV and that of an acquaintance to the Guptas.

Their narrative was the same: white monopoly capital, and not state capture by Zuma and the Guptas, was South Africa's biggest crisis. And both made Johann Rupert, billionaire businessman and chairman of Richemont, the face of #WMC. Manyi, a former bureaucrat who had famously said there was an 'over-supply' of coloured people in the Western Cape, became a regular commentator on the Guptas' ANN7 news channel. Mngxitama's articles started to appear in the Gupta-owned *The New Age* and he aggressively attacked so-called white monopoly capital, Rupert and white journalists on Twitter.

At the same time, Bell Pottinger was starting to draft media statements for organisations loyal to Zuma, like the ANCYL and MKMVA. On 6 February 2016, Geoghegan edited an MKMVA press statement, incorporating comments critical of the EFF in the statement.[5] In June that year she offered to supply 'talking points' for ANCYL leader Collen Maine's speech at a rally. Both organisations denied having received support from the PR firm.

The biggest and most aggressive pro-Gupta campaign was, however, not launched through the mouths of humans, but through a destructive and disgusting social-media campaign, targeting journalists at the forefront of exposing state capture. What experts later called a 'sock-puppet web', meaning an intricate network of fake social-media accounts, was set up to spread disinformation straight from Donald Trump's playbook. While the world was still coming to terms with the sophistication of Trump's dirty-tricks campaign to manipulate voter behaviour through social-media algorithms, someone was setting up a similar scheme to divert attention from state capture to white monopoly capital.

Rupert became the prime target. His late father, Anton, the tobacco kingpin, was an outspoken critic of the apartheid regime, but that didn't matter much to the architects of the disinformation campaign. The timing is curious: in March 2016, Rupert, one of the five richest people in Africa, called on Zuma to step down. This was after Zuma allegedly told a meeting of the ANC's NEC that Rupert had been behind the private sector's push to remove Van Rooyen as finance minister a few months earlier – a claim Rupert dismissed with contempt.[6]

Towards the latter part of 2016, Rupert received text messages from ANC sources, warning him that 'the Guptas have hired Bell Pottinger to push the "state capture" story onto you'.[7] Judging from the images distributed by the hundreds of sock puppets on Twitter during 2016, this was true. Rupert's photo featured in almost every Photoshopped image, portraying him as the face of white monopoly capital still pulling the strings of power in South Africa.

In many of these images, Rupert is portrayed controlling journalists like Ferial Haffajee (HuffPost SA), Peter Bruce (Tiso Blackstar) and Sam Sole (amaBhungane). In some, Rupert is shown walking his dog with the face of a journalist on it. Haffajee was Photoshopped sitting on his lap, and Vytjie Mentor, who blew the whistle on the Guptas, was Photoshopped sitting next to Rupert in his private jet. After having been a client of Bell Pottinger's for 18 years, Richemont terminated its contract and Rupert lashed out at his former PR firm for turning on him. 'We have never done business with the state ... ever. Firstly, I didn't trust the previous bunch, and I don't trust these guys. We have zero influence on the media or the [media] companies we are invested in. So it's getting a little tedious ...,' Rupert told the annual meeting of Remgro, the other company he chairs.[8]

Haffajee later wrote about the impact of these deceitful images:

I thought I knew myself better than the crafters of these images do, and so sometimes I've laughed them off when asked about the score of images that have linked me to the hashtag decrying #whitemonopolycapital (white monopoly capital) and which have labelled me variously a presstitute (media prostitute) and a lapdog of the Richemont chairman and South African billionaire Johann Rupert. But upon reflection, the instinct to feel ashamed and to worry about what my less digitally savvy family might think means this kind of trolling works.[9]

Towards the end of 2016, researcher Jean le Roux tracked 'suspicious Tweets' that were sent by Manyi and Esethu Hasane, a communications official for the then sports minister, Fikile Mbalula.[10] The Tweets were all in support of the #WMC narrative and they were re-Tweeted by fake Twitter bots with fake names like Ranier Pretorius, Christo Gama and Cylvia Khoza. Le Roux realised that hundreds of fake

Twitter accounts were linked and their activity patterns were the same, meaning it was likely that a few individuals were literally controlling hundreds of accounts and re-Tweeting the same narrative over and over again. Remember what Ms Geoghegan had said about repetition being all-important?

Geoghegan had denied being involved in setting up fake Twitter bots and sock puppets for the Guptas, but when Bell Pottinger finally apologised for their work on the account, CEO James Henderson mentioned 'a social media campaign that highlights the issue of economic emancipation in a way that we, having now seen it, consider to be inappropriate and offensive'.[11]

In late 2016 Lord Bell resigned as chairman of Bell Pottinger. He said he had warned the firm against the Guptas. 'I kept saying it was "smelly" ... and they ignored it.'[12]

By 2017 the dark arts behind the #WMC social media became more desperate as more detail about the Zuptas started to emerge. In April 2017, Bell Pottinger stepped down as spin doctors for Oakbay because of what they referred to as 'attacks' on the firm.[13] South Africans took to the streets to protest outside the PR firm's London offices and as it became clearer that there had been a dirty-tricks campaign, the firm's own social-media accounts were kept busy by aggrieved locals.

In the wake of the release of the #GuptaLeaks in May 2017, several websites claiming to expose senior journalists allegedly in cahoots with people like Rupert, Absa CEO Maria Ramos, Gordhan and Manuel started to pop up. The main site, called WMC Leaks, published a so-called intelligence report on Peter Bruce, editor-at-large at Tiso Blackstar, including surveillance photos of him and his family.

This was the first tangible proof that the drivers of the campaign would stop at nothing – not even breaking the law – in their attempts to sow doubt in the minds of readers who follow the #GuptaLeaks revelations. On 29 June 2016, a small group of Black First Land First protestors gathered outside Bruce's house, holding up posters with slogans like 'Peter

Bruce why hide white corruption?' on them. They also spray-painted the words 'Land or Death' on his garage door and physically abused *Business Day* editor Tim Cohen and eNCA analyst Karima Brown when they arrived to support Bruce.

With Bell Pottinger out of the picture, Mngxitama's role in the campaign amplified, and he and Black First Land First turned up the volume of their criticism of journalists. After the Bruce protest, Mngxitama warned other prominent editors and journalists that they would be next, prompting the South African National Editors' Forum to obtain a High Court interdict in July 2017 against Mngxitama and Black First Land First to prevent them from harassing, intimidating and assaulting journalists.

Henderson's apology and statement of 6 July 2017 came as a surprise. Bell Pottinger had fired Geoghegan and suspended another partner and two employees who had worked on the Oakbay account. Of all the 'dark arts' campaigns the firm had been involved in, it took a deeply cynical and damaging campaign to divert attention from Zuma's misrule for Bell Pottinger to say sorry. Senior management had been misled about what had been done, Henderson claimed. 'For it to be done in South Africa, a country which has become an international beacon of hope for its progress towards racial reconciliation, is a matter of profound regret and in no way reflects the values of Bell Pottinger,' he stated.[14]

What he neglected to say was that the #WMC campaign perverted an essential discussion South Africa should have with itself about the transfer of economic power to a broader section of society, the alleviation of pervasive poverty and closing the gap between the (mostly white) rich and (mostly black) poor. The campaign never intended to get answers to these critical questions: it was a deceitful attempt to protect Zuma and the Guptas from scrutiny.

The full details of the campaign are yet to emerge. In July 2017 News24 revealed that an Indian online reputation-management company was behind a number of the #WMC websites registered to spread disinformation. In September 2017 the UK Public Relations and Communications Association upheld a complaint by the DA against Bell

Pottinger for stirring racial tension in South Africa and terminated the PR firm's membership of the association for a minimum period of five years – the harshest punishment it can dish out. Bell Pottinger brought the PR and communications industry into disrepute, the association ruled.[15] Many of its clients terminated their accounts with the firm in the wake of the ruling. In September 2017 Henderson, the CEO, quit after massive public pressure and the firm went into business rescue.

In August, Manyi acquired ANN7 and *The New Age* from the Guptas for R450 million, financed through vendor funding. The news was met with much scepticism because Manyi had proven himself to be a staunch Gupta and Zuma loyalist. The jury is out whether he will indeed pay the Guptas for their media houses or whether he is merely a front.

CHAPTER 21

Zuma makes his move

'One of the clear benefits of the roadshows is that we are one of
very few countries that do not have to meet investors before issuing
an international bond. In other words, the South African government is able to raise amounts as high as $3-billion
within a matter of three to four hours.'

– Statement by the National Treasury, 28 March 2017

Landing at Heathrow in the early hours of Monday 27 March 2017, Lungisa Fuzile was a pretty tired man. The National Treasury's director general had been on a frantic chase from Pretoria down to the Eastern Cape and back again, delivering a prize bull to his farm and dropping off the transport trailer in Brits. His boss, Pravin Gordhan, had been on his back on Friday and Saturday, checking up on his progress: 'You'd better get to ORT in time ... there's no way you can miss this trip.'[1] When Fuzile arrived at OR Tambo International Airport, he sent a text to 'PG', as the minister is known, confirming he was on time for SAA's 20.30 flight to London. 'Why didn't you book on my flight, the 20.00 one?' Gordhan enquired. 'Because you would have kept me up all night with work!' the director general replied.[2]

The Treasury's most senior officials were to join forces with representatives from the private sector and the country's largest trade union movements on an international investors' roadshow, embarked on twice annually by Team South Africa. The previous years' roadshows helped stave off an almost certain downgrade of the country's investment status by the trio of international rating agencies, after Zuma's sudden dismissal of Nene. This year's roadshow was equally important – they needed to explain to investors what the Zuma government meant with the phrase 'radical economic transformation'. There were also increased fears about the Treasury's ability to insulate itself from political attacks and protect the fiscus. Investors and bond holders wanted to appraise themselves of the political situation – they also wanted an exit strategy should the rating agencies downgrade the country to junk status.

In the month following his budget speech in February 2017, Gordhan and his deputy, Jonas, had been on a national listening tour, explaining to all and sundry what the implications of the latest budget were. Gordhan enjoyed support from across the political spectrum, and civil society and markets considered him the most measured and sober political voice in government. But he was under pressure. The drums sounding a Cabinet reshuffle were beating louder and the court date with the Guptas loomed. The war between him and Moyane, the irascible apparatchik deployed by Zuma to SARS, was also beginning to take its toll, with Zuma poised to intervene between the two men. 'There's no need for anybody to intervene. Mr Moyane is the accounting officer and he's responsible to the minister,' Gordhan irritably said at a breakfast event at Deloitte in Johannesburg two days before his departure for London.[3]

In the build-up to the tabling of the budget, senior staff at the Treasury decided on a strategy to counter attacks on the institution, spearheaded by so-called 'paid Twitter'. These attacks were relentless and the tidal wave of animosity on social media grew bigger by the day. The Guptas' news outlets – most prominently ANN7, their satellite news channel – and 'paid Twitter' painted Gordhan and the Treasury as beholden to foreign interests, imperialism and white monopoly capital, and claimed they were acting outside the law. The Treasury, they said, was opposed to transformation and a bastion of vested interests, controlled by moneyed families, like the Ruperts and Oppenheimers, and had to be dismantled and returned to 'the people'.

Some of the most extraordinary assaults came from within Cabinet. Nomvula Mokonyane, the Minister of Water and Sanitation, and Bathabile Dlamini, the Minister of Social Development (both Zuma surrogates and prominent leaders in the ANC Women's League), attacked Gordhan for being stingy, uncommitted to 'transformation' and 'development', and unresponsive to the needs of the people.[4] Never mind the fact that Mokonyane's department had been run into the ground and was effectively bankrupt, or that Dlamini drew the ire of the Constitutional Court because she simply ignored directives from the country's highest arbiter and jeopardised the monthly payment of more than 17 million social grants. The mud seemed to stick.

Gordhan's lieutenants, consisting of his kitchen cabinet of trusted and experienced bureaucrats, decided to go on the attack. The normally staid and grey Treasury took to social media, ramping up its Twitter communications and attempting to dismantle the popular narrative that it was a 'state within a state', that it alone decides which ministers, 'get budget', for their programmes and that it is the real centre of power in government. Officials engaged role players and journalists to explain how the budgeting process actually works and that the Treasury cannot simply, on a whim, decide to withhold money from the national fiscus. They held briefings and workshops, and gave almost unprecedented access to the mechanics of compiling the budget. The attacks continued, but the Treasury wasn't deterred – even Tweeting some of those horrendous inspirational messages sometimes found on posters with leaping dolphins. It engaged with people on social media and distributed news and information it deemed important.

Gordhan pulled no punches at the press conference before the budget speech, making two references to the Guptas' attacks on him and answering questions with a determined honesty. Yes, he said, it does indeed matter who runs the Treasury – it's not a government department that you can simply bat around and hope for the best. 'There are a couple of institutions [in the state] which I would suggest, and I'm saying this in quotation marks, "you don't mess with". And Treasury is one of them,' he said, before adding, 'It takes many years to build an institution, to build confidence and trust, to build skills, culture, effectiveness, resilience. But it's very easy to break it down.'[5]

Gordhan's budget speech was the most political of his career as Minister of Finance. In it he tried to give substance to the amorphous term 'radical economic transformation', which Zuma and the ANC punted in the weeks leading up to the president's state of the nation address on 9 February 2017. Even though Zuma mentioned the term six times during his speech, he never defined it, so Gordhan saw an opportunity to frame the president's populist message in coherent and responsible fiscal prose, to take the initiative and to fortify the Treasury against future assaults. As he left the podium in the National Assembly, to rapturous and standing applause from the opposition and government benches alike, a few of his enemies remained seated – among them Dlamini, Mahlobo, Van Rooyen and Lindiwe Zulu (Minister of Small Business). Some grinned and looked around, bemused at the cheers Gordhan received as he made his way back to his front bench. Dlamini literally sat on her hands.

As the plane taxied to Heathrow's Terminal 2, Fuzile switched on his phone. It beeped immediately. There was a text from Jonas's chief of staff, warning him they might have to return to South Africa immediately. Then his phone rang; it was Gordhan's personal assistant: 'We're getting mixed messages. What should we do?' Fuzile was perplexed, but replied: 'Wait before you do anything. Let me talk to PG. You don't think we're about to get fired?' he joked with her. Another text message then came through, this time from Cassius Lubisi, his opposite number in the Presidency. It was long and officious: 'At the direction of His Excellency, President Jacob Zuma, I have been instructed to call you back to South Africa ...'

As Fuzile disembarked from the plane, Gordhan called him and asked where he was. 'I'm 30 minutes behind you. I think we should proceed with today's meetings. But let's talk at the hotel.'[6]

Arriving at their hotel, where a ballroom had been booked for the event, without a chance to freshen up – Gordhan and Fuzile immediately went into crisis mode. They had been given no information about why they were instructed to return from such a crucial international engagement. For the first time since his return to the Treasury 15 months before, Gordhan looked despondent. He usually thrives in a crisis and had already managed to stare down the Hawks, the NPA and some of his colleagues over the previous months. He didn't do the job for the money: he was financially secure and his children, one a doctor and the other a chartered accountant, were grown up. He was driven by his activist instincts to do good for his country. But now obstacles were being thrown in his path to achieve that.

Reports started coming though from South Africa about the reasons why Gordhan, Jonas (who hadn't yet left South Africa) and Fuzile were being ordered back. One narrative said they hadn't been given permission by Zuma, but then it emerged that an 'intelligence report' fingered the trio as being in cahoots with 'international bankers' to bring about 'regime change' in South Africa. Gordhan decided they would return on the same overnight flight that they had come on, but that Monday's commitments would be met. 'Look, the worst thing we can do is to cancel on those investors that are already travelling to meet us this morning,' Fuzile told Gordhan. 'We have to see the ratings agencies that are here and we have to talk to the people from New York. We can't tell the ratings agencies, "Stuff you!"'[7]

After checking reports on News24, Gordhan agreed, adding they would have to confront this issue 'head-on'. Fuzile then spoke to the Treasury team back in Pretoria, instructing them to arrange their return flights that evening and to cancel the second leg of the roadshow in New York. They also contacted investors who were about to travel to London to cancel their travel plans. Gordhan and Fuzile then freshened up before they met their teammates from business and labour, explaining what had happened and how the programme would change. Jabu Mabuza, president of Business

Unity South Africa, was incredulous: he had seen Zuma shortly before he left for London and there was no inkling of what was afoot.

Stakeholders and investors were baffled by the developments, coming off the back of the Treasury's concerted efforts to pacify jittery international markets. Their questions were pointed: how will government achieve its growth forecasts? Will it be able to balance its books on the spending and income side? And, importantly, who will take over the ANC leadership in December? Gordhan's mood improved during the day and he seemed more relaxed during a working lunch, answering questions about the country's political stability and fiscal outlook. 'He knows investors like him and he likes us. We asked him why has to go back, and he answered: "I do what my boss tells me,"' said one attendee.[8]

Back in South Africa, it was chaos. The rand – earlier buoyed by the flailing US markets and up on trading – fell by 3%, bonds tumbled and banking shares slid by 3%. Yolisa Tyantsi, Gordhan's spokesperson, couldn't confirm any details and referred all questions to the Presidency. Bongani Ngqulunga, Zuma's anonymous spokesperson, remained true to form and kept his cellphone turned off. It became clear Zuma was gearing up to fire Gordhan. The consistent attacks on the finance minister – from the jibes by the president directed at Gordhan, to the intimidation before the budget speeches and the vexatious charges by the Hawks – all pointed in the direction of an eventual Cabinet reshuffle. There was a train of thought that Zuma wouldn't dare fire Gordhan, as that would remove any pretence that he was beholden to the national interest rather than to other, familial and private interests. But the fight for access to state resources was bloody; it was a zero-sum game wherein good governance and something like credit ratings played no role.

Speculation and panic moved into the vacuum created by the lack of communication from government as South Africans readied themselves for another political shock. By then, hushed talk of a Cabinet reshuffle turned into louder discussions of who would replace Gordhan. But, to some, it still seemed far-fetched that Zuma was willing to go down the same route he had gone in December 2015. Economists immediately reacted, warning that rating agencies don't take kindly to political machinations like this, that government bonds would quickly be sold off and that the country's investment profile would risk another downgrade.

Senior staff at the Treasury's headquarters were in a state of panic, saying they were 'shocked' and 'in the dark'. A terse statement issued by the Presidency just before midday then confirmed the news: 'President Jacob Zuma has instructed the Minister of Finance, Mr Pravin Gordhan and Deputy Minister Mcebisi Jonas to cancel the international investment promotion roadshow to the United Kingdom and the United States and return to South Africa immediately.'[9]

Gordhan and Fuzile left London that night. They didn't sit together on the flight, but they did share the same fears about what the following day held. 'I found the whole affair offensive – it was almost like you had to live by the law of the jungle,' says Fuzile. 'There needs to be a semblance of normality and respect in government dealings ... but here you had a disrespectful leadership calling back the minister, the director general, businessmen and unionists, who had all put time aside from running their organisations to work with government and to prevent a downgrade and preserve our rating. I just knew: it was the end of PG and I realised I did not want to be part of this any longer.'[10]

He started composing his resignation letter in the middle of the night on the return flight. He didn't tell Gordhan.

The minister and his director general landed mid-morning on Tuesday, 28 March 2017, and were promptly greeted by a media scrum at OR Tambo's arrivals hall. Speculation was rife that the long-threatened Cabinet reshuffle was about to happen and that Molefe, who had been sworn in as an MP shortly before, was set to replace him. A message was relayed to the pair when they landed that Mantashe wanted to see them. They were driven in Gordhan's car to Luthuli House, the ANC's decrepit headquarters, and straight into another media scrum – assembled hacks were awaiting a statement after the death of struggle stalwart

Ahmed Kathrada in the early hours of the morning.

They met Mantashe in private. He wanted to know where Jonas was. They explained that he was in Pretoria, that he had never left. Zuma – the captured president – had been telling all and sundry that an 'intelligence report' claimed the minister, the deputy and the DG were in London agitating for the overthrow of government. Mantashe told them what Zuma had told the party's leaders and the alliance partners the day before: that he was going to fire both Gordhan and Jonas over the 'intel'. Fabricated stories based on falsified intelligence were being used to get rid of them, he said, in exactly the same way that the disbandment of the Scorpions had been justified (thanks to the Browse Mole Report), and how some of Zuma's political opponents were sidelined (through the Ground Coverage Report) and SARS was stripped (via the planted 'rogue unit' stories). They were stunned and angry, and told Mantashe so. Mantashe buried his head in his hands. 'South Africans aren't stupid,' Fuzile said. 'It [the planned reshuffle] smacked of desperation. We had been working on behalf of South Africa for a very, very long time. Why would we now do the opposite? It proved to me that I no longer belonged.'[11]

They left Luthuli House separately and went home for a change of clothing before returning to 40 Church Square, where they met with Jonas, calmed staff and reached out to investors, business and rating agencies. A discussion ensued whether or not they should go to the Union Buildings to present themselves to Zuma to tell him: 'We're back, as you requested.' They decided against that, however, preferring to help their team draft a statement on the importance of the roadshow.

That afternoon the most extraordinary scene played out when Gordhan, Jonas and Tyantsi exited the Treasury's head office and walked across Madiba Street to the High Court, where the finance minister's application for a declaratory order against the Guptas' Oakbay Investments was being heard. Gordhan sat in the back of the courtroom listening to proceedings, before slipping out to make a telephone call and walk back to the office through the throng of journalists trying to get a soundbite. 'Ye-e-e-s!' he smiled when asked if he was still finance minister, amid reports on ANN7 that the ANC's top six agreed he should be fired.

Late in the afternoon, the Treasury released a carefully crafted statement that a small team had pored over for hours, setting out the particulars of the international roadshow and explaining its importance. 'The ratings ... determine the cost at which SA will borrow the R730 billion it will need to meet its borrowing requirement for the next three years. Government on a weekly basis needs to borrow more than R13 billion in the domestic market. Of government's total borrowing requirement, USD6 billion needs to be raised from the international market over the next 3 years to partly meet government's foreign commitments.'[12]

That money is used to help finance public infrastructure, like roads, schools and hospitals. 'One of the clear benefits of the roadshows is that SA is one of very few countries that do not have to meet investors before issuing an international bond. In other words, the South African government is able to raise amounts as high as $3 billion within a matter of three to five hours. This has been the case for the last five years,' the statement read. The stakes were clear. And they were high.

Kathrada died in the early hours of the same day, 28 March 2017. The struggle veteran – a Treason and Rivonia trialist, and one of the last of the Mandela generation – was 87.

In April the previous year, Kathrada had written an open letter to President Zuma asking him to resign. He explained that he had kept quiet during the unfolding of his numerous scandals, believing it proper to resolve differences internally in the ANC, but that the Constitutional Court's Nkandla judgment forced him to break with that tradition. His death symbolised the passing of a so-called golden generation of leaders, like Nelson Mandela, Oliver Tambo and Walter Sisulu, and was greeted with despair. Funeral arrangements were announced almost immediately and he would be laid to rest, according to Muslim tradition, within 24 hours.

As Gordhan was making his way to the High Court that Tuesday afternoon, news broke that the Kathrada family did not want Zuma to attend the funeral. Relations between Zuma and Kathrada had soured after the letter, to which the president did not respond. It was a severe blow to Zuma that the ANC's president wasn't welcome at such a seminal moment in the history of the organisation. Kathrada was loved and respected by everyone within the liberation movement and occupied a position in the pantheon of ANC greats like Mandela, having served 26 years' imprisonment on Robben Island. It was a symbolic rebuke of Zuma's leadership and a rejection from beyond the grave. But worse was to come.

The funeral, at the Westpark Cemetery in Johannesburg on 29 March 2017, was held on an overcast and gloomy day, but proceedings honouring the life of one of the ANC's leading lights was anything but. The marquee tent was packed with ANC dignitaries, including former presidents Mbeki and Motlanthe, as well as ANC matriarch Winnie Madikizela-Mandela. The casket was draped in the ANC's flag, while former uMkhonto we Sizwe combatants kept a vigil. Almost the whole of the Cabinet attended, with its regular fortnightly meeting scheduled for that morning pushed back to the afternoon to enable ministers to attend. The leaders of the ANC in Gauteng, ardent critics of Zuma, were out in full force while Julius Malema scored a front-row seat, next to Madikizela-Mandela. Nkosazana Dlamini-Zuma also came to pay her respects.

Zuma was at the Union Buildings, following proceedings on television, and what he saw did not make him happy. Next to Barbara Hogan, Kathrada's widow and a former minister whom Zuma dismissed, sat Cyril Ramaphosa and his wife, Dr Tshepo Motsepe. Next to them sat Mbeki, Zuma's arch enemy, and his wife, Zanele, and to their right sat Graça Machel, Mandela's widow, and Zelda la Grange, his assistant. On Hogan's other side sat Motlanthe and his wife, Gugu Mtshali, Madikizela-Mandela and Malema. It was a battery of Zuma critics and opponents.

Motlanthe, stridently delivering the eulogy, quoted at length from Kathrada's letter, saying the struggle hero wasn't afraid to call on Zuma to resign. But, he lamented, Kathrada received no reply from the Presidency. He went on to warn that the ANC would 'disappear from the face of the earth' if it refuses to be introspective.[13]

During proceedings Gordhan sat quietly in the second row of mourners, in between Cabinet colleagues Lindiwe Sisulu and Aaron Motsoaledi, the respected health minister, privately preparing for what would be an acrimonious Cabinet meeting afterwards. But Neeshan Balton, the executive director of the Kathrada Foundation had other ideas. He told the assembled, representing the great and the good of the governing party, that Kathrada wanted to be the first to accompany Gordhan to court the previous year when he was charged by the Hawks. 'PG, where are you?' Balton asked, before Motlanthe, enthused and energised by the reaction to his denunciation of Zuma, pointed to where Gordhan was sitting. The Minister of Finance was overcome by emotion when Balton asked him to stand up. He choked back the tears as hundreds of people – ministers, party elders, provincial leaders, opposition politicians and friends alike – stood and gave him a thunderous ovation. He looked awkward being the centre of attention, taking a breath when standing up and giving a tentative salute, before he sat down and Balton continued.

'Irrespective of whether you are a minister or not in the days and weeks to come, you remain true to the values and principles that Ahmed Kathrada would be proud of,' Balton said while Gordhan dabbed at the tears in his eyes.[14] Mourners cheered and cheered. It was live on national television.

If Gordhan was emotional during the funeral, his determination to remain in his position was steely. Pressure was being put on him to resign, so as to prevent a repeat of the Nene disaster, but the minister's aides said there was no way he was stepping back. 'If Zuma wants PG out, he is going to have to fire him. He must own the decision,' one of Gordhan's advisors said, adding that Gordhan and Jonas would not 'walk away from this battle'.[15] Gordhan enjoyed enormous public support. But the Guptas' ANN7 news channel was already reporting his dismissal as fact.

CHAPTER 22

Treasury's walls finally breached

—

'Does it matter who sits in these chairs? Yes, it does matter.
Because it impacts on the policies and ideas that go to Cabinet.
It takes many years to build an institution, to build confidence
and trust, to build skills, culture, effectiveness, resilience.
But it's very easy to break it down.'

– Minister of Finance Pravin Gordhan, alongside Deputy Minister Mcebisi Jonas,

at a media conference before delivering the budget speech, Cape Town, 22 February 2017

The National Treasury's head office is an imposing fortress on the republican Church Square in Pretoria, in between the grand Palace of Justice (where the Rivonia Trial was held) and the Eerste Volksbank building and across the road from the NPA.

The building, completed in the early 1930s, was designed in the neo-classical style by famed architect Sir Herbert Baker, who was also in charge of designing the Union Buildings. Its thick outer walls, built on rock-solid, grey granite foundations, resembles something from *Game of Thrones*, with battlements and ramparts seemingly protecting the institution from would-be attackers. The outer windows at street level are secured by wrought-iron bars and the building is accessible only through a portcullis-like entrance.

Inside it smells of Brillo and floor polish, with brass railings, dark mahogany-panelled walls and polished balustrades – a reminder of the

253

building's previous incarnation as the first home of the South African Reserve Bank, who turned it over to the Treasury in 1988. Behind the defunct teller counters the old banking hall now serves as a dining facility. Wide staircases and a Depression-era lift lead upstairs, where polite bureaucrats staff the ministerial offices. The minister's boardroom has wood-panelled walls, with Africana art adorning the panel at the end of the long table, and a flagpole bearing the South African flag.

Under Mandela the Treasury was given a central role in efforts to construct a new South Africa. The new ANC government, however, first had to get to grips with the dire state of government accounts, and when Chris Liebenberg, the transitional finance minister, told Mandela he wanted out it fell to Manuel to carry out the will of the new president and the party, namely that the institution had to ensure financial sovereignty – that is, independence from Bretton Woods institutions, like the International Monetary Fund and the World Bank.

Manuel and erstwhile director general Maria Ramos set out to build a world-class institution and ensured the Treasury attracted civic-minded talent, a tradition carried on to this day. Gill Marcus became Manuel's deputy minister before she became Governor of the SARB; Lesetja Kganyago served as director general before he succeeded Marcus; Pravin Gordhan was commissioner of SARS for a decade before succeeding Manuel, and Nene was a member of Parliament's Standing Committee on Finance under Marcus's chair before he became chair and eventually finance minister.[1] The 'finance family', as the Treasury, the SARB, SARS and related institutions became known, developed a reputation for sound, robust and transparent financial management, an asset that has set South Africa apart from other developing nations. Manuel, Gordhan and Nene, and their respective teams, knew how fragile a country's reputation can be in the cut-throat and cruel world of international finance, and set out guarding and protecting it from the buffeting winds of local and international politics. This they did with great success for almost two decades.

When Manuel attended an economics conference in 1992, he was given three banknotes of 5 million zaires each, printed by President Mobutu

Sese Seko of Zaire. (When Mobutu paid his military with the worthless money, they rioted and helped hasten the dictator's fall.) Manuel gave one of the banknotes to Mbeki and one to Tito Mboweni, who was to become governor of the SARB, as a reminder of what could happen when bad governance and the undermining of institutions converge.[2] The Treasury, as Manuel was illustrating with the devalued Congolese banknotes, is therefore a key asset in the country's financial armoury. 'The role of the National Treasury is critical. It is the only government department that has a chapter in the Constitution dedicated to it. It cannot be changed at a whim and it must be protected,' said Ramos.[3]

Thursday 30 March 2017 was one of the busiest days of the year at the Treasury. Government's financial year end was less than 24 hours away, and staff were finalising departmental books. The next budgeting cycle was a month away. Gordhan was in the building. It was a normal working day. The minister was walking around, talking to bureaucrats and telling them to do their job, as they had become used to, and that they needed to be aware what was happening outside, with political storms raging. 'You can't ignore it, yes, but focus on what needs to be done,' the 'uncle' said to one. Gordhan had a reputation as a strict manager who demanded effective execution. Just because his head was on Zuma's chopping block didn't mean the Treasury's account of state finances should not be in mint condition.

Tension had been rising ever since news had broken on Monday that Zuma had ordered Gordhan back to the country and expectations that the finance minister was to be removed remained high. Information started emerging about the enormous disagreements among the ANC's 'top six' and within the Tripartite Alliance about the imminent reshuffle. While Treasury officials were imploring government departments to finalise their financial statements, Solly Mapaila, the SACP second deputy general secretary, dropped a bombshell at a press conference in Johannesburg: 'The SACP wishes to state that as the norm, the president informed us of his intention to effect a Cabinet reshuffle, replacing both the minister and deputy minister of finance. We recorded our objection to the intended reshuffle.[4]

Mapaila, who was emerging as one of Zuma's most strident critics, said that his party vehemently disagreed with Zuma's decision and, even though they might differ with Gordhan about economic policy, the Treasury must be handled with care: 'They [Gordhan and Jonas] have served our movement well and mustn't be harassed. We can't allow parasites in and have vultures circle it [the Treasury].' It was extraordinary: this was the first public confirmation from a political leader in the alliance of what Zuma's plans were and a clear indication that the SACP was now as opposed to Zuma as they had been to Mbeki circa 2006/07.

Senior officials at the Treasury had been bracing themselves for the worst since the beginning of the week. Gordhan spoke with a select few on Monday and tried to calm feelings on Tuesday, when he met with his kitchen cabinet. The expectation was that he would be axed on Tuesday, but Kathrada's death staved it off until after Wednesday's funeral. By Thursday an air of inevitability permeated through the Treasury. Analysts were starting to whisper that the groundwork had been done and that the markets had begun pricing in a Gordhan execution.

Late in the afternoon, a message was delivered by the Presidency to the ANC's officials, summoning them to the presidential residence for a meeting at 6.30 pm. The rand reacted immediately when the news broke, weakening from R12,80 to R13,09 to the dollar by 8 pm. Ramaphosa, Mantashe and the rest of the officials met Zuma in the same mansion where Mantashe and Motlanthe had told Mbeki, almost a decade before, that his time was up.

The top six were split: Ramaphosa, Mantashe and Mkhize were strongly against Zuma's decision and flatly opposed any plans to replace Gordhan with Brian Molefe. Both Duarte, Mantashe's deputy, and Mbete, the national chairperson, supported the president. The discussion lasted more than two hours, and although Zuma went into the meeting determined to rid himself of Gordhan – thrust on him by Ramaphosa and big business – there was strong resistance from his three opponents. By 8 o'clock, after an hour and a half of deliberations, a message slipped out from the Ramaphosa camp: 'The DP [deputy president] is holding firm. It looks like the old man might listen this time. We are holding out hope.'

At 12.14 that night, the Presidency released a statement announcing ten new ministerial and ten new deputy ministerial appointments. Both Gordhan and Jonas were omitted from Cabinet, as was Derek Hanekom, a veteran of the Mandela Cabinet and the one who proposed a motion of no confidence at the ANC's last NEC meeting. Gordhan was at home and received the news alongside the rest of the country. There was no phone call from the Presidency, no message to prepare him or thank him for his service. Just a general media statement with the news that he, alongside others, like Joemat-Pettersson (who had failed to push through the nuclear deal), had been booted from the executive. Zuma wielded his power brutally and ruthlessly.

ANN7 and its analysts were crowing about the Gordhan departure, which they had been predicting since Monday. Presenter Sindy Mabe struggled to contain her glee as Mzwanele Manyi and analyst Tshepo Kgadima extolled the virtues of the new finance minister, Malusi Gigaba, calling him a 'young lion' who would 'now drive the economy forward'. Manyi told viewers that Gigaba will 'surely' drop the court action against the Guptas, while Kgadima said Gordhan's image as an effective minister was a lie. The rand weakened further, retreating to R13,29. By midnight the rand was trading at R13,41 and analysts were warning about the effect that a fourth minister of finance in 15 months would have on the markets. The country reacted with shock. The following morning, while South Africans were on their way to work trying to digest events, an incredulous Mantashe went on Xolani Gwala's breakfast show on Talk Radio 702 and said he didn't agree with the decision and hadn't been consulted on the reshuffle: 'I can't use the word "consulted",' said Mantashe. 'The ANC was informed. We were given a list that was complete. I felt like this list had been developed somewhere else and given to us to legitimise … I am very uncomfortable, because …

ministers who did not perform were left untouched. He [Zuma] knows we are unhappy. He knows.'

Mantashe, the man who runs the ANC and without whose knowledge nothing in the organisation happens, was left floundering: 'The president of the ANC came with a list and gave it to us, he said we can comment if we want to, but these are the changes. I am telling you, our views on that list counted for naught.'

Later that morning, Ramaphosa was mobbed by reporters and confirmed Mantashe's comments: there had been no consultation on the formation of the new Cabinet, just a 'ready-made' list. The deputy president said he was 'greatly disturbed' and called Gordhan's dismissal 'unacceptable'. Ramaphosa said:

> I raised my concern and objection on the removal of the minister of finance largely because he was being removed based on an intelligence report that I believe contained unsubstantiated allegations. [This related to] the minister and his deputy going to London to mobilise financial markets against our country. Now that I find it totally, totally unacceptable [to think] that a person who has served our country with such distinction would do something like that.[5]

Little did Mantashe, Ramaphosa and Mkhize, who on Saturday morning echoed his colleagues' sentiments in a statement, know how powerless they were and how they would be forced to publicly recant their criticism of the all-powerful Zuma. In London, market commentators reacted with exasperation, warning that the president's actions would lead to multiple downgrades and that South Africa would be 'stripped of its valued investment grade status'. Kevin Daly of Aberdeen Asset Management said: 'There really is very little left of South Africa's reputation for sensible policymaking.'[6]

Gordhan and Jonas returned to 40 Church Square on Friday morning to clear their offices and greet staff. Before Gordhan addressed a media conference, his last task as finance minister, he and Jonas held a closed-door meeting with activists, including Sipho Pityana of the Save South Africa campaign, activist Mark Heywood and Zwelinzima Vavi, to share 'scary facts' with them about what could happen with pension funds managed by the Public Investment Corporation and what was going on at the Department of Water and Sanitation.[7]

Afterwards, when Gordhan and Jonas entered the vast room where the media conference was to take place, they were greeted by throngs of cheering Treasury staff singing '*Senzeni na?*' (What have we done?). Many were holding up placards with extracts from the Constitution and the Public Finance Management Act. Outside, thousands of protestors, mobilised on social media under the hashtag #OccupyTreasury, had gathered in Church Square to show their support for the Treasury. The sheer numbers that had gathered meant Fuzile had to brief Gigaba, the incoming minister, and a good friend of the Guptas, off-site.

Gordhan unshackled was a sight to behold. He challenged Zuma directly, saying he had tried his best to 'fix the blunders' of Nene's axing, which saw the rand fall from R13,40 to R15,40 to the dollar overnight. He was defeated but didn't hesitate to tell South Africans to 'organise and mobilise' against corruption and state capture. The message was clear: he had been fired because he was an obstacle to state capture, because he was an obstacle to Zuma. The now former minister launched into his detractors, saying the time had come for South Africans 'to connect the dots' and to see the pattern of 'particular interests' that were being protected and consolidated. He was scathing about the intelligence report that Zuma had presented to the ANC's leaders as a pretext to fire him, holding up printouts of a series of WhatsApp messages that constituted the so-called report. He said it was 'nonsense' and that allegations about him and Jonas plotting against their own country 'sicken[ed]' him. During question time he trained his guns, not for the first time, on reporters from the Guptas' ANN7, referring to the news channel and its proprietors' efforts to 'attack, malign and disgrace' the Treasury. 'This is not an assault on Treasury, it is an assault on the country and the values we stand for,' Jonas told staff.[8]

The country was in shock. Besides the protests on Church Square and the Union Buildings, a march on Parliament in Cape Town took place, and the DA and the EFF both mooted a vote of no confidence in Parliament. The Mandela and Kathrada foundations issued a joint media statement condemning the Cabinet reshuffle; Mbeki said Zuma needed to explain his decisions. As had been the case when Nene was fired, the markets' reaction was merciless: on 3 April 2017 Standard & Poor's downgraded South Africa's status to junk; Fitch followed suit a week later. The efforts of the Treasury, Gordhan, business and labour over the past 15 months had been swept aside. The country was now paying more to borrow and investors were leaving its shores. On the same day SARS, led by a grinning Moyane, who had now been delivered from Gordhan's intrusive oversight, announced the preliminary tax figures – a R30-billion shortfall, money that would now have to be borrowed at a premium.

But Zuma was triumphant. He batted away all opposition during a two-day meeting of the ANC's National Working Committee and forced Mantashe to apologise on behalf of himself, Ramaphosa and Mkhize for questioning the reshuffle and Gordhan's firing. At a carefully managed stage event where he launched new locomotives for Transnet, Zuma just grinned and laughed as journalists tried to ask him questions about the downgrades. Shortly after, the respected Treasury director general, Fuzile, quit.

The assault on the Treasury, which had been brewing for years and which burst out in the open when Nene was dismissed, culminated in the replacement of Gordhan with Gigaba, a perfumed and immaculately groomed career politician, adept at the game of survival, switching sides and smiling. He was also a good friend of the Guptas, visiting their Saxonwold home for celebrations,[9] helping to clear the decks at the boards of state-owned enterprises to enable Gupta-friendly appointments[10] and helping them acquire citizenship.[11] Impressionable, pliable and, more importantly, a Zuma man, Gigaba was a perfect fit for the job that Zupta needed doing, and a more palatable placement than Van Rooyen. 'He is rotten to the core,' Julius Malema told the media.[12]

The capture of the Treasury by rent-seekers, led and enabled by the president, was one of the seminal moments of the Zuma era. South Africans had by then become used to revelations by the media, as well as by state institutions like the Public Protector and the Auditor-General, to industrial-scale looting. The SAA, Prasa, Eskom and Transnet had become feeding troughs for connected cronyism and the state was being sucked dry by unscrupulous networks of criminal enterprises. Gordhan – along with his deputy minister and Treasury staff – had offered the only visible executive resistance in government and the ANC, who had shrunk and cowered before Zuma's brute force. Ramaphosa, Mantashe and Mkhize, for all their much vaunted commitment to the rule of law and constitutionalism, had done nothing but watch and meekly criticise, and then only for the record. The Treasury, battered and vilified, succumbed to a concerted campaign to deligitimise and demonise not only the institution's leaders, but also its constitutional and statutory role. With Gordhan, Jonas, Fuzile and a number of other experienced and senior Treasury officials out of the way, it had become easier to restart the process to spend billions on nuclear energy, use the Public Investment Corporation to prop up bankrupt SOEs, and manage and manipulate the state's annual spend of R840 billion on goods and services. There was a lot of taxpayers' money to be had, and it seemed that there was nobody left to guard it.

On Saturday 1 April, Gigaba gave his first press conference as minister. Meanwhile, Gordhan delivered a rousing message to hundreds of people packed into the Johannesburg City Hall, where a remembrance event was held for Kathrada. The former minister looked energised as he took to the podium, cheered on by his colleague Derek Hanekom and supported by ANC veterans like Manuel and Zola Skweyiya, a former minister and High Commissioner to London. He delivered his speech to an enthusiastic audience. 'When three senior party officials, the deputy president, the secretary general and the treasurer general, say in the space of 24 hours they don't know where this decision [to reshuffle the Cabinet] was made, we have a problem. And if anyone is thinking of taking us to a disciplinary committee, we'll ask these same questions at the next meeting of the NEC,' he said.[13]

Gordhan's message was unequivocal: mobilise. 'I will say to activists in the alliance, particularly, that now is the time to unite and fight against the weaknesses in our movement and to do everything possible so that the values of Mandela, Sisulu, Tambo and Kathrada are restored to our movement,' he said.

He was back to being an activist, challenging a government considered an enemy of the people.

PART 7

Endgame

CHAPTER 23

#GuptaLeaks

—

'*If you lose the state, you've lost the battle.*'

– amaBhungane managing partner Sam Sole at a Town Hall meeting to discuss

the Gupta leaks, Johannesburg, 27 July 2017

In November 1989, the now defunct 'alternative' Afrikaans newspaper *Vrye Weekblad* published an exposé that would change the course of history. The small newspaper, edited by legendary journalist Max du Preez, revealed how the apartheid police operated a death squad outside Pretoria called Vlakplaas. At Vlakplaas, anti-apartheid activists were intimidated, tortured and killed. *Vrye Weekblad*'s source was Captain Dirk Coetzee, the erstwhile commander of Vlakplaas, who revealed intimate details of the murderous operation to journalist Jacques Pauw.

The Vlakplaas revelations led to international condemnation of the apartheid state, which was on its last legs. They showed the extent of state-sanctioned criminality and led to a series of trials and commissions that would unravel the true nature of the dirty tricks deployed by the apartheid security apparatus.

In terms of impact and consequence, the arms deal was the first major scandal of democratic South Africa under the ANC. Over months and years, investigative journalists and whistle-blowers unearthed evidence of major skulduggery with the procurement of weaponry from European conglomerates that cost us anything between R40 billion and R70 billion, depending on who you believe. Former ANC chief whip and NEC member Tony Yengeni served prison time for failing to declare to Parliament a discount he received from an arms company on a Mercedes-Benz, and Zuma's financial advisor Schabir Shaik went to prison for, among other things, facilitating a R500 000 bribe for Zuma from French arms company Thales.

Although Zuma's term as president has felt like one long unfolding scandal, nothing could prepare South Africa for the leaking of over 300 000 emails and other documents from the Gupta family's business empire.

The #GuptaLeaks, as the series of reports by a plethora of journalists is known, became the biggest work of investigative journalism by South African hacks since *Vrye Weekblad*'s Vlakplaas exposés. The emails reveal the extent of state capture and destroy any notion that this was a dreamt-up concept by the so-called Western media, Zuma's opponents and 'white monopoly capital'. In Sole's words, they reveal how 'big and organised the assault on our sovereignty was'.[1]

But it didn't happen without some birth pains. For weeks, Sole, journalist Stefaans Brümmer and their colleagues from South Africa's first independent investigative journalism outfit, amaBhungane, together with other journalists from the *Daily Maverick*, had been trying to verify and safeguard the bombshell information leaked to them on a hard drive – and the whistle-blowers who had leaked it.

In their possession was the biggest data leak in the history of South African investigative journalism. But the information and the people who had leaked it had to be checked before they were prepared to publish. Asked about the process preceding the publication of the revelations, Sole said that they were in contact with the whistle-blowers who had provided the data, but weren't sure about its veracity. 'It looked very interesting, it looked real, but there was a whole process to check whether this was the real thing,' said Sole. 'We thought if somebody found out we had this before we got it out, there would be a real serious attempt to shut it down. We managed to deal with that.'

Meanwhile, however, unbeknown to these journalists, people they had 'trusted and let into the process' took a copy of the emails and leaked a selection of them to the *Sunday Times* and *City Press*.[2] On Sunday 28 May 2017, while the ANC's NEC was meeting in Pretoria, these newspapers led with stories headlined, respectively, 'Exposed: Explosive Gupta e-mails at the heart of state capture' and 'Zuma's Dubai exit plan'. In an editorial, the editors of amaBhungane and the *Daily Maverick* speculated that the 'misguided' people who had caused the emails to be leaked to the newspapers had tried to influence the NEC to recall Zuma. 'They failed,' the writers said.[3]

But, either way, the cat was out of the bag and there was no longer a reason to hold back on releasing the information. And over the next few months a series of revelations was unleashed on South Africa. In a highly competitive media industry, it is unusual for competing publications to cooperate when big scoops are at stake. But this story was too big for one title to do justice to it, so News24, the country's largest online publication, joined forces with amaBhungane and the *Daily Maverick* to process, investigate and publish the scandals emerging from the trove of documents. They were assisted by the data journalism organisation OpenUp and Finance Uncovered, a London-based investigative centre focusing on financial crime. Tiso Blackstar, the company that owns the *Sunday Times* and *Business Day*, dedicated a full-time team of reporters to work on the leaks and, three months later, more than 100 stories had been published by different media houses, detailing the depth of the rot South Africa had fallen into under Zupta rule. A website, gupta-leaks. com, was launched to showcase the reporting of the scandal through text, multimedia and video.

Despite the media activity, a state of inertia engulfed the law-enforcement agencies and three months after the first revelations from the leaks were published, no action had been taken by the police or the Hawks to secure the Guptas' computers' server or to conduct interviews with key witnesses or suspects. However, revelations about private-sector involvement in the Guptas' underhand business had led to the suspension of several executives and the establishment of forensic investigations at these companies and at SOEs.

Ashu Chawla is a busy man. The chief executive of the Gupta-owned Sahara Computers sends and receives hundreds of emails on a daily basis. Outside of his normal business correspondence, like receiving spreadsheets of computer sales and negotiating with suppliers of computer parts, Chawla also has other duties to fulfil for his demanding paymasters. These include organising extravagant weddings for Gupta family members, receiving and disseminating confidential government documents and organising passports and visas for family guests with senior Home Affairs officials.

If Chawla had known that his inbox would be leaked to the media, he may have been more circumspect about what he received and sent online. What is clear from the #GuptaLeaks is that Chawla is an important cog in the Gupta business machine. He is a trusted and loyal lieutenant who has come a long way with the family, having joined Atul Gupta's small computer company in the late 1990s. Chawla is often copied in on very sensitive communication that has no bearing on Sahara.

Opening Chawla's inbox is an overwhelming experience. It contains thousands of emails he received and sent over a five-year period. Among them are hundreds of pictures and messages relating to the wedding of the Guptas' niece, Vega Gupta, and Aakash Jahajgarhia at Sun City in 2013. Chawla was in correspondence with the three Gupta brothers and Duduzane Zuma.

A large part of the initial journalistic investigation entailed converting the emails and documents into a searchable format. It is not humanly possible to read through each and every email, which is why searching for the right people and topics was pivotal.

Of the huge number of initial stories that have now been published, these ten have caused the biggest fallout from the #GuptaLeaks so far. But this scandal is by no means over – the butterfly has just started to flap her wings.

1. Transnet and the locomotives bribe

The emails revealed that Gupta business partner Salim Essa signed what was effectively a kickback agreement with China South Rail, the company that won the tender to supply 359 locomotives to Transnet (the details have been covered in Chapter 8). Essa's Hong Kong-based Tequesta was 'contracted' by the Chinese for its 'familiarity with [the] regulatory, social, cultural and political framework' in South Africa.[4]

And what exactly did this mean? A clue could be found in the contract, which stipulated that Tequesta did not have to provide proof for its services rendered 'since it is understood that the project would not have materialised without the active efforts of Tequesta to provide the services listed above'. Which in plain English means: Tequesta got us the tender.

For its 'efforts', the company received an advisory fee of 21%, which translates to R3,8 billion plus a further R1,5 billion for two smaller Transnet tenders that China South Rail won.

Result: Following the exposé, Transnet appointed Werksmans Attorneys to conduct a forensic probe into the allegations.

2. The capture of Duduzane

One of the biggest revelations of the Gupta leaks was the extent to which Zuma's son Duduzane had become part of the Gupta empire and was acting as a proxy for his father in the machinery set up to capture the state. Besides the largesse that was bestowed on him, including a luxury apartment in Dubai and bankrolling his lavish wedding, at least two senior government appointments and a meeting with a controversial Russian oligarch prove his influence and role in the Zupta syndicate.

In December 2014, Duduzane was contacted by Russian investment firm Sistema with a request to organise a meeting between the company's chairman, Vladimir Yevtushenkov, and Jacob Zuma at the World Economic Forum in Davos in January 2015. This was a few months after Yevtushenkov was placed under house arrest for alleged money laundering, of which he was later cleared.[5] After the WEF conference, Duduzane was thanked by Sistema's managing director Evgeniy Chuikov for setting up the meetings and given a list of possible business opportunities between Sistema and the South African Government.[6]

On 29 June 2015, a secretive email was sent to Duduzane from someone called 'Business Man'. The email had attached to it the CV of Richard Seleke, the head of the Free State Provincial Department of Economic Development, Tourism and Environmental Affairs. The body of the email read: 'Evening sir, please find attached my CV and supporting documents. Regards, Richard.'[7] A few months later, Seleke was appointed by Cabinet, headed by Duduzane's father, as director general of public enterprises, overseeing SOEs Eskom, Denel and Transnet.

On 1 August 2015, Duduzane received the CV of Mosebenzi Zwane from Tony Gupta via email. At the time, Zwane was MEC for agriculture in the Free State and had benefited the Guptas through the Estina dairy farm project. Once again, sending a CV to Zuma Jr got the required outcome: on 23 September 2015, Zwane was appointed mining minister by Zuma (see Chapter 9 for more).[8]

Result: OUTA laid charges of treason, extortion, racketeering, fraud and forgery against Duduzane and the Gupta brothers following the #GuptaLeaks.

3. Bell Pottinger and fake news

The leaks have laid bare the mechanics of a public-relations campaign drafted in Britain by the notorious spin machine Bell Pottinger for their clients, the Gupta family and Duduzane Zuma, to counter negative press the family received in South Africa, particularly after the firing of Nene by Zuma in December 2015.

Briefing notes and emails showed how Duduzane met Bell Pottinger partner Victoria Geoghegan in January 2016 to strategise a campaign that highlighted 'economic apartheid' in South Africa and how Geoghegan bought into the narrative that South Africa's economy was run by a small group of white people. Geoghegan and her colleagues helped develop this narrative in speeches by leaders from the ANCYL and MKMVA – two organisations firmly in Zuma's corner.

The purpose of the campaign was to influence the 2016 local-government election in favour of the ANC and, in Duduzane's words, to 'turn the tide of our country's trajectory in the long term'.[9] Bell Pottinger was also contracted to assist with the 'setting up of a vehicle'[10] to be the public face of the narrative, which many believe led to the Guptas contracting with Andile Mngxitama and his Black First Land First organisation. In one instance, Mngxitama was briefed by the Guptas to write an article attacking a business publication.

The campaign had many shapes and ultimately culminated in an unsophisticated, crude social-media strategy to target so-called 'white monopoly capital' and its supporters in the media through fake Twitter bots and websites run from Israel and India.

Result: In July 2017 Bell Pottinger apologised to South Africa for their work for the Guptas, fired Geoghegan and suspended three employees. In August 2017, the UK regulatory body Public Relations and Communications Association conducted a hearing into Bell Pottinger after the DA lodged a formal complaint. The association found them guilty, which led to the resignation of CEO James Henderson. The firm went into business rescue in September 2017.

4. How the Free State government paid for the Sun City wedding

Unlike contact crimes, financial crimes, like corruption, fraud and money laundering, often don't have a direct, visible victim. It is hard to fathom the enormity and impact of government money being stolen or diverted when you don't see the face of neglect.

In the case of the Estina dairy project, the Gupta leaks showed exactly who suffered from the R200 million plus being paid to the Guptas for a failed farming project: the people of the Free State.

With a limited budget and agriculture as its only major source of economic activity, the province needs every cent of taxpayers' money to provide and deliver basic services to its residents. For years, the Free State health department, for example, has suffered to provide antiretrovirals and basic medical care for its citizens.

But in 2013, the provincial agriculture department, then led by Zwane, paid over R200 million to a Gupta front company called Estina, of which very little was invested back into the dairy farm near Vrede in the Free State.

The Gupta leaks show how the money was laundered through Dubai, some of it (R30 million to be precise) coming back to South Africa to pay for the lavish Gupta wedding at Sun City in April 2013.[11] The Guptas and their enablers – including audit firm KPMG, who didn't pick up the suspicious transactions and whose then CEO, Moses Kgosana, attended the wedding and gushed about it afterwards in emails to Atul Gupta – had no qualms diverting much-needed government money to a luxury family wedding.

Result: KPMG CEO Trevor Hoole and seven executives resigned in the wake of damaging findings by KPMG International that the firm lowered its standards for the Guptas. The firm further withdrew a forensic report into the so-called 'rogue unit' at SARS. Other private companies followed asset management firm Sygnia in dropping KPMG as its auditor. Business Leadership SA suspended KPMG as a member pending an investigation, and Moses Kgosana resigned from the board of Alexander Forbes.

5. Whites only and black monkeys
The Gupta leaks confirmed previous reports that had noted the racist attitudes of Gupta family members and staff towards black people.

The same family that contracted Bell Pottinger to craft a strategy that supposedly viewed 'white monopoly capital' as racism, insisted on white waiting staff and butlers at their niece's infamous Sun City wedding in 2013.[12] The family also demanded white-only masseuses to treat their guests at the wedding – a request that was turned down by the resort spa.

In 2012 Tony Gupta allegedly called black security guards at the family's Johannesburg home 'monkeys' after they did not respond to him.[13] This was detailed in complaints found in the emails.

Further proof of the Guptas' racial prejudices was found in an email concerning a tenant applicant for one of the Guptas' many properties, a flat in Cape Town. A Sahara staffer emailed Atul Gupta to say he had found a tenant but that 'he is Nigerian … Still looking for someone else'.[14] Atul Gupta responded, 'No to point one', in reference to the employee's remark about the potential tenant being Nigerian.

When the Guptas' mining company Tegeta wanted to hire an office administrator, director Ankur Sharma emailed Ashu Chawla, CEO of Sahara, that he was looking for a 'senior old white lady with good experience'.[15]

The Guptas rejected allegations of racism with 'contempt'.[16]

6. Multinational kickbacks

Two German multinational software companies, a Swiss-based crane builder and a Chinese company specialising in heavy-duty machines were ensnared in dodgy payments to obscure companies linked to the Guptas for tenders they had won at Transnet, the Gupta leaks revealed.

Software giant SAP paid almost R100 million to a Gupta-controlled company called CAD House, which specialises in selling 3D printers.[17] The purpose of the payments was not for SAP to purchase such printers, but rather as commissions to secure contracts from Transnet, which has annual revenue of about R60 billion. An analysis of financial statements shows that CAD House was effectively a front company for the Guptas, through which SAP payments were funnelled to other Gupta entities.

Between them, Liebherr-International AG (Switzerland) and Shanghai Zhenhua Heavy Industries (China) paid more than R100 million to Gupta companies after they had been awarded massive tenders by Transnet to supply cranes to the country's ports.[18] Shanghai Zhenhua built seven ship-to-shore cranes at Durban harbour at a cost of about R1,2 billion and transferred almost R55 million to a Gupta company registered in the United Arab Emirates (UAE). Liebherr, which delivered 22 cranes to Transnet, paid almost R55 million to another Gupta UAE front company, some of which was transferred to Gupta family members in the US.[19]

Also uncovered in the emails were apparent kickback agreements between German computer company Software AG and Global Softech Solutions, an IT services company that the Guptas were in the process of buying into. Software AG turned to the Guptas to try to secure tenders from Transnet, Sasol, MultiChoice, the Department of Correctional Services and Mangaung Municipality.[20]

Results: After the revelations came to light, SAP suspended four country managers and instituted an anti-corruption probe by an international law firm. Software AG launched an internal review.

7. A captured Presidency

The Gupta leaks reveal that at least four senior officials close to Zuma had interacted with or benefited from the Guptas.

Major General Mxolisi Dladla, head of Zuma's protection service and his long-time bodyguard, lived in a house owned by a Gupta company.[21] The Guptas also bought tickets for Dladla and his then wife, Presidency official Mogotladi Mogano, to go on holiday to the Maldives. Dladla and Mogano claimed they never used the tickets.[22]

Dladla assisted the Guptas with transport fitted with blue lights to the Sun City wedding. The transport was provided by a company owned by Phineas Manthata, a businessman who provides blue lights to the police service. Manthata paid R700 000 towards the purchase of a house for Dladla in 2012.[23]

Mogano was co-director of a dormant company with Tony Gupta and Duduzane Zuma. She says it never traded.[24] Mogano sent her CV to Tony Gupta for a job offer in 2011 and attended the Sun City wedding in 2013. She says her association with the Guptas did not influence her work, but that she had 'learnt from recent events to be more vigilant and judicious in professional relationships'.[25]

Lakela Kaunda, chief operating officer in the Presidency and trusted Zuma loyalist, entertained the idea of going into business with the Guptas, and sent Tony Gupta her company's details. She later declined the 'business opportunity' and says she is not involved with the family's enterprises.[26]

Delsey Sithole, Zuma's former private secretary and current director of events and protocol in the Presidency, received a small cash payment from the Guptas shortly after Zuma became president.[27] She was invited by the Guptas to their box at the 2010 Fifa World Cup, attended the Sun City wedding and sent Tony Gupta guest lists of Zuma's functions. The name of Sithole's husband, former SACP leader Justice Piitso, was included on the list of pro-Gupta commentators.[28]

8. All the President's men – and women

At least six of Zuma's Cabinet ministers were linked to the Guptas through the leaked emails. They are Malusi Gigaba (finance minister and former minister of home affairs and public enterprises); Mosebenzi Zwane (mining minister); Faith Muthambi (public service and administration minister, and former minister of communications); Ayanda Dlodlo (minister of communications); Des van Rooyen (cooperative governance minister and former finance minister) and Lynne Brown (public enterprises minister).

The emails revealed that Gigaba, at least through his legal advisor and home affairs officials, helped the Guptas obtain and fast-track visas for family and staff from India and Dubai. Gigaba isn't directly implicated, but home affairs staff refer in emails to an 'instruction' by him to move two officials to Mumbai and New Delhi to assist the Guptas.[29] Gigaba's advisor, Thamsanqa Msomi, emerges as a key helper of the Guptas inside home affairs.[30]

Of all the politicians and civil servants captured by the Guptas, Zwane is right up there. His entire career as mining minister has Gupta written all over it – from his appointment, where his CV landed up with Duduzane Zuma through the Guptas, to his private flights on the Gupta jet to secure Tegeta's purchase of the Optimum coal mine from Glencore. The Guptas also sponsored his visits to Dubai and even had his medical records in their possession, after they paid for him to visit India for medical treatment.[31] As Free State MEC for agriculture, Zwane approved the payment of over R200 million to the Guptas' failed dairy farm outside Vrede, his home town.

Muthambi may have broken the law by sending confidential Cabinet information to Tony Gupta and Chawla. The emails show how Muthambi discussed her previous portfolio, including proposed police and legislative changes, with the Guptas. This included sending a confidential memorandum by Telecommunications Minister Siyabonga Cwele to Chawla.[32]

Dlodlo was one of a plethora of politicians and civil servants to visit Dubai, where the Guptas stashed their cash and bought luxurious property. In December 2015, Dlodlo – then Deputy Minister of Public Service and Administration – stayed at the Oberoi, a five-star hotel in Dubai. Although the Guptas arranged her trip, arms deal 'playboy' Fana Hlongwane paid for her massages, room service, accommodation and car hire. Dlodlo didn't declare the trip to Parliament and said it was an 'arrangement between Fana and I', whom she had known since she was a child.[33]

Van Rooyen was caught in a lie by the leaks, which showed that the Guptas paid for his visit to Dubai shortly after he was appointed finance minister (for a few days) in December 2015. Van Rooyen had previously denied that the Guptas paid for the trip, but the emails prove that they sponsored his hotel stay at the Oberoi and his chauffeur-driven Jaguar.

Although Brown wasn't personally implicated in the emails, proof that her personal assistant, Kim Davids, visited Dubai courtesy of the Guptas was found in the leaks. The Guptas paid for Davids's stay at the Oberoi and for her chauffeur ride to the family's sprawling estate in Emirates Hills. Brown asked Davids to resign in the wake of the revelations.

9. Gupta Intelligence Agency
An Excel spreadsheet in the Gupta leaks with the title 'As1.xlsx' reveals that the family kept a close eye on their enemies and competitors. The document contains the flight records and ID numbers of several prominent South African businesspeople and others, including Manuel and Malema. The Guptas would have needed a deep throat in home affairs to provide them with this confidential information.

The businesspeople who were spied on were FirstRand founders Paul Harris, Laurie Dippenaar and GT Ferreira; Dimension Data chair Jeremy Ord; Investec CEO Stephen Koseff and Absa CEO Maria Ramos.

Results: Malema said he would take up the matter with the Inspector General of Intelligence. Ramos and Manuel said the breach of privacy amounted to criminal conduct and they were considering their legal options.[34]

10. All roads lead to Dubai

The other City of Gold, Dubai, is at the centre of the Gupta family's empire and efforts to capture the South African state. Although the family still has strong ties to India and has family there, Dubai has become their second home outside of India, if South Africa is their first.

The Gupta leaks have shown the extent to which the family is invested in Dubai – through expensive property, a string of companies and regular trips in their private jet. In July 2015, the family acquired a luxury mansion with ten bedrooms and 13 bathrooms in the exclusive Emirates Hills suburb for R331 million. In 2016 they bought an R18 million apartment in the exclusive Burj Khalifa building for Duduzane Zuma.

Included in the leaks are two unsigned letters written in Jacob Zuma's name to the vice president and prime minister of Dubai, Sheikh Mohammed Bin Rashid Al Maktoum, and the crown prince of Abu Dhabi, General Sheikh Mohammed Bin Zayed Al Nahyan, in which Zuma supposedly advises them that his family had decided to make the UAE their second home and asks to gain their 'patronage during our proposed residency in the UAE'.[35] Zuma has denied knowledge of the letters, although they were sent to Duduzane.

The leaks also show extensively how companies in Dubai were used as a 'laundromat' to wash money made from deals with South African entities through intricate consultancy or shareholding agreements.

The leaks contain proof of a flurry of visits to Dubai by South African politicians and state apparatchiks, particularly in and around December 2015 when Van Rooyen replaced Nene as finance minister, before he was abruptly replaced by Gordhan, and when the Optimum transaction went through. The modus operandi for all the visits was the same: they were booked into the Oberoi and had chauffeurs to drive them to and from the Guptas' mansion. The following people all visited Dubai in December 2015 and January 2016: Zwane, Dlodlo, Thato and Tshepiso Magashule (Free State premier Ace Magashule's sons); Hlongwane; Eskom's Anoj Singh; Van Rooyen; Davids; Denel chairman Dan Mantsha; Eskom boss Matshela Koko; Duduzane Zuma and Transnet CEO Siyabonga Gama.

If our criminal-justice system were functioning, a task team staffed with senior commercial-crimes investigators, prosecutors and analysts would have been appointed shortly after the leaks dropped at the end of May 2017. But while Zuma was controlling the state, it seemed almost impossible that a criminal empire so closely intertwined with his personal fortunes would be brought to book.

Nevertheless, the action taken by private companies and SOEs implicated in the Gupta leaks is a good start and could well trigger further civil and criminal action. Although we are still far from the state-capture trials, that must naturally follow Zuma's exit as head of state. There were also encouraging signs that not all senior ANC leaders had their heads in the sand about the enormity and impact of these revelations.

Speaking at the ANC's mid-year policy conference in Johannesburg, Mantashe said that individuals who were implicated should own up and come clean. He warned that 'regime change' rhetoric shouldn't be used to deflect attention away from allegations of corruption and state capture.[36] The ANC came out in support of a judicial commission of inquiry into state capture, although Zuma was still challenging former Public Protector Madonsela's damning report on the matter in court by mid-2017.

CHAPTER 24

Death race to December

▬

'*This shit is escalating. I can only hope that it doesn't
get worse before and after December.*'

– Tweet by Themba Maseko, former government spokesperson, 2 September 2017

'*Sadly, I think it is going to get worse.
It's not just about winning, it's about annihilation.*'

– Reply by Nomboniso Gasa, writer and activist

Steyn Speed, the veteran political operator and consummate party
man, was looking more worried than usual on Saturday night,
2 September 2017, as he paced up and down the corridor outside of
courtroom 9E at the High Court in downtown Johannesburg.

He has seen it all: as ANC spokesperson and a member of Luthuli
House's bureaucracy in 2006 and 2007, he helped manage the fallout
from the battle between Mbeki and Zuma before and after Polokwane.
He saw the Zuma takeover first-hand and left the party shortly after
that to try his hand at business, eventually landing up at Ramaphosa's
investment firm, Shanduka.

Now he has returned to the fold, following his boss, Ramaphosa,
back into active politics. He works as an advisor to the deputy president,
helping to manage his campaign for the ANC presidency and shaping
the message that CR17 – the social-media moniker that the Ramaphosa

campaign goes by – wants to repair the fractured ANC and stop the looting of state coffers.

The dirty-tricks campaign had started in all seriousness. Ramaphosa was attempting to interdict the editor of the Iqbal Survè-owned *Sunday Independent*, Steven Motale, from publishing salacious details of a series of email exchanges between Ramaphosa and as many as eight women. These emails purportedly show how Ramaphosa has been involved in numerous extramarital affairs, with one exchange allegedly revealing a miscarriage of a baby conceived by Ramaphosa.

Details of the impending front-page splash began circulating the day before, when Motale's email with his very detailed questions to Ramaphosa began doing the rounds on social media. The deputy president reacted angrily, issuing an elaborate statement on 2 September 2017, slamming the 'invasion of privacy'. The 'DP', as his advisors and support staff refer to him, said he was the latest victim of a concerted campaign to smear and discredit people who have taken a public stand against state capture and the looting of public resources. More worryingly, he saw the hand of state-intelligence agencies in the smears – agencies led by Mahlobo, the Minister of State Security and a key Zuma man:

> It is evident that there is a well-resourced, coordinated covert operation underway to prevent those responsible for wrongdoing from being held to account and for the integrity of our law enforcement agencies and other state institutions to be restored. This operation appears to have access to resources within intelligence circles with the capability to intercept communications and hack private emails. We now need to confront the likelihood that state agencies and resources are being abused to promote factional political agendas. We also need to confront the reality that those behind these agendas will go to any length to protect themselves and their interests. We need to ask who these people are. And on whose behalf they act.[1]

Just before Judge Bashier Vally dismissed Ramaphosa's application with cost, Speed wouldn't confirm or deny the authenticity of the emails

– just like his boss, who didn't make an explicit denial about their content in his statement. 'It could get worse,' Speed said. 'We're expecting it to get worse.'

After Vally handed down judgment – saying Ramaphosa hadn't provided him with a compelling enough argument about why he should stop publication – Andile Mngxitama, the loud-mouthed, Gupta-supporting leader of the fascist movement Black First Land First, crowed triumphantly: 'The buffalo is going down!' That with reference to Ramaphosa's known penchant for purchasing expensive breeding buffalo. Motale, surrounded by bodyguards, was hugged by Kenny Kunene, a socialite and convicted criminal, and mobbed by a team from the Guptas' ANN7. The *Sunday Independent* got the go-ahead to run the story and on Sunday morning, 3 September 2017, South Africans woke up to the headline, 'Ramaphosa "the Player": Cyril in bid to gag paper, womanising e-mail shock'.

The death race to December had kicked into overdrive. Speed had his work cut out for him.

When Ramaphosa agreed to the position of deputy president on Jacob Zuma's ticket at the ANC's elective conference in December 2012, many observers were surprised. Zuma's presidency had by then been tainted by allegations of corruption and malfeasance, and Deputy President Kgalema Motlanthe at the time decided to oppose Zuma as a matter of principle. It seemed odd that someone of Ramaphosa's stature – one of the Constitution's midwives and a successful businessman – would want to hitch a ride on the Nkandla wagon.

Ramaphosa had also been in the political wilderness for a decade and a half, after having been outmanoeuvred by Mbeki at the party's 1997 elective conference. Even though he had been elected to the NEC before assuming the deputy presidency in 2012, he had played no role in national politics, preferring to focus on building a vast business empire and dabbling in game farming. In 2009 Manuel, the finance minister who was sacrificed on the altar of Polokwane to appease Zuma's coalition, brought him back into the fold as deputy chair of the newly established National Planning Commission, a body that was to oversee the government-wide implementation of strategic initiatives.

But Ramaphosa had always wanted to be president. It was widely known that the ANC's former chief negotiator and chairperson of the Constituent Assembly – which oversaw the drafting of the Constitution – was Mandela's choice to succeed him. Mbeki thwarted those ambitions, but Zuma gave him another shot at realising his ambition. Ramaphosa dutifully played his part as the supporting act in the presidency, often receiving hospital passes in the form of e-tolls, the SAA and Eskom to sort out.

But Zuma, increasingly scheming and manipulative in his attempt to stay out of jail after his term of office ends, did not support Ramaphosa's plans to become the ANC president in 2017 and head of state in 2019, even though he has conceded that ANC tradition dictates that the deputy president is the natural presidential successor.

It's difficult to pinpoint precisely when Ramaphosa decided to actively start campaigning for the ANC presidency. His advisors had since mid-2016 been explaining that just because Ramaphosa had been rather mute in his condemnation of the Nkandla alterations, even after the subsequent findings by the Constitutional Court, and reticent about the ANC's disastrous results in the 2016 municipal elections and the Public Protector's report into state capture, one should not infer that he wasn't committed to challenging the corrupt status quo in the party and the authorities. 'It's all about timing,' one advisor countered when asked about Ramaphosa's apparent lethargy. 'If we get it wrong, it's over. When you want to kill the king, you have to make sure it's a head shot. Otherwise he'll take you out.'[2]

On 25 August 2016, Ramaphosa put his toe into the murky, shark-infested succession waters, delivering a eulogy at the funeral of the ANC stalwart and former sports minister, Makhenkesi Stofile. Speaking alongside Sipho Pityana, the outspoken chair of the Save South Africa movement, Ramaphosa said the ANC 'now more than ever' needs leaders who subscribe to the party's historical values of selflessness. 'We need people who will not succumb to the temptations of public office; who will not take for themselves what rightly belongs to the masses,' he told mourners.[3] While he was loath to openly criticise Zuma and his associates, he routinely railed against corruption and malfeasance, but always in such a manner that the president couldn't accuse him of any direct attacks.

This line of strategic water treading was brought to an abrupt end, however, when Zuma fired Gordhan on 31 March 2017. Ramaphosa came out strongly against the decision, condemning the Cabinet reshuffle as 'unacceptable'. He was forced to recant less than a week later, however, by the Zuma faction on the ANC's National Working Committee, who said he had broken party discipline by speaking out.

Ramaphosa's real coming out was in July 2017, during the SACP's national conference in Boksburg, when he delivered an impassioned speech – at least by his standards – saying 'the house is burning' and calling for a judicial commission of inquiry into state capture. This was a frontal attack on President Zuma, Duduzane Zuma and their friends and business partners, the Gupta family. 'We now know without any shred of uncertainty that billions of rands of public resources have been diverted into the pockets of a few. We also know that we as taxpayers in this country also paid for a lavish wedding that took place in Sun City. These are resources that rightly belong to the people of South Africa,' he said.[4]

It's clear that Ramaphosa wants the presidency, but it's unclear how desperate he is to move into the office. His opponents will stop at nothing to prevent him – even hacking into his private Gmail account if needs be. Polokwane 2007 was a dirty fight, but Nasrec 2017 is being fought in the gutters.

Dlamini-Zuma is the other main challenger for the post. A medical doctor and bureaucrat with no obvious charm or personality, she lacks the warmth and character of Ramaphosa, her main opponent in the build-up to the December conference. She, however, makes up for that in spades with institutional and ground-level support within the ANC, benefiting from the advantages given her by her former husband and the state, which provide her with security.

She has openly campaigned for the party top job ever since her return from Addis Ababa in March 2017, where she served a five-year term as head of the African Union Commission. Febe Potgieter-Gqubule, a former advisor at the African Union and her spokesperson, dismisses talk of Dlamini-Zuma as being a difficult person. 'I think she's an introvert and shy. But she also likes things done. When things don't get done, she speaks plainly, which people don't like. She is very approachable once you get to know her.'[5]

Dlamini-Zuma is one of the most experienced politicians in the country, having served as Minister of Health in Mandela's Cabinet, Minister of Foreign Affairs under Mbeki and Motlanthe, and Minister of Home Affairs under Zuma, before being packed off to East Africa. Besides being a party loyalist, she is considered a technocrat who knows the Byzantine ways of government inside out. She is credited with helping to turn around the flailing Department of Home Affairs, modernising and revamping internal processes and improving systems. She was largely overshadowed by Mbeki while she was Minister of Foreign Affairs, as the president preferred to conduct matters of international relations on his own, with Dlamini-Zuma often merely acting as a conduit for his ideas. Her record was marred by one of the first post-apartheid government scandals, when, in 1995, without following proper procedure, she allocated almost R15 million to playwright Mbongeni Ngema to produce a theatre production called *Sarafina II*. The Public Protector later found that the contract should not have been awarded and that Dlamini-Zuma's public pronouncements on the matter were false.

Her campaign is nothing like Ramaphosa's, who has a day job as the deputy president. Dlamini-Zuma has been free to roam the country, on the back of government security and transport (due to her status as former AU commissioner, considered equal to that of a former head of state[6]), and with the ANC Women's League and military veterans' association as chief organisers. She has regularly appeared on stage in KwaZulu-Natal, North West and Gauteng, delivering staid and lacklustre speeches to rack up support among ANC delegates ahead of the elective conference. Her message has centred on the Gupta- and Bell Pottinger-inspired theorem of radical economic transformation, cheerled by the disgraced Bathabile Dlamini, who leads the Women's League, and Carl Niehaus, the equally disgraced national spokesperson of the MKMVA. Dlamini-Zuma's campaign, although visible and active, seems to oscillate between radical populism and pragmatic realism, often trying to combine the two.

Dlamini-Zuma was sworn in as MP on 21 September 2017, giving rise to speculation that it might be a precursor to her being elevated to Cabinet. Of course, it also ensures a steady income for private citizen Dlamini-Zuma.

During a speech at the University of Pretoria's Gordon Institute of Business Science on 29 August 2017, she berated big business for not investing huge surplus funds in the economy while government was running a budget deficit. She did, however, acknowledge that government and the private sector need to find common ground to address poverty and unemployment. The written version of her speech – distributed afterwards – was almost totally different, though, attacking, as it did, the SARB's independence and slamming white monopoly capital and their 'imperialist backers'.

But whether Dlamini-Zuma really wants to be president or whether she's a Manchurian candidate remains to be seen. Whether she is addressing supporters or the general public, on the campaign trail in Soweto, or in front of business leaders, Dlamini-Zuma seems lethargic and uninterested. She does not engage her audience, she doesn't crack jokes or entertain any banter and she rarely speaks off the cuff. The former AU chair has been firm in her conviction that she's her own woman, and not kept by her former husband. Her lack of enthusiasm, though, suggests otherwise.

The months leading up to the elective conference were marked by tumult and dissent. The ANC's national policy conference in July ended in stalemate, with both the Ramaphosa and Dlamini-Zuma camps claiming ideological victory, while the growing internal revolt inside the ANC against Zuma came to a head in the motion of no confidence in August, with a significant number of ANC MPs voting in favour of the DA-led motion to remove Zuma.

The policy conference is held in the same year as the elective conference and is ostensibly convened to discuss the various policy positions the party is set to debate in December. In reality, however, it serves as a dress rehearsal for the leadership race, with policy discussions used as proxies to test support and determine weaknesses. The 2017 event pivoted on the question of white monopoly capital, the Gupta phrase introduced into the broad political lexicon by ANN7, polished by Bell Pottinger and conceived by Duduzane Zuma and Victoria Geoghegan. When Joel Netshitenzhe, the respected ANC policy guru, said at the conference that the Economic Transformation Commission rejected the characterisation of 'monopoly capital' as 'white', there was outrage and he was attacked from all sides – especially by the Gupta-ANN7-Manyi and Dlamini-Zuma axis – as ill-disciplined and untruthful. There were other ideological battlegrounds between the camps as well – land reform without compensation gained traction (with the caveat that it must happen within the bounds of the Constitution), as did the controversial mining charter, driven by the Guptarised Minister of Mineral Resources, Zwane.

Zuma, as is his wont, looked every bit in control of the party during the opening and closing addresses at Nasrec, even singing and dancing with Ramaphosa and inviting Dlamini-Zuma to join them. Dlamini-Zuma is Zuma's favoured candidate. And, although her camp could not claim victory at the conference, Zuma was buoyed by the strong support emanating from the provincial hinterlands, where his operatives in KwaZulu-Natal, the Free State and North West were mobilising strong support for Dlamini-Zuma at branch level.

But trouble was brewing. In Mpumalanga, premier David Mabuza was starting to grow restless, engaging in conversations with Paul Mashatile from Gauteng and fuelling speculation that he was keen to switch sides. In KwaZulu-Natal, the High Court declared the 2015 provincial elective conference null and void, which has far-reaching consequences for the national elective conference in December. Sihle Zikalala, a Zuma loyalist, served as provincial secretary since the disputed election, but now his predecessor, Senzo Mchunu, aligned to Ramaphosa, has been given a second bite at the cherry. KwaZulu-Natal is the biggest of all the ANC's regions and whoever controls the province has the shortest route to clinch the party's leadership. A divided KwaZulu-Natal spells trouble for Zuma's ambitions to entrench his dynasty and remain out of court.

The ANC was shaken by the parliamentary motion of no confidence tabled against the president on 8 August 2017. Although the motion was defeated by 198 votes to 177, the ANC failed to garner a majority of 200 plus one, and more than 30 ANC MPs voted with the opposition motion, which was conducted by secret ballot after a Constitutional Court challenge. Gordhan, Makhosi Khoza, an MP from KwaZulu-Natal, and Derek Hanekom, the fired Minister of Tourism, became the faces of the revolt, openly declaring their intention to vote with their conscience and decrying the continuing looting of state resources, endemic corruption in the state and party, and the feeding trough that SOEs had become. All three were subsequently harassed by the party. Manuel was asked by the Hawks to provide a statement in connection with the SARS High-Risk Investigations Unit, with Gordhan saying, 'they will probably charge us'.[7] Khoza, who resigned from the party on 21 September 2017 saying the ANC 'won't self-correct',[8] was charged with ill-discipline, while Hanekom was asked by Mantashe to provide reasons why he should not be removed as chairperson of the ANC's National Disciplinary Committee. Zuma and the rent-seekers brook no opposition, whether it is rooted in the rule of law or not.

The ANC elects its president every five years, with delegates drawn from the party's nine provinces who cast their votes for the top six positions and the NEC, the party's highest decision-making body.

The regional delegations consist of branch delegates and are proportional to the number of members and branches in those provinces that are 'in good standing', in other words whose membership fees are paid up. These branches are audited by the office of the secretary general, who tallies and finalises the number of delegates each province is allowed to send to the conference. It is these delegates – an electoral college of about 4 000 members – who then have voting rights at the conference and who determine who South Africa's next president will be.

Although the public and the media see Ramaphosa decrying rent-seeking and state capture in his campaign, and they witness the dour Dlamini-Zuma rattling off speeches in support of radical economic transformation, the real campaign is being fought away from the glare of cameras and prying journalists. The war for the post-Zuma era is being waged in hundreds of ANC branches dotted all over the country, out of sight and in closed meetings, where the threat of whole branches and provinces being bought off is very real. Mantashe, who has said he has no ambitions for higher office but whose name has been pencilled in on various slates, is in charge of branch auditing. This is done to ensure that there is no gerrymandering ahead of the conference. Any triumph needs to be built off the back of painstaking and repeated lobbying at branch level, trying to convince many who are willing to sell their vote to the highest bidder in order to get access to the rich network of patronage constructed by Zuma and his lieutenants in government and elsewhere. But it can also be done by buying whole branches or establishing 'ghost branches' that are there on paper, but which don't actually exist.

The key to a December win therefore lies at branch level in the provinces. But there are already fears of widespread collusion and corruption in the cooking of membership figures. Zweli Mkhize, the ANC's treasurer general, ordered investigations into the bulk buying of membership in KwaZulu-Natal, the Eastern Cape, Limpopo and Mpumalanga. In KwaZulu-Natal alone, the party was looking at the forging of 200 000 membership forms[9] – more than enough to skew proportional representation and sway the elective conference.

Zuma is pulling hard for Dlamini-Zuma, believing that if she wins he can cut a deal with her, so that the 18 charges of corruption and fraud (relating to 783 suspicious payments to him) go away. He also relies heavily on sentiment, and his former wife is close to his late wife Kate Mantsho's twins, Duduzane and Duduzile. A Dlamini-Zuma presidency, brought about by Zuma's support, will also enable Zuma to consolidate the dynasty he has established, including the expansive network of patronage. But there are no guarantees. Once Dlamini-Zuma ascends to the presidency, as Zuma hopes she will, she may well decide to clean up the rotten recesses of the Zuma executive and let the law run its course.

Ramaphosa meanwhile poses a clear and present danger to Zuma. He has built his campaign on a zero-tolerance approach to corruption and state capture, and has in the months since Gordhan's removal become increasingly vocal about the rot that has set in, in both party and state.

Zweli Mkhize has emerged as a dark horse, being touted as the 'unity candidate'. He seems to be the preferred choice for a number of provincial ANC chairmen, including Mpumalanga's David Mabuza and Gauteng's Paul Mashatile, who is alleged to be exploring different options from Ramaphosa and Dlamini-Zuma. And with Mkhize's clout in KwaZulu-Natal (he is a former premier) he might just throw a spanner in the works at Nasrec.

The elective conference will also be influenced by other minor candidates, such as Lindiwe Sisulu, a politician with lofty struggle credentials, and Baleka Mbete, Speaker of Parliament, who will play the gender card and test the ANC's verbal commitment to gender parity and female empowerment. If both or one of them is able to muster strong support, they will be able to play kingmaker (or queen maker) by pledging their support to either of the main candidates.

Besides these candidates, Minister in the Presidency Jeff Radebe and former ANC treasurer general Mathews Phosa have also launched official campaigns, with the latter being more vocal about change than the former, who is the longest-serving Cabinet member.

The smear campaign against Ramaphosa, however, which burst out into the open on the pages of the *Sunday Independent* in early

September, may indicate that 'Team NDZ' is taking strain and that it has to resort to nefarious tactics to bring down its opponent. And with rumours abounding that conditions might be created for the conference to be postponed, South Africa could be plunged into a period of political instability if the leadership race deteriorates any further. The Dlamini-Zuma camp, relying on Zuma's institutional and underhand support, has shown itself capable of playing a dirty and destructive game. If Ramaphosa is serious about clinching the leadership for himself he will arguably have to employ the same tactics.

Conventional wisdom seems to suggest that Nasrec will be a shoot-out between Ramaphosa and Dlamini-Zuma: the change candidate versus the incumbent's choice. Key points to consider:

- ❏ It has become increasingly clear that both major camps are following a winner-takes-all strategy, with very little room for compromise or rapprochement.
- ❏ But both need the support of various key players and influencers, and that's where horse-trading could get interesting.
- ❏ The so-called 'premier league', consisting of the premiers of KwaZulu-Natal, Free State, North West and Mpumalanga, seem to be at loggerheads, which means some provinces' support could be up for grabs.
- ❏ KwaZulu-Natal seems to be split, which is bad news for the Dlamini-Zuma campaign. The province remains the biggest and most influential in the ANC.
- ❏ Zweli Mkhize further dilutes the KwaZulu-Natal vote. He may prove to be the candidate that breaks the deadlock.
- ❏ The ANC's organisational structure is not federal in nature, which means delegates are technically not bound to regional or provincial decisions who to support or vote for.
- ❏ The self-sustaining and sprawling network of patronage and corruption in government and the ANC will seek to ensure its survival post Nasrec 2017. This means cutting deals with whichever candidate seems most likely to win.

❏ A unity result – which incorporates members of both the winners' and losers' camps – will represent a lifeline for the patronage network.

A clear and unambiguous Ramaphosa win could give the ANC a chance to repair the enormous damage state capture and corruption have done to the party. There is however widespread agreement that a victory by Dlamini-Zuma might entrench the status quo and could accelerate the party's undoubted decline. Whoever triumphs in December has the monumental challenge of saving the ANC from breaking down before the 2019 elections. To do this, the successful candidate will have to systematically rebuild democratic institutions left reeling after an eight-year Zunami that has taken Africa's oldest liberation movement to the brink of collapse. There is no consensus whether this is even possible. If the ANC fails, the country's future is in the hands of a brave new generation of young, diverse politicians and civil-society leaders who have previously succeeded in putting ideological differences aside to save South Africa.

Notes

Chapter 1: The coalition of the wounded

1 Party in Polokwane as Zuma sweeps to victory, IOL, 18 December 2007, https://www.iol.co.za/news/politics/party-in-polokwane-as-zuma-sweeps-to-victory-383197.

2 Transcript: Zwelinzima Vavi, head of COSATU, *Financial Times*, 12 December 2007, https://www.ft.com/content/e36a72a2-a8cf-11dc-ad9e-0000779fd2ac.

3 The people have taken back the party, *Sunday Independent*, 23 December 2007.

4 *The State v Schabir Shaik And Others*, 31 May 2005.

5 Blade Nzimande, The revolution is on trial: The 1996 Class Project behind the aloofness of style, *Umsebenzi*, vol. 6, no. 22, 5 December 2007, http://www.sacp.org.za/pubs/umsebenzi/2007/vol6-22.html.

6 Vavi: We'll take over the ANC, *Mail & Guardian*, 9 March 2007.

7 Department of Finance Budget Review, 22 June 1994.

8 See Nelson Mandela Foundation, 18 May 2017, https://www.nelsonmandela.org/news/entry/invitation-to-cover-mandelas-economic-legacy-dialogue.

9 Ibid.

10 Ibid.

11 William Mervin Gumede, *Thabo Mbeki and the battle for the soul of the ANC*, London and New York: Zed Books, 2007, p. 208.

12 Blade Nzimande, The revolution is on trial: The 1996 Class Project behind the aloofness of style, *Umsebenzi*, vol. 6, no. 22, 5 December 2007, http://www.sacp.org.za/pubs/umsebenzi/2007/vol6-22.html.

13 Sapa, Cosatu wants Zuma back as deputy, IOL, 16 August 2005, http://www.iol.co.za/news/politics/cosatu-wants-zuma-back-as-deputy-250987.

14 Sapa, Vavi 'smells victory' for Zuma, IOL, 5 September 2006, http://www.iol.co.za/news/south-africa/vavi-smells-victory-for-zuma-292447.

15 Transcript: Andrew Geoghegan, The World Today, 21 December 2007, http://www.abc.net.au/worldtoday/content/2007/s2125227.htm.

NOTES

Chapter 2: Cracks in the coalition

1 Sapa, Zuma charming, but a constitutional danger, says DA, *Mail & Guardian*, 10 December 2009, https://mg.co.za/article/2009-12-10-zuma-charming-but-a-constitutional-danger-says-da.

2 Jonny Steinberg, Julius Malema: The man who scarred South Africa, *The Guardian*, 10 February 2012, https://www.theguardian.com/world/2012/feb/10/julius-malema-south-africa-anc.

3 The Africa Confidential Interview: AC interviews Jacob Zuma, Africa Confidential, March 2006, https://www.africa-confidential.com/special-report/id/34/Jacob_Zuma.

4 Sapa, Reuters, Zuma lays into the Scorpions, *Mail & Guardian*, 21 September 2006, https://mg.co.za/article/2006-09-21-zuma-lays-into-the-scorpions.

5 Henry Cloete, Zuma 'persecuted like Christ', News24, 30 November 2008, http://www.news24.com/SouthAfrica/Politics/Zuma-persecuted-like-Christ-20081130?cpid=3.

6 Mike Cohen, South Africa to retain 'conservative' fiscal policy, Bloomberg, 29 April 2009.

7 Zuma sworn in as South African president, *Financial Times*, 10 May 2009, https://www.ft.com/content/05261106-3c88-11de-8b71-00144feabdc0.

8 ANC warns union, IOL, 28 May 2009, http://www.iol.co.za/news/politics/anc-warns-union-444738.

9 Lizel Steenkamp, *Vavi warsku korrupte politieke elite lei SA na 'n 'roofdierstaat'*, *Beeld*, 27 August 2010.

10 The Constitutional Court later found the awarding of the mining rights by the Department of Mineral Resources to ICT to have been illegal and irregular. ArcelorMittal also dropped plans to buy the company.

11 Anna Majavu, Elite 'spitting in faces of poor', *Sowetan*, 28 October 2010, http://www.sowetanlive.co.za/news/2010/10/28/elite-spitting-in-faces-of-poor.

12 Andisiwe Makinana, Malema issues warning to 'white monopoly', IOL, 20 June 2011, http://www.iol.co.za/news/politics/malema-issues-warning-to-white-monopoly-1085559.

13 Malema a leader in the making – Zuma, News24, 26 October 2009, http://www.news24.com/SouthAfrica/Politics/Malema-a-leader-in-the-making-Zuma-20091026.

14 Carien du Plessis and Warren Gwilt, ANC puts heat on Malema, IOL, 10 April 2010, http://www.iol.co.za/news/politics/anc-puts-heat-on-malema-480111.

15 ANC statement, 10 April 2010.

16 Carien du Plessis and Xolani Mbanjwa, Malema takes on Zuma, *Pretoria News*, 12 April 2010.

17 Cosatu CEC Political Discussion Paper, *The Alliance at a crossroads – the battle against a predatory elite and political paralysis*, September 2010, http://www.cosatu.org.za/docs/discussion/2010/dis0903.pdf.

18 Ibid.

19 Malema 'storms' NGC, *Saturday Star*, 25 September 2010, http://www.iol.co.za/news/south-africa/kwazulu-natal/malema-storms-ngc-681565.

20 Carien du Plessis, Malema attacks 'dictator' Zuma, *City Press*, 30 March 2012, http://city-press.news24.com/politics/malema-attacks-dictator-zuma-20120330.

21 No quick fix at Cosatu's Vavi meeting, IOL, 7 April 2014, http://www.iol.co.za/news/politics/no-quick-fix-at-cosatus-vavi-meeting-1562428.

22 Sam Mkokeli, Tripartite Alliance is dead, says Motlanthe, *Business Day*, 2 November 2015.

Chapter 3: The Mangaung whitewash

1 Chester Makana, SACP upset by 'vote buying', *The Star*, 21 November 2012, http://www.iol.co.za/the-star/sacp-upset-by-vote-buying-1427563.

2 Baldwin Ndaba, Vote-buying accusations levelled at EX-MEC, *The Star*, 26 November 2012.

3 Mia Lindeque, 'Blue light driver' sentenced to five years, Eyewitness News, 28 January 2015, http://ewn.co.za/2015/01/28/VIP-driver-sentenced-to-five-years-in-prison.

4 North West ANC secretary escapes assassination attempt, *City Press*, 30 November 2015, http://www.news24.com/Archives/City-Press/North-West-ANC-secretary-escapes-assassination-attempt-20150430.

5 Greg Marinovich and Thapelo Lekgowa (Newsfire), Mangaung: 'Forces of Change' delegates claim police brutality, *Mail & Guardian*, 20 December 2012, https://mg.co.za/article/2012-12-20-anc-north-west-cops-detain-and-beat-forces-of-change-delegates.

6 Gugu Phandle, Struggle for freedom still has long, hard road ahead, *Daily Dispatch*, 21 July 2014, http://www.dispatchlive.co.za/opinion/2014/07/21/struggle-for-freedom-still-has-long-hard-road-ahead/.

7 James Myburgh, Mangaung: Lessons from Polokwane, Politicsweb, 23 October 2012, http://www.politicsweb.co.za/opinion/mangaung-lessons-from-polokwane.

8 Ibid.

9 Zuma scolds 'clever' blacks, *City Press*, 3 November 2012, http://www.news24.com/Archives/City-Press/Zuma-scolds-clever-blacks-20150429.

10 Sipho Khumalo and Wendy Jasson da Costa, Mixed feelings on Ramaphosa bid, *The Mercury*, 18 December 2012, http://www.iol.co.za/news/politics/mixed-feelings-on-ramaphosa-bid-1442096.

11 Marietjie Gericke, Ramaphosa: 'Totally unacceptable' for JZ to fire Gordhan, Netwerk24, 31 March 2017, http://www.news24.com/SouthAfrica/News/ramaphosa-upset-but-wont-resign-20170331.

12 Derrick Spies, Ramaphosa 'launches' campaign with attack on Zuma, Guptas,

News24, 23 April 2017, http://www.news24.com/SouthAfrica/News/
ramaphosa-launches-campaign-with-attack-on-zuma-guptas-20170423.

13 Ibid.

Chapter 4: Pay back the money

1 Chris Roper, The day we broke Nkandla, *Mail & Guardian*, 4 December 2013,
   https://mg.co.za/article/2013-12-04-the-day-we-broke-nkandla.

2 The Presidency, Construction work at President Zuma's residence, 3 December
   2009.

3 Mandy Rossouw, Zuma's R65m Nkandla splurge, *Mail & Guardian*, 4 December
   2009, https://mg.co.za/article/2009-12-04-zumas-r65m-nkandla-splurge.

4 Sipho Masondo, What is VBS Mutual Bank? Everything you need to know, *City
   Press*, 23 September 2016, http://city-press.news24.com/News/
   what-is-vbs-mutual-bank-everything-you-need-to-know-20160922.

5 Gwen Mahlangu-Nkabinde, letter to Zuma titled Nkandla: Security installations
   at the private residence of His Excellency President Jacob Zuma, 5 November
   2010.

6 Matuma Letsoalo and Charles Molele, Bunker time: Zuma's lavish Nkandla
   upgrade, *Mail & Guardian*, 11 November 2011, https://mg.co.za/
   article/2011-11-11-bunker-time-for-zuma.

7 R200m splurge on Zuma homestead, *City Press*, 29 September 2012, http://www.
   news24.com/Archives/City-Press/R200m-splurge-on-Zuma-homestead-20150430.

8 Hansard, unrevised transcript, 15 November 2012.

9 Ibid.

10 Public Protector, Secure in Comfort, 19 March 2014, http://www.pprotect.org/
    library/investigation_report/2013-14/SECURE%20IN%20COMFORT.pdf.

11 Sam Sole and Lionel Faull, Who paid the R20m for Zuma's Nkandla houses?,
    Mail & Guardian, 6 June 2014, https://mg.co.za/article/2014-06-06-who-paid-the-
    r20m-for-zumas-nkandla-houses.

12 Gwen Mahlangu-Nkabinde, letter to Zuma titled Nkandla: Security installations at
    the private residence of His Excellency President Jacob Zuma, 5 November 2010.

13 Nickolaus Bauer, 'No evidence' public money spent on Nkandla, *Mail &
    Guardian*, 27 January 2013, https://mg.co.za/article/2013-01-27-no-evidence-
    public-money-spent-on-nkandla.

14 Ibid.

15 Thuli Madonsela, opposing affidavit, *The Minister of Police v The Public
    Protector*, 12 November 2013.

16 Public Protector, media statement, Public Protector welcomes Security Cluster
    Ministers' withdrawal of their court bid against her, 14 November 2013.

17 10 things worth knowing about Madonsela's Nkandla report, *City Press*,

19 March 2014, http://www.news24.com/Archives/City-Press/10-things-worth-knowing-about-Madonselas-Nkandla-report- 20150430.

18 Babalo Ndenze and Moloko Moloto, Zuma queries differences in Nkandla reports, *The Mercury*, 4 April 2014.

19 Ngwako Modjadji, President responds on Nkandla – finally, *The Citizen*, 15 August 2014.

20 Head rolls for Nkandla but …, *City Press*, 28 December 2014, http://www.news24.com/Archives/City-Press/Head-rolls-for-Nkandla-but-20150429.

21 Thomas Hartleb, Madonsela misled SA on Nkandla – ANC, News24, 30 July 2015, http://www.news24.com/SouthAfrica/News/Madonsela-misled-SA-on-Nkandla-ANC-20150730.

22 Annika Larsen, Zuma proposes Nkandla solution, eNCA, 2 February 2016, http://www.enca.com/south-africa/zuma-proposes-nkandla-solution.

23 ANC MPs turn on Zuma, *City Press*, 14 February 2016, http://city-press.news24.com/News/anc-mps-turn-on-zuma-20160213-2.

24 Nkandla matter traumatised SA – Zuma's lawyer, News24, 9 February 2016.

25 Camilla Bath, Stand-out quotes from the #Nkandla Concourt face-off, Eyewitness News, 9 February 2016, http://ewn.co.za/2016/02/09/Constitutional-Court-Nkandla-Stand-out-quotes.

26 *EFF v Speaker of the National Assembly and Others*, Constitutional Court, 31 March 2016.

Chapter 5: Meet the Guptas

1 Tshidi Madia, South Africans hate the Guptas because they are Indian – MKMVA, News24, 19 June 2017, http://www.news24.com/SouthAfrica/News/south-africans-hate-the-guptas-because-they-are-indian-mkmva-20170619.

2 Pieter-Louis Myburgh, *The Republic of Gupta: A story of state capture*, Cape Town: Penguin Books, 2017.

3 Thabo Mbeki, Book associating me with the Guptas is fake news, *Mail & Guardian*, 27 April 2017, https://mg.co.za/article/2017-04-27-thabo-mbeki-associating-me-with-the-guptas-is-fake-news.

4 Susan Comrie, The rise (and fall?) of Duduzane Zuma, *City Press*, 10 April 2016, http://city-press.news24.com/News/the-rise-and-fall-of-duduzane-zuma-20160409-2.

5 'I would've been further if my name wasn't Zuma', *City Press*, 6 March 2011, http://www.news24.com/SouthAfrica/Politics/I-would-have-been-further-if-my-surname-wasnt-Zuma-20110305-2.

6 #GuptaLeaks, Duduzane Zuma, kept and captured, amaBhungane and Scorpio, 1 June 2017, http://amabhungane.co.za/article/2017-06-01-guptaleaks-duduzane-zuma-kept-and-captured.

7 Mondli Makhanya, The answer is in the emails, *City Press*, 18 June 2017, http://www.news24.com/Columnists/Mondli-Makhanya/the-answer-is-in-the-emails-20170616.

8 Pieter-Louis Myburgh, *The Republic of Gupta: A story of state capture*, Cape Town: Penguin Books, 2017.

9 Pieter-Louis Myburgh, Exclusive: Zuma friend's R550m bonanza, News24, 14 August 2016, http://www.news24.com/SouthAfrica/News/exclusive-zuma-friends-r550m-bonanza-20160814.

10 amaBhungane, Keeping it in the family, *Mail & Guardian*, 19 March 2010, http://amabhungane.co.za/article/2010-03-19-keeping-it-in-the-family.

11 Mandy Rossouw, Unease over Zuma's Gupta ties, *Mail & Guardian*, 23 July 2017, https://mg.co.za/article/2010-07-23-unease-over-zumas-gupta-ties.

12 Ibid.

13 Kalim Rajab, From our vault: Message to Cabinet – it is NOT just a wedding, *Daily Maverick*, 6 May 2013, https://www.dailymaverick.co.za/opinionista/2013-05-06-message-to-cabinet-it-is-not-just-a-wedding/#.WZGGozMjGM8.

14 Ibid.

15 Mandy Rossouw, Welcome to the Gupta club, *Mail & Guardian*, 23 July 2010, https://mg.co.za/article/2010-07-23-welcome-to-the-gupta-club.

16 Qaanitah Hunter and Sibongakonke Shoba, 'Zuma told me to help Guptas', *Sunday Times*, 20 March 2016.

17 State of Capture, A report of the Public Protector, 14 October 2016, http://cdn.24.co.za/files/Cms/General/d/4666/3f63a8b78d2b495d88f10ed060997f76.pdf.

18 Ibid.

19 Hlengiwe Nhlabathi, 'Punished for snubbing the Guptas', *City Press*, 9 October 2016, http://www.news24.com/SouthAfrica/News/punished-for-snubbing-the-guptas-20161008.

20 Ibid.

21 ANN7 fires 5 more journalists, News24, 4 August 2016, http://www.news24.com/SouthAfrica/News/ann7-fires-5-more-journalists-20160804.

22 amaBhungane, Guptas 'backed' Maine's R140k-a-month bond, amaBhungane Centre for Investigative Journalism, 1 May 2016, http://amabhungane.co.za/article/2016-05-01-00-guptas-backed-oross-r140k-a-month-bond.

23 Sapa, New Age publisher arrested, *Mail & Guardian*, 27 September 2010, https://mg.co.za/article/2010-09-27-new-age-publisher-arrested.

24 Moipone Malefane, Mzilikazi wa Afrika, Nkululeko Ncana and Stephan Hofstatter, Zuma faces ANC revolt over Guptas, *Sunday Times*, 27 February 2011.

25 Carien du Plessis and Andisiwe Makinana, Malema takes a swipe at Gupta family, *Cape Times*, 28 February 2011, https://www.iol.co.za/news/politics/malema-takes-a-swipe-at-gupta-family-1033211.

26 Sapa, Malema slammed for Gupta claims, IOL, 3 March 2011, https://www.iol.co.za/news/politics/malema-slammed-for-gupta-claims-1035558.

27 Jacques Pauw, NIA 'spied' on Guptas, *City Press*, 18 September 2011, http://city-press.news24.com/Politics/News/NIA-spied-on-Guptas-20110917.
28 Pieter-Louis Myburgh, *The Republic of Gupta: A story of state capture*, Cape Town: Penguin Books, 2017.
29 Erika Gibson, *SMS'e wys Jacob Zuma weet*, Netwerk24, 21 January 2015, http://www.netwerk24.com/Nuus/SMSe-wys-Jacob-Zuma-weet-20150121.
30 Scorpio and amaBhungane, #GuptaLeaks: How captured ambassador lobbied the Dutch, News24, 11 June 2017, http://www.news24.com/SouthAfrica/News/guptaleaks-how-captured-ambassador-lobbied-the-dutch-20170611-2.

Chapter 6: Poison ivy and Russian blood

1 Pain forces Jacob Zuma to leave duties, *City Press*, 8 June 2014, http://www.news24.com/SouthAfrica/News/Pain-forces-Jacob-Zuma-to-leave-duties-20140608.
2 Sapa, Zuma admitted to hospital, *Drum*, 7 June 2014, http://www.news24.com/Drum/Archive/zuma-admitted-to-hospital-20170728-2.
3 Carien du Plessis, Ill Jacob Zuma driven down red carpet, *City Press*, 17 June 2014, http://www.news24.com/SouthAfrica/Politics/Ill-Jacob-Zuma-driven-down-red-carpet-20140617.
4 Stephen Grootes, Zuma's health: The erosion begins, *Daily Maverick*, 22 June 2014, https://www.dailymaverick.co.za/opinionista/2014-06-22-zumas-health-the-erosion-begins/#.WZGQ9zMjGM8.
5 Bongani Mthethwa, Sibongakonke Shoba, Matthew Savides and Sibusiso Ngalwa, Zuma 'poison plot', *Sunday Times*, 22 February 2015.
6 Dirco, President Zuma to undertake a working visit to the Russian Federation, 23 August 2014.
7 Jacob Zuma's mysterious mission to Russia, *City Press*, 31 August 2014, http://www.news24.com/Archives/City-Press/Jacob-Zumas-mysterious-mission-to-Russia-20150429.
8 Bongani Mthethwa, Sibongakonke Shoba, Matthew Savides and Sibusiso Ngalwa, Zuma 'poison plot', *Sunday Times*, 22 February 2015.
9 The trillion rand thank you, *Africa Confidential*, vol. 58, no. 9, 28 April 2017.
10 Ibid.
11 Bongani Hans, Zuma poison claims 'malicious gossip', *The Mercury*, 23 February 2015,https://www.iol.co.za/news/south-africa/kwazulu-natal/zuma-poison-claims-malicious-gossip-1822012.
12 Glynnis Underhill, The death of Ntuli-Zuma's bodyguard: So many questions, after all these years, *Daily Maverick*, 11 March 2015, https://www.dailymaverick.co.za/article/2015-03-11-the-death-of-ntuli-zumas-bodyguard-so-many-questions-after-all-these-years/#.WZGWBTMjGM8.
13 Author's interview with direct source, September 2017.

Chapter 7: Who will guard the guardians?

1 Pieter-Louis Myburgh, Exclusive: Molefe slammed Hawks boss over Prasa probe, News24, 8 March 2017, http://www.news24.com/SouthAfrica/News/exclusive-molefe-slammed-hawks-boss-over-prasa-probe-20170308.

2 Pieter-Louis Myburgh, Exclusive: Prasa locomotives contractor paid ANC 'fundraisers', News24, 10 March 2017, http://www.news24.com/SouthAfrica/News/exclusive-prasa-locomotives-contractor-paid-anc-fundraisers-20170310.

3 Madibeng investigated by former convicted thief, Kormorant, 28 June 2013, http://kormorant.co.za/2645/madibeng-investigated-by-former-convicted-thief/.

4 New dawn for NPA, says Nxasana, SA News, 11 October 2014, http://www.sanews.gov.za/south-africa/new-dawn-npa-says-nxasana.

5 Sapa, Black Lawyers Association welcomes new NDPP appointment, TimesLive, 1 September 2013, https://www.timeslive.co.za/news/south-africa/2013-09-01-black-lawyers-association-welcomes-new-ndpp-appointment/.

6 Glynnis Underhill, New NPA boss Nxasana seeks clarity on Mdluli case, *Mail & Guardian*, 18 October 2013, https://mg.co.za/article/2013-10-17-new-npa-boss-nxasana-seeks-clarity.

7 Sapa, Nxasana says he's victim of plot, *The Citizen*, 18 August 2014.

8 3 top NPA leaders charged with perjury, *City Press*, 10 August 2014, http://www.news24.com/Archives/City-Press/3-top-NPA-leaders-charged-with-perjury-20150430.

9 Jenna Etheridge, Zuma lied under oath about me willingly leaving office – Nxasana, News24, 13 April 2017, http://www.news24.com/SouthAfrica/News/zuma-lied-under-oath-about-me-willingly-leaving-office-nxasana-20170413.

10 Sam Sole, She's the boss: Jiba's stunning comeback, *Mail & Guardian*, 21 August 2015, https://mg.co.za/article/2015-08-20-shes-the-boss-jibas-stunning-comeback.

11 amaBhungane, How Panday wriggled off the hook, 8 October 2015, http://amabhungane.co.za/article/2015-10-08-how-panday-wriggled-off-the-hook.

12 Hanlie Retief, Booysen's tell-all book reveals web of deceit, *City Press*, 18 September 2016, http://www.news24.com/SouthAfrica/News/booysens-tell-all-book-reveals-web-of-deceit-20160917.

13 Jessica Pitchford, *Blood on their hands: General Johan Booysen reveals his truth*, Johannesburg: Pan Macmillan, 2016.

14 Affidavit by Colonel Kobus Demeyer Roelofse, Anti-corruption task team, 2 March 2012, http://www.politicsweb.co.za/documents/a-report-on-the-mdluli-investigation--col-kobus-ro.

15 Sent to die, *Sunday Times*, 23 October 2011.

16 Charl du Plessis and Adriaan Basson, Mdluli: Paper denies police bribes, *City Press*, 17 May 2012, http://www.news24.com/SouthAfrica/Politics/Mdluli-Paper-denies-police-bribes-20120517.

17 Ibid.

18 Stephan Hofstatter, Mzilikazi wa Afrika and Rob Rose, Shoot to kill: Inside a South African police death squad, *Sunday Times*, 11 December 2011, https://www.timeslive.co.za/news/south-africa/2011-12-11-shoot-to-kill-inside-a-south-african-police-death-squad/.

19 Mpho Raborife, Suspended KZN Hawks boss goes on early retirement, News24, http://www.news24.com/SouthAfrica/News/suspended-kzn-hawks-boss-goes-on-early-retirement-20170228.

20 Mandy Wiener, Hollowing out the state: Johan Booysen speaks out, *Daily Maverick*, 18 September 2016, https://www.dailymaverick.co.za/article/2016-09-18-hollowing-out-the-state-johan-booysen-speaks-out/#.WZLLEDMjGM8.

21 Ibid.

22 Letter from Anwa Dramat to the Minister of Police, Nkosinathi Nhleko, 24 December 2014, https://cdn.mg.co.za/content/documents/2015/01/09/dramatletter.pdf.

23 Franny Rabkin, A brief history of the dishonourable and dishonest Berning Ntlemeza, *Business Day*, 14 September 2016, https://www.businesslive.co.za/politics/2016-09-14-a-brief-history-of-the-dishonourable-and-dishonest-berning-ntlemeza/.

24 Jeanette Chabalala, Former Gauteng Hawks head blames Mdluli for ending his career, News24, http://www.news24.com/SouthAfrica/News/former-gauteng-hawks-head-blames-mdluli-for-ending-his-career-20170323.

25 Karabo Ngoepe and Tshidi Madia, Breaking – ConCourt rules for McBride, News24, 6 September 2016, http://www.news24.com/SouthAfrica/News/breaking-concourt-rules-for-mcbride-20160906.

26 Court judgment, *Helen Suzman Foundation and Freedom Under Law* v *Minister of Police and Others*, 17 March 2017, North Gauteng High Court.

27 Mpho Raborife, Ntlemeza's lawyer tells him to hand over car, cellphone, News24, 24 April 2017, http://www.news24.com/SouthAfrica/News/ntlemezas-lawyer-tells-him-to-hand-over-car-cellphone-20170424.

28 Jenna Etheridge, Taxpayers fork out over R11m for suspended Phiyega, Mdluli, News24, 27 June 2017, http://www.news24.com/SouthAfrica/News/taxpayers-fork-out-over-r11m-for-suspended-phiyega-mdluli-20170627.

29 Mzilikazi wa Afrika, *Nothing left to steal: Jailed for telling the truth*, Cape Town: Penguin 2014.

30 Gia Nicolaides, Phiyega calls for Marikana findings to be set aside, Eyewitness News, 26 April 2016, http://ewn.co.za/2016/04/26/Phiyega-calls-for-Farlam-Commissions-findings-to-be-set-aside.

31 Angelique Serrao, Senior police officers found guilty of defending Phiyega, News24,http://www.news24.com/SouthAfrica/News/senior-police-officers-found-guilty-of-defending-phiyega-20170127.

Chapter 8: Zupta-owned enterprises

1 State of Capture, A report of the Public Protector, 14 October 2016.

2 Mzilikazi wa Afrika and Kyle Cowan, Guptas courted president's aide, Lakela Kaunda, *Sunday Times*, 11 June 2017, https://www.timeslive.co.za/sunday-times/news/2017-06-11-guptas-courted-presidents-aide-lakela-kaunda/.

3 Affidavit by Mabel Petronella Mentor to the SAPS, 9 May 2016.

4 Ibid.

5 'Incompetent' Hawks have finally found me – Vytjie Mentor, *The Citizen*, 8 November 2016, https://citizen.co.za/news/south-africa/1338808/incompetent-hawks-finally-found-vytjie-mentor/.

6 Affidavit by Mabel Petronella Mentor to the SAPS, 9 May 2016.

7 South African Airways add flights to Mumbai, Flysaa.com, 8 May 2012, https://www.flysaa.com/za/en/flyingSAA/News/South-African-Airways-announces-additional-flights-to-Mumbai.html.

8 Sasha Planting, SAA's CEO, two general managers resign, Moneyweb, 8 October 2012, https://www.moneyweb.co.za/archive/unconfirmed-saa-ceo-quits/.

9 South African Airways and India's Jet Airways sign code share agreement, Flysaa.com, 16 April 2013, https://www.flysaa.com/za/en/flyingSAA/News/South_African_Airways_and_Indias__Jet_Airways_sign_code_share_agreement.html.

10 John Croft, South Africa fines Jet Airways in 'Guptagate', *Aviation Week*, 9 May 2013, http://aviationweek.com/blog/south-africa-fines-jet-airways-guptagate.

11 South African Airways plans to pull out of India, *The Hindu*, 31 January 2015, http://www.thehindu.com/business/Industry/south-african-airways-plans-to-pull-out-of-india/article6843011.ece.

12 Ziyanda Ngcobo, The Gupta family 'categorically' denies meeting Mentor, Eyewitness News, 15 March 2013, http://ewn.co.za/2016/03/15/The-Gupta-family-categorically-denies-meeting-with-Mentor.

13 Amanda Khoza and Lizeka Tandwa, Zuma has 'no recollection' of Mentor – Presidency, News24, 15 March 2016, http://www.news24.com/SouthAfrica/Politics/zuma-has-no-recollection-of-mentor-presidency-20160315.

14 Affidavit by Mabel Petronella Mentor to the SAPS, 9 May 2016.

15 Vytjie Mentor, *No holy cows: Moments in my political life 2002–2017*, self-published, 2017.

16 State of Capture, A report of the Public Protector, 14 October 2016.

17 Mbeki's rising star will take time to cool off, *Pretoria News*, 15 March 2010.

18 Lionel Faull, Vinayak Bhardwaj, Matuma Letsaolo, Sam Sole and Stefaans Brümmer, Transnet tender boss's R50-billion double game, *Mail & Guardian*, 3 July 2014, https://mg.co.za/article/2014-07-03-transnet-tender-bosss-r50-billion-double-game.

19 Ibid.

20 Salim Essa bio, #GuptaLeaks, 21 July 2017, http://www.gupta-leaks.com/

information/salim-essa-bio/.

21 Sam Sole, Craig McKune and Stefaans Brümmer, The 'Gupta owned' state enterprises, amaBhungane Centre for Investigative Journalism, 24 March 2016, http://amabhungane.co.za/article/2016-03-24-the-gupta-owned-state-enterprises.

22 amaBhungane and Scorpio, #GuptaLeaks: Guptas and associates score R5.3bn in locomotives kickbacks, amaBhungane Centre for Investigative Journalism, 1 June 2017, http://amabhungane.co.za/article/2017-06-01-guptaleaks-guptas-and-associates-score-r53bn-in-locomotives-kickbacks.

23 State of Capture, a report of the Public Protector, 14 October 2016.

24 Sam Sole, Craig McKune and Stefaans Brümmer, How to eat a parastatal like Transnet – chunk by R600m chunk, *Mail & Guardian*, 16 September 2016, https://mg.co.za/article/2016-09-16-00-how-to-eat-a-parastatal-chunk-by-r600m-chunk.

25 amaBhungane and Scorpio, #GuptaLeaks: Guptas and associates score R5.3bn in locomotives kickbacks, amaBhungane Centre for Investigative Journalism, 1 June 2017, http://amabhungane.co.za/article/2017-06-01-guptaleaks-guptas-and-associates-score-r53bn-in-locomotives-kickbacks.

26 Ibid.

27 Ibid.

28 Ibid.

29 Pieter-Louis Myburgh, Exclusive: Transnet's new Chinese locomotives 'fail first test', News24, 23 January 2017, http://www.news24.com/SouthAfrica/News/exclusive-transnets-new-chinese-locomotives-fail-first-test-20170123.

30 amaBhungane and Matuma Letsoalo, Jacob Zuma links to 'untouchable' SAA boss, *Mail & Guardian*, 7 November 2014, https://mg.co.za/article/2014-11-06-jacob-zuma-links-to-untouchable-saa-boss.

31 Ibid.

32 *Isolezwe*, 17 December 2015.

33 Matthew le Cordeur, SAA Airbus swap deal goes Nene's way, Fin24, 21 December 2015, http://www.fin24.com/Companies/Industrial/breaking-saa-airbus-swap-deal-goes-nenes-way-20151221.

34 Sabelo Skiti, The big junk joke, *Sunday Times*, 9 April 2017.

35 Sam Sole, How Denel was hijacked, amaBhungane Centre for Investigative Journalism, 30 May 2016, http://amabhungane.co.za/article/2016-05-30-how-denel-was-hijacked.

36 Ibid.

37 amaBhungane, *Daily Maverick* and News24, #GuptaLeaks: How the Guptas screwed Denel, 10 June 2017, http://www.news24.com/SouthAfrica/News/guptaleaks-how-the-guptas-screwed-denel-20170610.

38 Sam Sole, How Denel was hijacked, amaBhungane Centre for Investigative Journalism, 30 May 2016, http://amabhungane.co.za/article/2016-05-30-how-denel-was-hijacked.

39 amaBhungane, *Daily Maverick* and News24, #GuptaLeaks: How the Guptas screwed Denel, News24, 10 June 2017, http://www.news24.com/SouthAfrica/News/guptaleaks-how-the-guptas-screwed-denel-20170610.

40 Genevieve Quintal, Denel's partner in Asia insolvent, says Lungisa Fuzile, *Business Day*, 18 May 2017, https://www.businesslive.co.za/bd/companies/2017-05-18-denels-partner-in-asia-insolvent-says-lungisa-fuzile/.

41 Liesl Peyper, Gigaba maintains he opposes Denel-VR Laser deal, Fin24, 26 May 2017, http://www.fin24.com/Companies/Industrial/gigaba-maintains-he-opposes-denel-vr-laser-deal-20170526.

Chapter 9: How to hijack a mine

1 Marc Rich apartheid's most important sanctions-buster, Open Secrets, 17 July 2013, http://opensecrets.org.za/marc-rich-open-secret/.

2 Ibid.

3 amaBhungane and Scorpio, #GuptaLeaks: How Eskom was captured, Fin24, 9 June 2017, http://www.fin24.com/Economy/Eskom/guptaleaks-how-eskom-was-captured-20170609.

4 Eugenie du Preez, Glencore blames Eskom deal for Optimum woes, Fin24, 5 August 2015, http://www.fin24.com/Companies/Mining/Glencore-blames-Eskom-deal-for-Optimum-woes-20150805.

5 Susan Comrie, Eskom stonewalls on Glencore's Optimum, *City Press*, 1 November 2015, http://city-press.news24.com/Business/Eskom-stonewalls-on-Glencores-Optimum-20151030.

6 Ibid.

7 Sam Sole and Susan Comrie, How Brian Molefe 'helped' Gupta Optimum heist, amaBhungane Centre for Investigative Journalism, 16 May 2017, http://amabhungane.co.za/article/2017-05-16-exclusive-how-brian-molefe-helped-gupta-optimum-heist.

8 Sam Sole, Craig McKune and Stefaans Brümmer, The 'Gupta owned' state enterprises, *Mail & Guardian*, 24 March 2016, https://mg.co.za/article/2016-03-24-00-the-gupta-owned-state-enterprises.

9 Sam Sole and Susan Comrie, How Brian Molefe 'helped' Gupta Optimum heist, amaBhungane Centre for Investigative Journalism, 16 May 2017, http://amabhungane.co.za/article/2017-05-16-exclusive-how-brian-molefe-helped-gupta-optimum-heist.

10 SA Council of Churches, State of capture: Much more than corruption', 18 May 2017.

11 Ombudsman favours Molefe over Saxonwold shebeen story, *Cape Times*, 1 March 2017.

12 Sam Sole and Susan Comrie, How Brian Molefe 'helped' Gupta Optimum heist,

amaBhungane Centre for Investigative Journalism, 16 May 2017, http://
amabhungane.co.za/article/2017-05-16-exclusive-how-brian-molefe-helped-gupta-
optimum-heist.

13 Sally Evans, #GuptaLeaks: The 'Gift' that keeps on giving, amaBhungane Centre
for Investigative Journalism, 5 June 2017, http://amabhungane.co.za/
article/2017-06-05-guptaleaks-the-gift-that-keeps-on-giving.

14 Ibid.

15 Sam Sole and Susan Comrie, How Brian Molefe 'helped' Gupta Optimum heist,
amaBhungane Centre for Investigative Journalism, 16 May 2017, http://
amabhungane.co.za/article/2017-05-16-exclusive-how-brian-molefe-helped-
gupta-optimum-heist.

16 Ibid.

17 Franz Wild and Paul Burkhardt, Zuma's son took stake in Tegeta 3 wks before
Optimum buy, Fin24, 7 March 2016, http://www.fin24.com/Companies/Mining/
zumas-son-took-stake-in-tegeta-3-wks-before-optimum-buy-20160307.

18 Jan de Lange, *Molefe keer Cyril se pel om myn te koop*, Rapport, 23 July 2017.

19 State of Capture, A report of the Public Protector, 14 October 2016.

20 Susan Comrie, How Eskom bailed out the Guptas, *City Press*, 12 June 2016, http://
city-press.news24.com/News/how-eskom-bailed-out-the-guptas-20160612.

21 amaBhungane and Scorpio, #GuptaLeaks: Guptas pushed Eskom for R1.68bn
prepayment, amaBhungane Centre for Investigative Journalism, 1 June 2017,
http://amabhungane.co.za/article/2017-06-01-guptaleaks-guptas-pushed-eskom-
for-r168bn-prepayment.

22 Yolandi Groenewald, Charges to be laid against Eskom's Anoj Singh, Fin24,
20 July 2017, http://www.fin24.com/Economy/Eskom/
charges-to-be-laid-against-eskoms-anoj-singh-20170720.

23 State of Capture, A report of the Public Protector, 14 October 2016.

24 Susan Comrie, Sam Sole and Stefaans Brümmer, Gupta mine grab: How Brown
misled Parliament, amaBhungane Centre for Investigative Journalism, 18 May
2017, http://amabhungane.co.za/article/2017-05-18-exclusive-gupta-mine-grab-
how-brown-misled-parliament.

25 Ibid.

26 Brian Molefe, media statement, 11 November 2016, http://www.fin24.com/
Economy/Eskom/full-statement-eskom-ceo-brian-molefe-quits-20161111.

27 Koko faces disciplinary action over R1bn contracts, Fin24, 19 July 2017, http://
www.fin24.com/Economy/Eskom/koko-faces-disciplinary-action-over-r1bn-
contracts-20170719.

28 Andisiwe Makinana, Why Ben Ngubane quit, *City Press*, 18 June 2017, http://
www.news24.com/SouthAfrica/News/why-ben-quit-20170617.

29 Why Eskom crushed R2.1bn Optimum fine to just R255.4m, Fin24, 19 July 2017,
http://www.fin24.com/Economy/Eskom/why-eskom-crushed-r21bn-optimum-
fine-to-just-r2554m-20170719.

30 Liesl Peyper, Brian Molefe the biggest winner of Eskom's bonus bill, Fin24, 19 July 2017, http://www.fin24.com/Economy/Eskom/brian-molefe-the-biggest-winner of-eskoms-bonus-bill-20170719.

31 Sabelo Skiti, Kyle Cowan and Mzilikazi wa Afrika, Eskom suspends Gupta-linked finance chief Anoj Singh, TimesLive, 27 July 2017, https://www.timeslive.co.za/ news/south-africa/2017-07-27-breaking-eskom-suspends-gupta-linked-cfo-anoj-singh/.

Chapter 10: 'I am Hlaudi Motsoeneng, baby!'

1 How Hlaudi Motsoeneng lied in SABC application: 4 E's and an F in 'matric', *City Press*, 16 July 2014.

2 Louis Flanagan, Snake pit at SABC exposed, *The Star*, 12 May 2008, https://www. iol.co.za/news/south-africa/snake-pit-at-sabc-exposed-400093.

3 Angelique Serrao and Jeanette Chabalala, King Hlaudi's rise to power, News24, 23 September 2016, www.news24.com/SouthAfrica/News/investigation-king-hlaudis-rise-to-power-20160923.

4 Ibid.

5 Ibid.

6 Ibid.

7 How Hlaudi Motsoeneng lied in SABC application: 4 E's and an F in 'matric', *City Press*, 16 July 2014.

8 When Governance and Ethics Fail, report of the Public Protector, February 2014.

9 Ibid.

10 Angelique Serrao and Jeanette Chabalala, King Hlaudi's rise to power, News24, 23 September 2016, www.news24.com/SouthAfrica/News/investigation-king-hlaudis-rise-to-power-20160923.

11 Ibid.

12 Ibid.

13 Sibongakonke Shoba, Thabo Mokone and Carlos Amato, How the SABC turned into Hlaudi House, *Sunday Times*, 3 July 2016.

14 Angelique Serrao and Jeanette Chabalala, King Hlaudi's rise to power, News24, 23 September 2016, www.news24.com/SouthAfrica/News/investigation-king-hlaudis-rise-to-power-20160923.

15 Ibid.

16 Hlaudi was the 'go-to' man at the SABC – former CEO, News24, 8 December 2016, www.news24.com/News/ South Africa/News/hlaudi-was-the-go-to-to-man-at-the-sabc-former-ceo-20161208.

17 SABC: Metro FM decision is leadership at its best, Eyewitness News, 6 December 2012, ewn.co.za/2012/12/06/SABC-shows-new-muscle-with--Metro-FM-decision.

18 Ibid.

19 Sapa, SABC bans Zuma fish & chips ad, News24, 27 November 2012, www.
    news24.com/SouthAfrica/News/SABC-bans-Zuma-fish-chips-ad-20121127.
20 SABC stands by its decision on fish and chips ad, SABC News, 29 November 2012,
    http://www.sabc.co.za/SABC/newsblog/index.html/a/a5b5e2804d9f8fff934cf3e570
    eb4ca2/SABC-stands-by-its-decision-on-fish-and-chips-ad-20121129
21 Author's interview with former SABC board member, August 2017.
22 Glynnis Underhill and Ruwaydah Harris, SABC calls for 70% happy news, *Mail
    & Guardian*, 30 August 2013.
23 Charl Blignaut and Lloyd Gedye, How Hlaudi sold the SABC, *City Press*,
    11 December 2016.
24 Ibid.
25 A timeline of the Ellen Tshabalala affair – DA, Politicsweb, 3 December 2014,
    www.politicsweb.co.za/documents/a-timeline-of-the-ellen-tshabalala-affair--da.
26 When Governance and Ethics Fail, a report of the Public Protector, February
    2014.
27 Babalo Ndenze, Inquiry told of interference in SABC affairs, *The Herald*,
    9 December 2016.
28 Rebecca Davis, Supreme Court of Appeal judgment: A confirmation of Public
    Protector's powers, *Daily Maverick*, 8 October 2015.
29 Rahima Essop, Hlaudi Motsoeneng's salary increases by almost R1m, Eyewitness
    News, 23 September 2015, ewn.co.za/2015/09/23/Hlaudi-Motsoenengs-salary-
    increases-to-almost-R1m.
30 A timeline of the Ellen Tshabalala affair – DA, Politicsweb, 3 December 2014,
    www.politicsweb.co.za/documents/a-timeline-of-the-ellen-tshabalala-affair--da.
31 Prince Chauke and Norman Masungwini, Meet Zuma's nyatsi!, *Sunday Sun*,
    16 November 2014.
32 Ibid.
33 Applause as Motsoeneng cleared of all charges, News24, 12 December 2015,
    http://www.news24.com/SouthAfrica/News/applause-as-motsoeneng-cleared-of-
    all-charges-20151212-of-all-charges-20151212.
34 Pontsho Pilane, 90% local content: I'm Hlaudi Motsoeneng, baby!, *Mail &
    Guardian*, 20 May 2016.
35 Jan Gerber, SABC institutes legal proceedings against Motsoeneng, Aguma,
    News24, 1 August 2017, http://www.news24.com/SouthAfrica/News/sabc-
    institutes-legal-proceedings-against-motsoeneng-aguma-20170801.
36 Leeto Khoze and Mia Lindeque, SABC will no longer broadcast footage of violent
    protests, Eyewitness News, 27 May 2016, http://ewn.co.za/2016/05/27/SABC-will-
    no-longer-broadcast-footage-displaying-violent-protests.
37 Thandeka Gqubule, founding affidavit in *Gqubule and Others* v SABC,
    Constitutional Court, 15 July 2016.
38 Ibid.
39 Paul Herman, You can question anyone, except Zuma – Hlaudi to SABC

journalists, News24, 18 July 2016, http://www.news24.com/SouthAfrica/News/
you-can-question-anyone-except-zuma-hlaudi-to-sabc-journalists-20160718.

40 Thandeka Gqubule, founding affidavit in *Gqubule and Others v SABC*,
Constitutional Court, 15 July 2016.

41 Lukhanyo Calata, SABC's decisions fly in the face of what many, like the Cradock
4, sacrificed, *City Press*, 27 June 2016, http://city-press.news24.com/Voices/
sabcs-decisions-fly-in-the-face-of-what-many-like-the-cradock-4-sacrificed-
20160627.

42 Ibid.

43 Paul Herman, SABC Acting Group CEO Jimi Matthews quits, News24, 27 June
2016, http://www.news24.com/SouthAfrica/News/sabc-ceo-jimi-matthews-quits-
20160627.

44 Mzilikazi wa Afrika, Hlaudi gives Zuma's daughter R167m contract, *Sunday
Times*, 10 July 2016.

45 Paul Herman, Breaking: SABC board members announce resignation in
Parliament, News24, 5 October 2016, http://www.news24.com/SouthAfrica/
News/breaking-sabc-board-members-announce-resignation-in-parliament-
20161005.

46 Mayibongwe Maqhina, Gupta New Age breakfasts cost SABC R20m, IOL,
14 June 2017, https://www.iol.co.za/news/politics/gupta-new-age-breakfasts-cost-
sabc-r20m-9783128.

47 Bekezela Phakathi and Philani Nombembe, Hlaudi's reign of terror exposed, *The
Herald*, 13 December 2016.

48 Ra'eesa Pather, Motsoeneng not fit to hold any position in SABC, says Western
Cape High Court, *Mail & Guardian*, 12 December 2016.

49 Mpho Sibanyoni, I'm not to blame for SABC mess – Hlaudi, *Sowetan*, 20 April
2017.

Chapter 11: Zuma's Parliament

1 Strengthening the fight against crime, *ANC Today*, Vol. 8, No. 3, 25–31 January
2008, http://www.anc.org.za/docs/anctoday/2008/ato3.htm#art1.

2 Sapa, ANC delaying Nkandla committee – DA, News24, 14 April 2014, http://
www.news24.com/elections/news/anc-delaying-nkandla-committee-da-20140414.

3 Parliamentary Monitoring Group, 23 April 2014.

4 Ibid.

5 Ibid.

6 See Andrew Feinstein, *After the party: A personal and political journey inside the
ANC*, Johannesburg and Cape Town: Jonathan Ball Publishers, 2009.

7 Sapa, Can Parliament stand up to Zuma on Nkandla?, eNCA, 15 August 2014,
http://www.enca.com/zuma-confident-parliament-will-deal-nkandla.

8 Questions for oral reply: The president, Hansard, 21 August 2014, https://pmg.
org.za/hansard/18600/.
9 See https://www.youtube.com/watch?v=EENSokNzTio.
10 Ad Hoc Committee, President's submission in response to Public Protector's
report on Nkandla: Public Protector's report on Nkandla security upgrades,
Parliamentary Monitoring Group, 25 September 2014, https://pmg.org.za/
committee-meeting/17595/.
11 Ad Hoc Committee, President's submission in response to Public Protector's
report on Nkandla: Nkandla Security Upgrades: Public Protector and SIU reports:
Consideration, Parliamentary Monitoring Group, 25 September 2014, https://pmg.
org.za/committee-meeting/17596/.
12 President's state-of-the-nation address, Hansard, 12 February 2015, https://pmg.
org.za/hansard/20613/.
13 Ibid.
14 Ibid.
15 Ibid.
16 Ibid.

Chapter 12: Dismantling SARS

1 Written parliamentary answer by the Minister of Finance, March 2016.
2 Johann van Loggerenberg with Adrian Lackay, *Rogue: The inside story of SARS's
elite crime-busting unit*, Johannesburg and Cape Town: Jonathan Ball Publishers,
2016.
3 Pieter du Toit, Moyane's endgame at Sars: 'I've come to clear the air', HuffPost
SA, 27 January 2017, http://www.huffingtonpost.co.za/pieter-du-toit/moyanes
-endgame-at-sars-ive-come-to-clear-the-air_a_21663341/.
4 David Hausman, Reworking the Revenue Service: Tax collection in South Africa,
1999–2009, Innovations for successful societies, https://successfulsocieties.
princeton.edu/sites/successfulsocieties/files/Policy_Note_ID125.pdf.
5 Pieter du Toit, No fears of a tax revolt – Gordhan, HuffPost SA, 26 March 2017,
http://www.huffingtonpost.co.za/2017/03/26/no-fears-of-a-tax-revolt-gordhan_a_
22012517/.
6 Ibid.
7 SARS, tax statistics 2016, see http://www.sars.gov.za/About/SATaxSystem/Pages/
Tax-Statistics.aspx.
8 Jane Doherty, Increasing tax revenue and its impact on financing public health
care in South Africa, RESYST Working Paper 6, http://resyst.lshtm.ac.uk/sites/
resyst.lshtm.ac.uk/files/docs/reseources/Working%20paper%206.pdf.
9 Ibid.
10 Ibid.

11 Johan Van Loggerenberg with Adrian Lackay, *Rogue: The inside story of SARS's elite crime-busting unit*, Johannesburg and Cape Town: Jonathan Ball Publishers, p. 10.

12 Karen Maughan, NPA charges of tax evasion are 'improper', claims Zuma, *Cape Times*, 4 June 2008.

13 See Antoinette Slabbert, Zuma's Nkandla tax headache, Moneyweb, 23 December 2013, https://www.moneyweb.co.za/archive/zumas-nkandla-tax-headache/.

14 Zuma must pay R63.9m in Nkandla tax benefits: DA, News24, 7 July 2016, http://www.news24.com/SouthAfrica/Politics/zuma-must-pay-r639m-in-nkandla-tax-benefits-da-20160707.

15 Ferial Haffajee, How the taxman was broken, *City Press*, 9 April 2017, http://www.news24.com/SouthAfrica/News/how-the-taxman-was-broken-20170409-2.

16 Jan Gerber, SARS investigating Zuma's Nkandla fringe benefit tax, Fin24, 24 May 2017, http://www.fin24.com/Economy/sars-investigating-zumas-nkandla-fringe-benefit-tax-20170524.

17 Media release: SARS did not comment on President Zuma's tax matters, South African Revenue Service, 25 May 2017, http://www.sars.gov.za/Media/MediaReleases/Pages/25-May-2017---SARS-did-not-comment-on-president-Zuma-tax-matters-.aspx.

18 Ferial Haffajee, How the taxman was broken, *City Press*, 9 April 2017, http://www.news24.com/SouthAfrica/News/how-the-taxman-was-broken-20170409-2.

19 Malcolm Rees, Cigarette bust links to Fastjet SA directors, Moneyweb, 2 August 2013, https://www.moneyweb.co.za/archive/cigarette-bust-links-to-fastjet-sa-directors/.

20 *Sunday Tribune*, 16 February 2014, https://www.pressreader.com/south-africa/sunday-tribune/20140216/281492159217732.

21 Staff reporter, White monopoly capital is persecuting us – Edward Zuma, *The Citizen*, 23 October 2016.

22 Pauli van Wyk, *Zuma-man dalk skotvry, kul inkomstediens glo uit R1,8 miljard*, *Beeld*, 19 February 2015.

23 Piet Rampedi, Mzilikazi wa Afrika, Stephan Hofstatter and Malcolm Rees, SARS bugged Zuma, *Sunday Times*, 12 October 2014.

24 Mzilikazi wa Afrika, Piet Rampedi and Stephan Hofstatter, Taxman's rogue unit ran brothel, *Sunday Times*, 19 November 2014.

25 Sars head vows action on Zuma bugging report, Fin24, 14 October 2014, http://www.fin24.com/Economy/Sars-head-vows-action-on-Zuma-bugging-report-20141014.

26 Max du Preez, The Sars dossier that could spell trouble for Zuma and friends, News24, 1 March 2016, http://www.news24.com/Columnists/MaxduPreez/the-sars-dossier-that-could-spell-trouble-for-zuma-and-friends-20160301.

Chapter 13: The day everything changed

1 Author's interview with Lungisa Fuzile, 25 July 2017.
2 Ibid.
3 Ibid.
4 President Jacob Zuma addresses the business community, SABC Digital News, 9 December 2015, https://youtu.be/M2XYp4lg5MQ.
5 South Africa's rand holds its own despite rating downgrade, Reuters, 7 December 2015, http://af.reuters.com/article/africaTech/idAFKBN0TQ0JH20151207.
6 Jan de Lange, *Anglo American: Nog 4 350 in SA verloor hul werk*, *Beeld*, 9 December 2015.
7 Niel Joubert, *Sakeklimaat bly onseker*, *Beeld*, 4 December 2015.
8 Author's interview with Lungisa Fuzile, 25 July 2017.
9 Ferial Haffajee, 4 days in December, *City Press*, 4 December 2016, http://www.news24.com/SouthAfrica/News/4-days-in-december-20161204-3.
10 State of Capture, a report of the Public Protector, 14 October 2016.
11 Mzilikazi wa Afrika, Sabelo Skiti, Thanduxolo Jika, Seven days in a row!, *Sunday Times*, 30 October 2016.
12 Ferial Haffajee, 4 Days in December, *City Press*, 4 December 2016, http://www.news24.com/SouthAfrica/News/4-days-in-december-20161204-3.
13 Thanduxolo Jika and Sabelo Skiti, The dark heart of state capture, *Sunday Times*, 23 October 2016.
14 State of Capture, a report of the Public Protector, 14 October 2016.
15 Genevieve Quintal and Fadia Salie, Guptas: We never met with Mcebisi Jonas, Fin24, 10 March 2016, http://www.fin24.com/Economy/guptas-we-never-ever-met-with-mcebisis-jonas-20160310.
16 Paul Herman, President Zuma appointed me – Van Rooyen denies Gupta hiring, News24, 12 September 2017, http://www.news24.com/SouthAfrica/News/president-zuma-appointed-me-van-rooyen-denies-gupta-hiring-20170912.
17 Thanduxolo Jika, Exposed: Explosive Gupta e-mails at the heart of state capture, *Sunday Times*, 28 May 2017, https://www.timeslive.co.za/sunday-times/news/2017-05-28-exposed-explosive-gupta-e-mails-at-the-heart-of-state-capture/.
18 Ferial Haffajee, 4 Days in December, *City Press*, 4 December 2016, http://www.news24.com/SouthAfrica/News/4-days-in-december-20161204-3.
19 Author's interview with Lungisa Fuzile, 25 July 2017.
20 Ferial Haffajee, 4 Days in December, *City Press*, 4 December 2016, http://www.news24.com/SouthAfrica/News/4-days-in-december-20161204-3.

Chapter 14: Gents, finally …

1 Fadia Salie, Nene removal sends shockwaves through South Africa – As it happened, Fin24, 10 December 2015, http://www.fin24.com/Economy/live-nene-

removal-sends-shock-waves-throughout-sa-20151210.

2 Ibid.

3 Dane McDonald and Fadia Salie, Markets react aggressively to Nene axing, Fin24, 10 December 2015, http://www.fin24.com/Markets/Equities/ markets-react-aggressively-to-nene-axing-20151210.

4 Ibid.

5 Colleen Goko, Panic on bonds market over Nene's dismissal, *The Times*, 10 December 2015.

6 The John Robbie Show, Talk Radio 702, 10 December 2015.

7 The Redi Thlabi Show, Talk Radio 702, 10 December 2015.

8 Siseko Njobeni, Sacci wants Zuma to come clean on Nene, Fin24, 10 December 2015, http://www.fin24.com/Economy/sacci-wants-zuma-to-come-clean-on-nenes-sacking-20151210.

9 Genevieve Quintal, Rand's fall not Zuma's fault – ANC youth leader, News24, 11 December 2015, http://www.news24.com/SouthAfrica/News/rands-fall-not-zumas-fault-anc-youth-leader-20151211.

10 Alec Hogg, Calculating Zuma's R500bn #Nenegate blunder – rand depreciation excluded, Fin24, 7 March 2016, http://www.fin24.com/BizNews/calculating-zumas-r500bn-nenegate-blunder-rand-depreciation-excluded-20160307.

11 Liesl Peyper, PIC lost over R100bn when Zuma fired Nene – CEO, Fin24, 10 May 2016, http://www.fin24.com/Economy/pic-lost-over-r100bn-when-zuma-fired-nene-ceo-20160510.

12 Author's interview with Lungisa Fuzile, 25 July 2017.

13 Thanduxolo Jika and Sabelo Skiti, The dark heart of state capture, *Sunday Times*, 23 October 2016.

14 Author's interview with Lungisa Fuzile, 25 July 2017.

15 Thanduxolo Jika and Sabelo Skiti, Financial company given confidential package prepared for Zuma's Cabinet, *Sunday Times*, 20 November 2016.

16 Matthew le Cordeur, Gordhan reassures markets, rand firmer – As it happened, Fin24, 14 December 2015, http://www.fin24.com/Economy/live-sa-reacts-to-gordhans-reappointment-as-finance-minister-20151214.

17 Pauli van Wyk, Pravin Gordhan: *'Ons neem nou beheer'*, Netwerk24, 14 December 2015.

18 Wim Pretorius, SAA memo: What they didn't want you to know, News24, 17 December 2015, http://www.fin24.com/Companies/Industrial/saa-memo-what-they-didnt-want-you-to-know-20151217.

19 National Treasury, SAA concluding swap transaction with Airbus as directed by finance minister, statement, 21 December 2015, see http://www.politicsweb.co.za/news-and-analysis/saa-to-go-ahead-with-swap-transaction-with-airbus.

20 Trevor Manuel, Trevor Manuel responds to Lindiwe Zulu, *City Press*, 20 December 2015, http://city-press.news24.com/Voices/trevor-manuel-responds-to-lindiwe-zulu-20151220.

Chapter 15: The State vs Pravin Gordhan

1 Pauli van Wyk, *Pravin Gordhan onder kruisverhoor oor 'rogue unit'*, Netwerk24, 25 February 2016.
2 Genevieve Quintal, Van Rooyen was highly qualified for finance job, says Zuma, Fin24, 22 February 2016, http://www.fin24.com/Economy/van-rooyen-was-very-qualified-for-finance-job-zuma-20160222.
3 Bruce Whitfield, The Midday Report, Talk Radio 702, 24 February 2016, http://www.702.co.za/articles/11777/bruce-whitfield-one-on-one-with-minister-pravin-gordhan-on-today-s-budget.
4 Statement by the Minister of Finance, National Treasury, 26 February 2016, http://www.treasury.gov.za/comm_media/press/2016/2016022601%20-%20Ministers%20Statement.pdf.
5 Ibid.
6 Author's interview with Lungisa Fuzile, 25 July 2017.
7 Emsie Ferreira, Hawks run out of patience with tardy Gordhan, IOL, 15 March 2016, https://www.iol.co.za/news/politics/hawks-run-out-of-patience-with-tardy-gordhan-1998131.
8 Statement by the Minister of Finance, 30 March 2016, http://www.treasury.gov.za/comm_media/press/2016/2016033001%20-%20Hawks%20Response%20Statement.pdf.
9 Statement by the Minister of Finance, 17 May 2016, http://www.treasury.gov.za/comm_media/press/2016/2016051701%20Statement%20By%20The%20Minister.pdf.
10 Gordhan could soon be arrested – report, News24, 15 May 2016, http://www.news24.com/SouthAfrica/News/gordhan-could-soon-be-arrested-report-20160515.
11 Ahmed Areff, Allegations of Gupta comments about Gordhan arrest 'lies' – family, News24, 16 May 2016, http://www.news24.com/SouthAfrica/News/allegations-of-gupta-comments-about-gordhan-arrest-lies-family-20160516.
12 Statement by the Minister of Finance, 17 May 2016, http://www.treasury.gov.za/comm_media/press/2016/2016051701%20Statement%20By%20The%20Minister.pdf.
13 Pierre de Vos, Gordhan: Is there any case to answer?, Constitutionally Speaking, 11 October 2016, http://constitutionallyspeaking.co.za/gordhan-is-there-any-case-to-answer.
14 Pieter du Toit, *Die mark lieg nie; SA stuur op krisis af*, Netwerk24, 24 May 2016.
15 Dewald van Rensburg, How Guptas called in the cavalry, *City Press*, 18 December 2016, http://www.fin24.com/Economy/how-guptas-called-in-the-cavalry-20161216.
16 Statement by the Minister of Finance, National Treasury, 24 August 2016, http://www.treasury.gov.za/comm_media/press/2016/2016082401%20-%20Final%20Statement%20by%20Minister.pdf.

17 Pierre de Vos, Twitter, 25 August 2016, https://twitter.com/pierredevos/status/768687447056220160.
18 Gordhan plot all about power, SOEs and tenderpreneurs – economist, Fin24, 25 August 2016, http://www.fin24.com/Economy/gordhan-plot-all-about-power-soes-and-tenderpreneurs-economist-20160825.
19 Ernest Mabuza, Bizos: I fear for the future of justice and law in SA, www.businesslive.co.za, 15 August 2016.
20 Angelique Serrao and Adriaan Basson, Guptas are attacking me, Gordhan tells Treasury staff, News24, 26 August 2016, http://www.news24.com/SouthAfrica/News/guptas-are-attacking-me-gordhan-tells-treasury-staff-20160826.
21 Statement on Eskom contracts, National Treasury, 29 August 2016, http://www.treasury.gov.za/comm_media/press/2016/2016082901%20-%20Statement%20on%20Eskom%20Contracts.pdf.
22 Finance minister meets new SAA board, National Treasury, 9 September 2016, http://www.treasury.gov.za/comm_media/press/2016/2016090901%20-%20Minister%20Press%20Statement%20on%20Minister%20Meeting%20with%20new%20SAA%20Board.pdf.
23 Mpho Raborife, Days of not holding gvt officials accountable are over – NPA boss, News24, 11 October 2016.
24 Summons issued against Minister Gordhan, National Treasury, 11 October 2016, http://www.treasury.gov.za/comm_media/press/2016/20161011%20-%20Ministry%20Media%20Statement%20on%20Hawks%20summons.pdf.
25 Matthew le Cordeur, Business Leader of the Year Gordhan calls for justice over SARS unit, Fin24, 8 November 2016, http://www.fin24.com/Economy/sa-business-leader-of-2016-gordhan-calls-for-justice-over-sars-unit-20161108.

Chapter 16: The rise of civil society

1 ANA, Helen Suzman Foundation says break-in not 'ordinary', *Mail & Guardian*, 21 March 2016, https://mg.co.za/article/2016-03-21-helen-suzman-foundation-says-break-in-not-ordinary.
2 Chantelle Benjamin, Urgent court application made to enforce court ruling on Dramat's reinstatement, *Mail & Guardian*, 26 January 2015, https://mg.co.za/article/2015-01-26-urgent-court-application-made-to-enforce-court-ruling-on-dramats-reinstatement.
3 Franny Rabkin, A brief history of the dishonourable and dishonest Berning Ntlemeza, *Business Day*, 14 September 2016, https://www.businesslive.co.za/politics/2016-09-14-a-brief-history-of-the-dishonourable-and-dishonest-berning-ntlemeza.
4 Marc Davies, The agents are coming: Four phases of a 'colour revolution' according to the ANC, HuffPost SA, 6 July 2017, http://www.huffingtonpost.

co.za/2017/07/05/the-agents-are-coming-four-phases-of-a-colour-revolution-acco
_a_23017225.

5 Public Affairs Research Institute, Betrayal of the promise: How South Africa is
   being stolen, State Capacity Research Project, May 2017, http://pari.org.za/
   betrayal-promise-report.

6 Jan Gerber, We have 'connected the dots' against Zuma – OUTA, News24,
   28 June 2017, http://www.news24.com/SouthAfrica/News/we-have-connected-the-
   dots-against-zuma-outa-20170628.

7 Natasha Marrian, Plan to launch 'broad front' against state capture, *Business
   Day*, 17 July 2017, https://www.businesslive.co.za/rdm/politics/2017-07-17-plan-to-
   launch-broad-front-against-state-capture.

8 Amil Umraw, The National Foundations dialogue doesn't want to replace
   activism, HuffPost SA, 5 May 2017, http://www.huffingtonpost.co.za/2017/05/05/
   the-national-foundations-dialogue-initiative-doesnt-want-replac_a_22070972.

9 Abram Mashego, #GuptaLeaks: Why NPA won't act, *City Press*, 13 August 2017,
   http://www.news24.com/SouthAfrica/News/guptaleaks-why-npa-wont-act-
   20170813-2.

Chapter 17: Ten trials that changed our history

1 Sapa, ANC takes issue with deputy chief justice, *Mail & Guardian*, 15 January
   2008, https://mg.co.za/article/2008-01-15-anc-takes-issue-with-deputy-chief-justice.

2 Ibid.

3 Ibid.

4 Attack on the judiciary, *Advocate,* vol. 21, no. 1, April 2008, p 32, http://www.
   sabar.co.za/law-journals/2008/april/2008-april-vol021-no1-p32a.pdf

5 ANC statement on meeting with Chief Justice and Deputy Chief Justice, anc.org.
   za, 17 January 2008, http://www.anc.org.za/content/anc-statement-meeting-chief-
   justice-and-deputy-chief-justice.

6 Matuma Letsoalo, Mandy Rossouw and Sello S Alcock, ANC boss accuses judges
   of conspiracy against Zuma, *Mail & Guardian*, 4 July 2008, https://mg.co.za/
   article/2008-07-04-anc-boss-accuses-judges-of-conspiracy-against-zuma.

7 Sapa, Mantashe defends criticism of judiciary, *Mail & Guardian*, 16 July 2008,
   https://mg.co.za/article/2008-07-16-mantashe-defends-criticism-of-judiciary.

8 Mpumelelo Mkhabela, Full interview: ANC's Mantashe lambasts judges,
   Sowetan, 18 August 2011, http://www.sowetanlive.co.za/news/2011/08/18/
   full-interview-ancs-mantashe-lambasts-judges.

9 Mahlatse Gallens, Zuma slates opposition for challenging 'majority' decisions in
   courts, News24, 30 June 2017, http://www.news24.com/SouthAfrica/News/
   zuma-slates-opposition-for-challenging-majority-decisions-in-courts-20170630.

10 Ibid.

11 Ibid.

12 Sabelo Ndlangisa, Queen of the house of blues: Now Mbete wants to be president, *Sunday Times*, 9 July 2017, https://www.timeslive.co.za/sunday-times/news/2017-07-08-queen-of-the-house-of-blues-now-mbete-wants-to-be-president.

Chapter 18: Losing the vote

1 Karabo Ngoepe, ANC will rule until Jesus comes, Zuma says again, News24, 5 July 2016, http://www.news24.com/elections/news/anc-will-rule-until-jesus-comes -zuma-says-again-20160705.

2 Crispian Olver, State capture at a local level: A case study of Nelson Mandela Bay, Public Affairs Research Institute, November 2016, http://pari.org.za/is-this-how-the-anc-lost-nelson-mandela-bay.

3 Sapa, Zuma: If ANC goes down, so will SA, News24, 27 November 2014, http://www.news24.com/SouthAfrica/Politics/Zuma-If-ANC-goes-down-so-will-SA-20141127.

4 Mmanaledi Mataboge and Qaanitah Hunter, Gwede Mantashe admits ANC could lose power, *Mail & Guardian*, 19 December 2014, https://mg.co.za/article/2014-12-18-gwede-mantashe-admits-anc-could-lose-power.

5 Max du Preez, Zuma – SA's one-man wrecking-ball, *Pretoria News*, 30 December 2014, https://www.iol.co.za/pretoria-news/opinion/zuma---sas-one-man-wrecking-ball-1799819.

6 Qaanitah Hunter, Urban blacks lose confidence in Zuma, *Sunday Times*, 3 April 2016.

7 Marianne Merten, Afrobarometer: Trio of polls show shifting attitudes but voters would still opt for ANC, *Daily Maverick*, 19 May 2016, https://www.dailymaverick.co.za/article/2016-05-19-afrobarometer-trio-of-polls-show-shifting-attitudes-but-voters-would-still-opt-for-anc/#.WZrFc_kjGM8.

8 Theuns Kruger, ANC loses control of metro billions, *City Press*, 23 August 2016, http://city-press.news24.com/Voices/ancs-big-loss-20160819.

9 Greg Nicolson, Thoko Didiza: I feel part of Tshwane, *Daily Maverick*, 23 June 2016.

10 Barry Bateman and Queenin Masuabi, '2016 elections [a] historic moment for SA', Eyewitness News, 6 August 2016, http://ewn.co.za/2016/08/06/Maimane-describes-2016-local-elections-as-historic-moment-for-SA.

Chapter 19: Stalingrad and state capture

1 A full transcript of Thuli Madonsela's interview with Jacob Zuma can be found at, for example, Politicsweb, 2 November 2016, http://politicsweb.co.za/

documents/thuli-madonselas-interview-of-jacob-zuma-full-tran.

2 Andrew England, South Africa: The power of the family business, *Financial Times*, 8 March 2016, https://www.ft.com/content/abd6e034-e519-11e5-a09b-1f8b0d268c39.

3 Thanduxolo Jika, Qaanitah Hunter and Sabelo Skiti, How Guptas shopped for new minister, *Sunday Times*, 13 March 2016, http://archive.timeslive.co.za/sundaytimes/stnews/2016/03/13/How-Guptas-shopped-for-new-minister.

4 ANA, ANC slams *Sunday Times* over Gupta story, IOL, 13 March 2016, https://www.iol.co.za/news/politics/anc-slams-sunday-times-over-gupta-story-1997134.

5 Guptas offered me ministerial role: Vytjie Mentor, eNCA, 15 March 2016, http://www.enca.com/south-africa/guptas-offered-me-ministerial-role-vytjie-mentor.

6 Statement by Deputy Minister of Finance Mr Mcebisi Jonas (MP), National Treasury, 16 March 2016, http://www.treasury.gov.za/comm_media/press/2016/2016031601%20-%20Statement%20by%20Deputy%20Minister%20Jonas.pdf.

7 Hlengiwe Nhlabathi, Guptas confronted Jonas over his 'factional relations' against Zuma, *City Press*, 3 November 2016, http://city-press.news24.com/News/guptas-confronted-jonas-over-his-factional-relations-against-zuma-20161102.

8 Pauli van Wyk, Ajay Gupta denies under oath that he offered Jonas finance minister job, *Mail & Guardian*, 10 February 2017, https://mg.co.za/article/2017-02-10-ajay-gupta-i-have-never-met-deputy-finance-minister-mcebisi-jonas.

9 The references to Thuli Madonsela's interview with Jacob Zuma in this chapter are in an addendum to the Public Protector's State of Capture report, in the author's possession.

10 State of Capture, A report of the Public Protector, 14 October 2016.

Chapter 20: Fake news and dirty tricks

1 Amanda Khoza, Zuma on Nenegate 'stooges' and never saying surrender, News24, 21 December 2016, http://www.news24.com/SouthAfrica/News/zuma-on-nenegate-stooges-and-never-saying-surrender-20161221.

2 Joseph Cotterill and David Bond, Bell Pottinger reputation muddied by South African scandal, *Financial Times*, 7 July 2017, https://www.ft.com/content/6fa8c2d4-6327-11e7-8814-0ac7eb84e5f1.

3 Crofton Black and Abigail Fielding-Smith, Fake news and false flags, The Bureau of Investigative Journalism, 2 October 2016, http://labs.thebureauinvestigates.com/fake-news-and-false-flags.

4 Sabelo Skiti and Sibongakonke Shoba, Inside the Zuma PR machine, *Sunday Times*, 19 March 2017.

5 Monica Laganparsad, #GuptaEmails: Inside the £100 000 a month media spin

machine, News24, 1 June 2017, http://www.news24.com/SouthAfrica/News/guptaemails-inside-the-100-000-a-month-media-spin-machine-20170531.

6 Pieter du Toit, *Rupert aan Zuma: 'Vir kinders se toekoms, bedank'*, Netwerk24, 23 March 2016, http://www.netwerk24.com/Nuus/Politiek/rupert-aan-zuma-vir-kinders-se-toekoms-bedank-asb-20160323.

7 Pieter du Toit, How Rupert was warned about Bell Pottinger: 'They're behind it.', HuffPost SA, 26 January 2017, http://www.huffingtonpost.co.za/2017/01/25/how-rupert-was-warned-about-bell-pottinger-theyre-behind-it_a_21662494.

8 Marc Hasenfuss, Johann Rupert vexed by 'spin campaign', *Business Day*, 2 December 2016, https://www.businesslive.co.za/bd/national/2016-12-02-johann-rupert-vexed-by-spin-campaign.

9 Ferial Haffajee, The Gupta fake news factory and me, HuffPost SA, 6 June 2017, http://www.huffingtonpost.co.za/2017/06/05/ferial-haffajee-the-gupta-fake-news-factory-and-me_a_22126282.

10 Paid Twitter: Manufacturing dissent, helping Guptas, *Daily Maverick*, 10 November 2016, https://www.dailymaverick.co.za/article/2016-11-10-paid-twitter-manufacturing-dissent-helping-guptas/#.WaVkTvkjGM8.

11 James Henderson, 'We were misled, we are deeply sorry' – read Bell Pottinger's full statement, *Business Day*, 6 July 2017, https://www.businesslive.co.za/bd/national/2017-07-06-we-were-misled-we-are-deeply-sorry--read-bell-pottingers-full-statement.

12 Sam Burne James, 'I kept saying it was smelly': Lord Bell claims Bell Pottinger ignored his concerns over Gupta work, *PR Week*, 11 July 2017, http://www.prweek.com/article/1439079/i-kept-saying-smelly-lord-bell-claims-bell-pottinger-ignored-concerns-gupta-work.

13 Bell Pottinger cuts ties with Guptas' Oakbay – report, Fin24, 12 April 2017, http://www.fin24.com/Companies/Investment-Holdings/bell-pottinger-cuts-ties-with-guptas-oakbay-report-20170412.

14 James Henderson, 'We were misled, we are deeply sorry' – read Bell Pottinger's full statement, *Business Day*, 6 July 2017, https://www.businesslive.co.za/bd/national/2017-07-06-we-were-misled-we-are-deeply-sorry--read-bell-pottingers-full-statement.

15 Jan Cronje, Bell Pottinger expelled from PR body for Gupta work, Fin24, 4 September 2017, http://www.fin24.com/Companies/Advertising/breaking-bell-pottinger-expelled-from-pr-body-for-gupta-work-20170904.

Chapter 21: Zuma makes his move

1 Author's interview with Lungisa Fuzile, 25 July 2017.

2 Ibid.

3 Mia Lindeque, Gordhan: No need for Zuma to intervene in Moyane matter,

Eyewitness News, 24 March 2017, http://ewn.co.za/2017/03/24/overstated-sars-treasury-relationship-important-gordhan.

4 Babalo Ndenze and Thanduxolo Jika, Fiscal fight: 'Zuma ministers' want Treasury to 'share the cake', *Sunday Times*, 12 February 2017.

5 Pieter du Toit, Gordhan: There are some institutions that you just shouldn't mess with, HuffPost SA, 22 February 2017, http://www.huffingtonpost.co.za/2017/02/22/gordhan-there-are-some-institutions-that-you-just-shouldnt-mes_a_21719278.

6 Author's interview with Lungisa Fuzile, 25 July 2017.

7 Ibid.

8 Mfuneko Toyana and Sujata Rao, South Africa's Zuma recalls Gordhan from international roadshow, rand falls, Reuters, 27 March 2017, http://www.reuters.com/article/us-safrica-gordhan-idUSKBN16Y0XM.

9 Finance Minister and National Treasury Director General to return from Investor road show, National Treasury, 27 March 2017, see http://www.news24.com/SouthAfrica/News/gordhan-jonas-ordered-to-return-to-sa-presidency-20170327.

10 Author's interview with Lungisa Fuzile, 25 July 2017.

11 Ibid.

12 NT: Statement on National Treasury's international roadshow, Polity, 28 March, 2017, http://www.polity.org.za/article/nt-statement-on-national-treasurys-international-roadshow-2017-03-28.

13 Mpho Raborife, Kathrada never got a response from Zuma – Motlanthe, News24, 29 March 2017, http://www.news24.com/SouthAfrica/News/kathrada-never-got-a-response-from-zuma-motlanthe-20170329.

14 Govan Whittles, Embattled Gordhan honoured with standing ovation at Kathrada funeral, *Mail & Guardian*, 29 March 2017, https://mg.co.za/article/2017-03-29-embattled-gordhan-honoured-with-standing-ovation-at-kathrada-funeral.

15 Pieter du Toit, Gordhan dares Zuma: Fire me, because I'm not going anywhere, HuffPost SA, 29 March 2017, http://www.huffingtonpost.co.za/2017/03/28/gordhan-dares-zuma-fire-me-because-im-not-going-anywhere_a_22016095.

Chapter 22: Treasury's walls finally breached

1 Pippa Green, SA's sundered finance team was years in the making, *Business Day*, 10 April 2017, https://www.businesslive.co.za/bd/opinion/2017-04-10-sas-sundered--finance-team-was-years-in-the-making.

2 Ibid.

3 Author's interview with Maria Ramos, 3 August 2017.

4 Kyle Cowan, SACP: We cannot be a state run by gangsters, TimesLive, 30 March 2017.

5 Ramaphosa says Gordhan's axing is unacceptable, eNCA, 31 March 2017, https://

www.enca.com/media/video/ramaphosa-says-gordhan-s-axing-is-unacceptable.

6 Jonathan Wheatley, Zuma's game of chicken with markets sees Gordhan go, *Financial Times*, 31 March 2017, https://www.ft.com/content/10a1f2a2-1489-11e7-b0c1-37e417ee6c76.

7 Ferial Haffajee, Gordhan shares 'scary facts' with activists in closed-door meeting, HuffPost SA, 31 March 2017, http://www.huffingtonpost.co.za/2017/03/31/gordhan-shares-scary-facts-with-activists-in-closed-door-meeti_a_22020240.

8 As it happened: Zuma Cabinet reshuffle, News24, 31 March 2017, see http://www.fin24.com/Economy/outa-seeks-legal-action-on-gordhan-axing-20170331.

9 Lameez Omarjee, Gigaba admits: I celebrated Diwali with the Guptas, Fin24, 4 April 2017, http://www.fin24.com/Economy/gigaba-admits-i-celebrated-diwali-with-the-guptas-20170404.

10 Kyle Cowan, Graeme Hosken, Sikonathi Mantshantsha and Genevieve Quintal, Toxic network: Gigaba and Brown eased Gupta allies in, *Business Day*, 6 June 2017, https://www.businesslive.co.za/bd/national/2017-06-06-toxic-network-gigaba-and-brown-installed-gupta-cronies-at-state-owned-companies.

11 Graeme Hosken and Katharine Child, Gigaba granted SA citizenship to the Guptas, *Business Day*, 13 June 2017, https://www.businesslive.co.za/bd/national/2017-06-13-gigaba-granted-sa-citizenship-to-the-guptas.

12 TimesLive, Malema: 'Gigaba is rotten to the core', YouTube, https://www.youtube.com/watch?v=5YIgAb_IXfw.

13 Pieter du Toit, How Pravin Gordhan became the catalyst for the resistance, HuffPost SA, 2 April 2017.

Chapter 23: #GuptaLeaks

1 Sam Sole, #GuptaLeaks town hall meeting, 27 July 2017.

2 Stefaans Brümmer, Sam Sole and Branko Brkic, Editorial: The #GuptaLeaks revealed, *Daily Maverick*, 1 June 2017, https://www.dailymaverick.co.za/article/2017-06-01-editorial-the-guptaleaks-revealed.

3 Ibid.

4 amaBhungane and Scorpio, #GuptaLeaks: Guptas and associates score R5.3bn in locomotives kickbacks, amaBhungane Centre for Investigative Journalism, 1 June 2017, http://amabhungane.co.za/article/2017-06-01-guptaleaks-guptas-and-associates-score-r53bn-in-locomotives-kickbacks.

5 Sistema's chairman, Vladimir Yevtushenkov, under house arrest, Rogtec, 17 September 2014, http://www.rogtecmagazine.com/blog/sistema-s-chairman-vladimir-yevtushenkov-under-house-arrest.

6 Genevieve Quintal, Duduzane's role as Russia fixer emerges, *Business Day*, 2 June 2017, https://www.businesslive.co.za/bd/national/2017-06-02-duduzanes-role-as-russia-fixer-emerges/.

7 amaBhungane and Scorpio, #GuptaLeaks: Duduzane Zuma, kept and captured, amaBhungane Centre for Investigative Journalism, 1 June 2017, http://amabhungane.co.za/article/2017-06-01-guptaleaks-duduzane-zuma-kept-and-captured.

8 Ibid.

9 Scorpio, #GuptaLeaks: How Bell Pottinger sought to package SA economic message, amaBhungane Centre for Investigative Journalism, 6 June 2017, http://amabhungane.co.za/article/2017-06-06-guptaleaks-how-bell-pottinger-sought-to-package-sa-economic-message.

10 Ibid.

11 amaBhungane and Scorpio, #GuptaLeaks: The Dubai laundromat – how millions from dairy paid for Sun City wedding, amaBhungane Centre for Investigative Journalism, 30 June 2017, http://amabhungane.co.za/article/2017-06-29-guptaleaks-the-dubai-laundromat.

12 amaBhungane and Scorpio, #GuptaLeaks: Emails offer further proof of Gupta racist attitudes, *Daily Maverick*, 9 June 2017, https://www.dailymaverick.co.za/article/2017-06-09-scorpio-and-amabhungane-guptaleaks-emails-offer-further-proof-of-gupta-racist-attitudes/#.WZ7Il_kjGM8.

13 Angelique Serrao, #GuptaEmails: Tony Gupta allegedly called Saxonwold security guards 'monkeys', News24, 1 June 2017, http://www.news24.com/SouthAfrica/News/guptaemails-tony-gupta-allegedly-called-saxonwold-security-guards-monkeys-20170601.

14 #GuptaLeaks: More racism exposed in email, News24, 28 June 2017, http://www.news24.com/SouthAfrica/News/guptaleaks-more-racism-exposed-in-email-20170627.

15 Ibid.

16 Ibid.

17 amaBhungane and Scorpio, #GuptaLeaks: Software giant SAP paid Gupta front R100m 'kickbacks' for state business, News24, 11 July 2017, http://www.news24.com/SouthAfrica/News/guptaleaks-software-giant-paid-gupta-front-r100m-kickbacks-for-state-business-20170711.

18 amaBhungane and Scorpio, #GuptaLeaks: More multinationals ensnared in Transnet kickback web, amaBhungane Centre for Investigative Journalism, 17 July 2017, http://amabhungane.co.za/article/2017-07-16-guptaleaks-more-multinationals-ensnared-in-transnet-kickback-web.

19 Ibid.

20 amaBhungane and Scorpio, #GuptaLeaks: Another software giant implicated in 'kickback' payments, News24, 25 July 2017, http://www.news24.com/SouthAfrica/News/guptaleaks-another-software-giant-implicated-in-kickback-payments-20170725.

21 #GuptaLeaks: The captured presidency, News24, 19 July 2017, http://www.news24.com/SouthAfrica/News/guptaleaks-the-captured-presidency-20170718.

22 Ibid.

23 Exclusive: Guptas' blue lights mystery solved through #GuptaLeaks, News24, 14 August 2017, http://www.news24.com/SouthAfrica/News/exclusive-guptas-blue-lights-mystery-solved-20170814.

24 #GuptaLeaks: The captured presidency, News24, 19 July 2017, http://www.news24.com/SouthAfrica/News/guptaleaks-the-captured-presidency-20170718.

25 Ibid.

26 Ibid.

27 Ibid.

28 Ibid.

29 amaBhungane and Scorpio, #GuptaLeaks: Did Gigaba and officials grease Gupta gears?, amaBhungane Centre for Investigative Journalism, 1 June 2017, http://amabhungane.co.za/article/2017-06-01-guptaleaks-did-gigaba-and-officials-grease-gupta-gears.

30 Qaanitah Hunter and Kyle Cowan, E-mails reveal Gigaba adviser as Guptas' 'man on the inside', TimesLive, 31 May 2017, http://www.heraldlive.co.za/news/2017/05/31/e-mails-reveal-gigaba-adviser-guptas-man-inside.

31 Thanduxolo Jika, How Guptas paid for minister's trip to India for medical treatment, *Sunday Times*, 2 July 2017, https://www.timeslive.co.za/sunday-times/investigations/2017-07-01-how-guptas-paid-for-ministers-trip-to-india-for-medical-treatment.

32 Thanduxolo Jika, Exposed: Explosive Gupta e-mails at the heart of state capture, *Sunday Times*, 28 May 2017, https://www.timeslive.co.za/sunday-times/news/2017-05-28-exposed-explosive-gupta-e-mails-at-the-heart-of-state-capture/.

33 Siphe Macanda, Gupta fixer paid for minister's Dubai stay, SowetanLive, 5 June 2017, http://www.sowetanlive.co.za/news/2017/06/05/gupta-fixer-paid-for-minister-s-dubai-stay.

34 #GuptaLeaks: Guptas spied on Manuel, Malema and bank bosses, News24, 25 June 2017, http://www.news24.com/SouthAfrica/News/guptaleaks-guptas-spied-on-manuel-malema-and-bank-bosses-20170624.

35 amaBhungane and Scorpio, #GuptaLeaks: Duduzane Zuma's UAE residency confirmed, amaBhungane Centre for Investigative Journalism, 3 June 2017, http://amabhungane.co.za/article/2017-06-03-guptaleaks-duduzane-zumas-uae-residency-confirmed.

36 Mahlatse Gallens and Tshidi Madia, Own up, Mantashe warns those implicated in #GuptaLeaks, News24, 30 June 2017, http://www.news24.com/SouthAfrica/News/own-up-mantashe-warns-those-implicated-in-guptaleaks-20170630.

Chapter 24: Death race to December

1 Statement by Deputy President Cyril Ramaphosa on invasion of privacy, The

Presidency, 2 September 2017, http://www.thepresidency.gov.za/press-statements/
statement-deputy-president-cyril-ramaphosa-invasion-privacy?page=29#!slide.

2 Interview with Pieter du Toit, October 2016, quoted on condition of anonymity.

3 Eulogy by Deputy President Cyril Ramaphosa at the funeral of Makhenkesi
Stofile, 25 August 2016, http://www.thepresidency.gov.za/speeches/
eulogy-deputy-president-cyril-ramaphosa-funeral-reverend-arnold-makhenkesi-
stofile%2C.

4 Greg Nicholson, SACP congress: 'The house is burning', *Daily Maverick*, 12 July
2017.

5 Liesl Pretorius, Dlamini-Zuma's a clever player, but can she live with herself?,
HuffPost SA, 16 August 2017, http://projects.huffingtonpost.co.za/articles/
dlamini-zumas-a-clever-player-but-can-she-live-with-herself/.

6 Khanyisile Ngcobo, Dlamini-Zuma's VIP protection based on 'threat and security
assessment', police say, *The Citizen*, 14 April 2017.

7 Boris Groendahl (Bloomberg), Gordhan: 'They will probably charge us', News24,
1 September 2017, http://www.fin24.com/Economy/gordhan-they-will-probably
-charge-us-20170901.

8 Garreth van Niekerk, Makhosi Khoza resigns from the ANC, HuffPost SA, 21
September 2017, http://www.huffingtonpost.co.za/2017/09/21/makhozi-khoza-
resigns-starts-her-own-party_a_23217442/.

9 Govan Whittles, ANC probes fake membership plot, *Mail & Guardian*, 7 July
2017.

Acknowledgements

To write a book of history in real time, while editing a digital publication, requires enormous discipline and sacrifices from our loved ones and friends.

To Cecile, Janetha, Michiel, Schalk and Lukas, thank you for giving up your husbands and dads to allow them to write this book. We hope that it will in some way contribute to the growth and improvement of our beloved South Africa. We love you dearly.

To our Media24 bosses, Andreij Horn and Charlene Beukes, thank you for allowing us to write this book while the news was breaking. Your support has been invaluable.

Eugene Ashton and Jeremy Boraine from Jonathan Ball Publishers just wouldn't let go of the idea of this book. After many glasses of good red wine, they finally convinced us to tackle this mammoth task. We guess you were right, gents.

To our colleagues at News24 and HuffPost SA, thank you for supporting us throughout the research and writing process. It gave us huge comfort knowing the show would go on without us being around.

We have drawn heavily on the work of South Africa's amazing crop of investigative, political and news journalists. If it weren't for you, we would have been in much deeper shit by now.

And we, as journalists, couldn't have told these stories if it weren't for the brave and selfless whistle-blowers in government, the ANC and the private sector. You are the unsung heroes of the Zuma years.

To Mandy Rossouw, who pushed over the first domino that ultimately led to exposing our naked emperor: may your soul rest in peace.

Adriaan Basson & Pieter du Toit

Index

Mashatile, Paul 28, 286
Masondo, Amos 215
Mataboge, Kabelo 30
Matakata, Yolisa 93
Matisonn, John 132
Matojane, Elias 91, 92, 93, 191
Matona, Tshediso 111
Matsepe-Casaburri, Ivy 122
Matthews, Jimi 129, 130, 131
Matuba, Meokgo 200
Mavuso, Vusi 131
Mazibuko, Lindiwe 24, 41, 137, 138
Mbalula, Fikile 9, 10, 15, 72, 93, 94, 95, 207, 238
Mbeki, Thabo *xii*, 7, 8, 9, 10, 12, 13, 14, 15, 17, 18, 19, 23, 32, 57, 60, 102, 114, 121, 123, 134, 135, 136, 189, 194, 195, 197, 201, 213, 216, 251, 255, 256, 260, 279, 281, 282, 284
Mbeki, Zanele 251
Mbete, Baleka *xvi*, 9, 28, 52, 135, 138, 141, 142, 143, 144, 200, 208, 256, 289
Mboweni, Tito 12, 255
McBride, Robert 90, 92, 152, 178, 179
McCarthy, Leonard 204
Mchunu, Senzo 287
McKinsey 105
Mdluli, Richard *xviii*, 3, 81, 82, 83, 85, 87, 88, 89, 90, 92, 94, 122, 201
Mentor, Mabel Petronella 'Vytjie' *xvii*, 97, 98, 99, 101, 102, 215, 223, 225, 227, 228, 230, 238
Metcash 147
Metro FM 124
Meyer, Jacques 153
Mhlongo, Welcome 82
MI6 65
Mkhize, Buhle 105
Mkhize, Zweli *xi*, 9, 28, 171, 172, 173, 256, 258, 260, 261, 288
uMkhonto we Sizwe 86, 251
uMkhonto we Sizwe Military Veterans' Association (MKMVA) 56, 64, 237, 270, 285
Mkhwebane, Busisiwe 222, 223

Mlambo-Ngcuka, Phumzile 9
Mlambo, Dunstan 202
Mmemezi, Humphrey 29, 30
Mngxitama, Andile 236, 237, 240, 281
Mobutu Sese Seko 255
Modise, Joe 232
Modise, Thandi 9, 28
Mogajane, Dondo 160
Mogano, Mogotladi 274
Mogoeng, Mogoeng *xix*, 53, 55, 200, 203, 208, 209
Mokhari, William 202
Mokhobo, Lulama 124
Mokoena, France Oupa 113, 114
Mokoena, Sophie 122, 123
Mokonyane, Nomvula 175, 211, 244
Mokotedi, Prince 92
Molefe, Brian *xx*, 64, 101, 105, 110, 111, 112, 113, 114, 116, 117, 118, 119, 184, 248, 256
Molosi, Itumeleng 51, 55
Monetary Policy Committee 20
Moneymine 42, 50
Moodley, Roy 60
Moody's 185
Moonoo, Vinesh 91
Mopeli, Kenneth 122
Morajane, Tshepo *v*
Moscow 69
Moseneke, Dikgang 197, 198
Motale, Steven 280, 281
Mothapo, Moloto 137
Mothiba, Lesetja 95
Mothle, Billy 204
Motlanthe, Kgalema 9, 19, 25, 26, 27, 28, 29, 30, 31, 33, 195, 198, 251, 252, 256, 281, 284
Motsepe, Patrice 161, 172
Motsepe, Tshepo 251
Motshekga, Mathole 44, 51, 135
Motsoaledi, Aaron 252
Motsoeneng, Hlaudi *xix*, 29, 120–133, 205
Moyane, Tom *xx*, 79, 145, 146, 150, 151, 152, 153, 154, 177, 180, 182, 243, 260
Mozambique 150
Mpisi Trading 149